9th Edition

Business Buyout Agreements

Plan Now for All Types of Business Transitions

**Attorneys Bethany K. Laurence
& Anthony Mancuso**

NINTH EDITION	JUNE 2022
Editor	BETHANY K. LAURENCE
Book Design	SUSAN PUTNEY
Proofreading	CATHLEEN SMALL
Index	VICTORIA BAKER
Printing	SHERIDAN

Names: Laurence, Bethany K., 1968-, author. | Mancuso, Anthony, author.
Title: Business buyout agreements : plan now for all types of business
   transitions / Bethany K Laurence, J.D. & Anthony Mancuso.
Description: 9th ed. | Berkeley, CA : Nolo, [2022] | Includes index.
Identifiers: LCCN 2022000295 (print) | LCCN 2022000296 (ebook) | ISBN
   9781413329650 (paperback) | ISBN 9781413329667 (ebook)
Subjects: LCSH: Sale of business enterprises--Law and legislation--United
   States--Popular works.
Classification: LCC KF1659 .M36 2022 (print) | LCC KF1659 (ebook) | DDC
   346.73/0652--dc23/eng/20220330
LC record available at https://lccn.loc.gov/2022000295
LC ebook record available at https://lccn.loc.gov/2022000296

This book covers only United States law, unless it specifically states otherwise.

Please note

Accurate, plain-English legal information can help you solve many of your own legal problems. But this text is not a substitute for personalized advice from a knowledgeable lawyer. If you want the help of a trained professional—and we'll always point out situations in which we think that's a good idea—consult an attorney licensed to practice in your state.

Acknowledgments

Many thanks to Jake Warner, Terri Hearsh, Susan Putney, Mike Mansel, Walter Gibbons, and Nolo for helping us produce and publish this small business book through many transitions.

About the Authors

Anthony Mancuso is a corporations and limited liability company expert. He graduated from Hastings College of the Law in San Francisco, studied advanced business taxation at Golden Gate University in San Francisco, and is an active member of the California State Bar. Mr. Mancuso is the author of Nolo's bestselling titles on forming and operating corporations (both profit and nonprofit) and limited liability companies. His titles include *Incorporate Your Business*, *How to Form a Nonprofit Corporation* (national and California editions), *Form Your Own Limited Liability Company*, *The Corporate Records Handbook*, and *LLC or Corporation?* His books and software have shown more than a quarter of a million businesses and organizations how to form an LLC or a corporation. He also is a licensed helicopter pilot and performs as a guitarist. He currently works for Google.

Bethany K. Laurence joined Nolo as a legal editor in 1997. She holds a law degree from University of California, Hastings College of the Law, a B.A. degree from Boston University (Phi Beta Kappa, magna cum laude), and is a member of the California State Bar. Ms. Laurence has combined her legal and financial expertise to edit many Nolo books. Over the years she has been the editor of *Form Your Own Limited Liability Company*, *Tax Savvy for Small Business*, and *The Small Business Start-Up Kit*, and she was the co-author of *Save Your Small Business: 10 Crucial Strategies to Survive Hard Times or Close Down & Move On* and *Bankruptcy for Small Business Owners: How to File for Chapter 7*. Prior to joining Nolo, Ms. Laurence worked for CCH, Inc. (a division of Wolters Klewer, Inc.). Over the last decade she has been active on the board of directors of several educational nonprofit organizations.

Table of Contents

Appendixes

Your Legal Companion for Creating a Buyout Agreement

Any new business owner knows there is an insane number of tasks involved in launching a business. Just getting your business license, government filings, and finances in order can wear you down, never mind readying the heart of your business: how to market and sell your goods or services.

If you're looking at this book, though, you know that you really should plan for more than running your business day to day. You should think about the long term, too. And part of that is considering what you want to happen when an owner leaves the business.

It may seem odd to think about ownership changes when you're just starting out, but sooner or later, an owner will leave—maybe to pursue other interests, maybe for other reasons. It's impossible to know what your business will look like in five or ten years. To protect your investment, you need a plan to deal with these transitions. Without an exit plan, if you want out of the business in three years, you might have to leave your money and hard work behind. And without buyout provisions, what if a co-owner, out of the blue, threatens to liquidate the company if you don't meet a buyout price you can't afford—who wins? To avoid disagreements (maybe even lawsuits) and keep the business going smoothly, you need a buyout agreement that spells out the owners' rights and obligations when an ownership transition occurs.

You might want to think of a buyout agreement as a type of prenuptial agreement. Just as a prenup specifies what will happen to shared property if one spouse wants out of a marriage, a buyout agreement lets everybody know what each owner's rights will be if someone wants or needs to leave the business. Nobody has to worry about, or fight about, the consequences of a "breakup"—it has all been agreed to.

In this book, you'll learn:

- when and how to allow an owner to request a buyout
- when a buyout should be required (for example, after disability, divorce, bankruptcy, retirement, or death)
- how to restrict who can buy into the company
- how to value the business and each owner's share
- how to set up payment terms to make future buyouts affordable, and
- how to provide the funds for future buyouts.

Creating a buyout agreement may sound like a task you should hand over to a lawyer—after all, you've got a lot on your plate already. But the truth is you can prepare one yourself easily using the agreement that comes with this book. The book will help you pick the options in the agreement that best suit your business situation. Then you can open the agreement on this book's companion page on Nolo.com (see Appendix A for the link) and fill in some blanks—just as if you went to a lawyer's office, where they use fill-in-the-blanks agreements every day. (And if you do hire a lawyer to create your buyout agreement, you'll be ahead of the game because you'll understand the key issues. A little knowledge may save you a lot on the lawyer's bill.)

The important part of creating a buyout agreement is making personal decisions about your business. A lawyer can't do that for you. Only you can decide, for instance, whether you want you and your co-owners to have the ability to force a buyout, and under what circumstances, at what price, and according to what payment terms.

We provide the legal and tax information you need to make these decisions. We even include a worksheet where you can record your choices and thoughts as you go through the issues in the book with your co-owners. Along the way, there may be areas where your situation is complicated enough that you should seek advice from a lawyer or tax accountant. We'll let you know when you need outside help.

When you're done, you'll know that you've done the most important thing you can do when starting a business: ensured that if and when you don't want to (or can't) continue in the business, you'll have an exit strategy in place so that you can get your money without a lawsuit. And if another owner wants to leave, you'll be able to keep the business going with you at the helm.

We hope that this book, with its step-by-step process for creating a buyout agreement that makes sense for your business, will help you relax and get to the good part: making your business a success.

An Overview of Buyout Agreements

The first days and months of a new business are busy times. The last thing you have time for is worrying about what will happen when you or another owner wants to get out of the business—or becomes disabled, gets divorced, or dies. Unfortunately, it's a huge mistake to ignore the fact that, sooner or later, your business will lose owners and perhaps gain new ones. After all, do you know what you'll be doing five or ten years from now? You can't be sure that the business will fulfill all of your financial and emotional needs and that you'll want to stay involved forever. You can be sure about one thing, however: You will leave your business at some point, whether it is to start another company, become an employee somewhere else, move, retire, or, god forbid, become disabled or die when you're not expecting it.

If you are the owner who leaves first, you don't want to leave your investment and hard work behind. You need a way to convert your business interest into money that you can take with you. To make sure this happens, you and your co-owners may want to agree that the company or the co-owners will buy out an owner who wants or needs to leave—at least under certain circumstances.

Or, if it turns out that you are the owner who wants to stay with the company for the long haul, losing an owner or gaining a new one may throw you off course. When ownership interests change hands, conflicts often arise that can upset the functioning of a small, closely managed company. If you doubt this even for a minute, quickly skim the following questions:

- What if one of your co-owners demands you buy him out for an unreasonable price, at a time when the company is under financial strain?

- What if your longtime friend and business partner gets Alzheimer's disease? Can you buy out his share? Can the person's caretaker force you to buy the share?

- What if one of your co-owners becomes alcohol or drug dependent or loses her professional license? Can she be expelled?

- What if a co-owner gets divorced and her ex-husband ends up with part ownership because of the divorce settlement?

- What if the majority owner of your company wants to sell his share to a stranger?
- What if an older co-owner wants to give half of his interest to his notoriously irresponsible son, who has never worked for the company, and elect him to the board?

The answer to all these dilemmas is the same. If you haven't made a sound agreement to anticipate and deal with these issues before they happen, you're taking a risk that friction will arise between owners who will remain at the company and a new owner or a departing owner. Much of the time, this tension occurs because the continuing owners do not want to be forced to work with and share control of the company with an unqualified, inactive, or unlikable new owner. (After all, most small business owners own their own businesses because they want to run things their way, or at least share management with co-owners with whom they can comfortably and easily deal.)

When such owner-to-owner tension arises, it can lead to serious personal and business discord, which might even be fought out in court or result in the demise of your company. Put bluntly, if you do not have a buyout agreement, here is what may happen:

- If a stranger is allowed to buy the interest of a departing co-owner, or a family member of a deceased or divorced owner receives an interest, the new owner may be inexperienced or untrustworthy; this could end up hurting the company's bottom line.
- If a co-owner is forced to file for personal bankruptcy or defaults on a personal loan secured by his ownership interest in the business, you may be stuck co-owning the company with a bankruptcy trustee or creditor. This can create business delays and prevent you from getting bank loans.
- If a co-owner—or the co-owner's inheritors—want to be bought out, you and your co-owners may argue endlessly over what price should be paid for the interest that is changing hands, resulting in an angry deadlock that spills over into business operations.
- If you leave the company or die, you or your survivors may be stuck with a small business interest that no outsider wants to buy and for which no insider (co-owner) will give you a decent price.

To avoid these conflicts, you and your co-owners should arrange matters so you'll be able to collectively control who will own and manage the company in the future. In other words, if someone wants to buy into the company, you and the other owners can have a say. If an owner wants to give his share to his kids, you and the other owners may want to say no. If an owner wants to retire but hold on to his interest, you and the other owners may want to rearrange things. That's why it's best to set some ground rules ahead of time. Enter the buyout agreement (sometimes also called a buy-sell agreement or a business continuity agreement).

Much like a prenuptial agreement, a buyout agreement gives owners a way to deal with ownership disruptions in a way that won't wreck their business, by providing preestablished rules for transferring interests. After all, you probably started your own business to work with people you enjoy and to control your own destiny. A buyout agreement will make sure it stays that way.

Of course, planning in advance to contend with likely disputes is not the same thing as saying you can prevent change—for good or bad, your company's ownership situation is almost sure to be different five years hence. But you can plan for transitions with a buyout agreement—to make the transition process as positive and as smooth as possible—and put your mind at ease.

What a Buy-Sell, or Buyout, Agreement Can Do

Contrary to popular belief, a buy-sell agreement is not about buying and selling companies. A buy-sell agreement is a binding contract—between you and your co-owners—that controls when an owner can sell his interest, who can buy an owner's interest, when the company or co-owners must buy another owner's interest, and what price will be paid for that interest. In this book, we use the terms "buy-sell agreement" and "buyout agreement" interchangeably.

Guarantee a Buyer for Your Ownership Interest

At a time when many people demand that their work be both profitable and personally meaningful, you may decide that the business is not working out for you as you expected, or you may no longer get along with one of your co-owners, or you may even have to move to another city because your spouse takes a new job. Whatever the reason, you'll no doubt want to turn the value of your share of the business into cash—to provide you with retirement funds, seed money for another project, or even a down payment on a vacation house.

The Problem

If at some point you want to leave the business but your co-owners won't pay a fair price for your interest, without a buy-sell agreement you could be stuck with a share of the company, instead of having cash to spend or invest elsewhere. Why?

Your co-owners may not want to part with the money it would take to buy you out—at least not at the price you want. And you're not likely to have luck selling to a third party either. It's often impossible to find an interested buyer for part ownership of a company, especially if you're trying to sell a minority interest.

It shouldn't come as a surprise that it can be quite difficult to sell a less-than-100% share of a small business. A minority share gives an owner little or no control over how the business is run. Think of it this way: If your dream has been to own and run your own business, would you be likely to settle for a tiny piece of someone else's? Probably not—if you are like most people.

The Solution

If the time comes when you want or need to sell your ownership interest, having a buyout agreement that provides for forced buyouts can end up protecting you and your family from financial hardship and hard feelings. A buyout agreement can give you the right to force the company or the co-owners to buy you out under certain circumstances, and at a set price. A buy-sell agreement typically gives owners this right when any of the following occur:

- An owner decides to move on to something else or to retire after a certain period of time.
- An owner becomes disabled and is no longer able to actively participate in the company.
- An owner dies, and the estate representative or inheritors want to sell his interest back to the company or the continuing owners.

For instance, if you have to move out of state for family reasons and want to sell your ownership interest, or you become disabled and can no longer work, your agreement could require your company or co-owners to buy your share from you. In effect, this type of provision "makes a market" for your interest where one might not naturally exist.

Or, if you die unexpectedly, requiring the company to buy back your interest from your estate provides financial stability for your heirs—assuming they would inherit your chunk of the company after you die.

EXAMPLE: Dean, Ivan, and Winter, coworkers in a large cosmetics company, quit their jobs to form a natural cosmetics corporation. Unfortunately, although they spend a lot of time developing a business plan and organizing their business, they do not create an agreement or a mechanism to fund a buyout, should one of them want to sell out.

Three years after the corporation was formed and just when it is beginning to earn substantial profits, Ivan dies, soon after his fiftieth birthday. His wife and two children each inherit an equal number of his shares. But his wife is strapped for cash, and his kids, just entering college, also need money. Neither his wife nor the kids are interested in continuing the business. Dean and Winter don't feel the company can afford to pay the true value of Ivan's shares to his family, and they know that Ivan's heirs probably can't find an outside buyer. They plead poverty and initially refuse to buy the shares. Ivan's wife and kids are stuck. Dean and Winter finally agree to buy their shares for far less than they were really worth, by making small payments to the family over five years.

This is not an uncommon situation in small businesses. Often, when an owner dies, the last thing family members want to do is pick up the business where the owner left off. But families who are grieving the loss of a loved one may also suffer financially, from living expenses, funeral costs, and estate taxes. In that case, it's really necessary for an inheritor who does not want to carry on the business to be able to offer her interest to the company and the remaining owners of the company and be guaranteed that they'll buy it for a fair price.

We look at the ways a buy-sell agreement can provide forced buyout rights in Chapter 3, "Providing the Right to Force Buyouts."

Control Who Can Own an Interest in the Company

When the shoe is on the other foot, and you're the one who wants to stay while another owner leaves, you'll want some guidelines in place to keep the ownership and control of your company stable and the business solvent. This may happen when a co-owner is not getting along and wants to sell out or simply feels like doing something else.

The Problem

As discussed above, an outsider who gains an ownership interest could disrupt business as usual and trigger major problems in any small company's management. For example, a new owner with different goals might not see eye to eye with the existing owners on the election of the management team (board of directors, general partners, or limited liability company managers) or the approval of important management decisions. And since unanimous agreement of all owners is required for certain decisions, a new owner could hold up important company actions.

Even worse, an unwanted outsider in a corporation, especially one who buys or inherits a large block of shares, can gain control by electing herself to the board of directors. Once a person becomes a board member, that person becomes an equal participant on the board. Let's look at how an unwelcome outsider can disrupt a company's management.

EXAMPLE: Cousins Xavier and Yolanda incorporate a small business, with Xavier receiving 55% of the corporation's shares and Yolanda 45%. Each cousin serves as a director of the corporation. A few years later, Xavier and Yolanda have a falling out over whether to significantly expand the business. To escape from the resulting tension, Xavier sells his 55% interest to Richard, a wealthy investor Yolanda doesn't even know, and sets off to spend his days sailing the sunlit Caribbean.

Richard elects himself to the board of directors to fill Xavier's seat. He immediately proposes laying off several loyal employees in order to maximize short-term profits, with an eye toward making a quick and lucrative sale of the company. This horrifies Yolanda, who is interested in the long-term health and growth of the business. Richard and Yolanda quickly reach an impasse in corporate decision making, and Yolanda files a minority-shareholder lawsuit, trying to unseat Richard. This escalates their personal and professional conflicts, with the result that the company's day-to-day operations practically come to a standstill.

Likewise, in an unincorporated business, an outsider can sometimes take control automatically by becoming a majority owner in the partnership or limited liability company (LLC).

The Solution

When an owner is contemplating selling or giving away his interest, a good buyout agreement steps in to give the continuing owners some control over the transaction, often regulating who can buy the departing owner's interest and at what price, or, sometimes, whether the owner can sell his interest at all. The agreement gives the continuing owners the tools to prevent outsiders from buying in.

Usually a buyout agreement gives the company and its owners the opportunity to buy out an owner who stops working for the company. By so doing, it eliminates the possibility that active owners will be forced to share profits with an inactive owner. A buyout agreement can also give owners the right to purchase an owner's interest after he dies rather than allow his inheritors to become owners.

In fact, a typical buyout agreement gives the company and the owners the right to buy out an owner (that is, force an unwilling owner to sell) in all of these situations:

- The owner becomes disabled and is no longer able to actively participate in the company.
- The owner's ex-spouse stands to receive an ownership interest in the company as part of a divorce settlement.
- The owner's interest is in danger of being confiscated by creditors (because of a personal bankruptcy or foreclosure of a debt).
- The owner decides to retire from active participation in the company.
- The owner dies.

We discuss these options in Chapter 2, "Limiting the Transfer of Ownership Interests," and Chapter 3, "Providing the Right to Force Buyouts."

Set a Price for a Buyout

An important part of adopting a well-thought-out buyout agreement is setting a price at which ownership interests will be transferred. Without having an established price for the company in advance—or at least a formula for setting the price—lengthy disputes and lawsuits can arise over the value of an ownership interest. Not only are these disagreements almost sure to result in personal ill will, but they may even disrupt the ongoing business to the point that the company loses its edge and is in danger of failing.

However, it can be difficult to value a small or family-owned business. Sure, you can add up the value of property, equipment, and accounts receivable, but what about the value of your customer lists and your business's reputation—sometimes known as the "going concern" value? Should these assets get factored into the equation? And, of course, whatever number you come up with, a departing business partner could have a different idea of the company's worth: The departing owner could be thinking of a price based on the increasing profits over the last three years, while you may be fearful that the owner's departure is going to hurt sales or make the business's future uncertain.

We discuss setting a price for buyouts in Chapter 6.

Arrange a Payment Method for a Buyout

Likewise, a company that doesn't plan *how* it will pay a departing owner (or that person's family members) can be in for trouble. Having to come up with a large lump-sum payment out of the blue can cause a company to drown in financial hot water. These issues can be extremely problematic if a payment schedule is not determined until the time when the ownership interest has to be bought back. For instance, if an owner wants the company to buy back his interest and pay for it on the spot, the company may need to borrow the cash (of course, some can't) or liquidate assets to make the payment.

Fortunately, a good buyout agreement can set forth the mechanics of a buyout—including specific payment terms. A buy-sell agreement can provide that a departing owner (or the owner's family members) can be paid in installments, perhaps from company revenues, over a period of years, which will be more affordable for the continuing owners than a lump-sum payment.

We discuss payment methods for buyouts in Chapter 7.

Fund a Buyout

To cover the possibility of an owner's death or disability, one common funding method is to require the purchase of life or disability insurance for each of the business owners—and then use the policy proceeds to buy an owner out if an owner dies or becomes disabled. Without a funding mechanism, in some cases your company's only other option might be to liquidate or file for bankruptcy—something you surely want to avoid.

EXAMPLE: Imagine the same circumstances as the above example, except this time Dean, Ivan, and Winter create a buy-sell agreement at the outset. The agreement protects the owners' inheritors by requiring the corporation to buy back an inheritor's interest at a price based on a professional appraisal. It also provides that the buyout will be funded with company-purchased life insurance. The life insurance proceeds will keep the remaining owners from having to take out loans or sell assets to execute the buyout. Thanks to the buy-sell agreement, Ivan's wife and kids receive a reasonable sum for their shares, at no financial strain to the company.

In addition to, or in combination with, funding a buyout with insurance, if you plan ahead, departing owners can be partially compensated with deferred compensation or retirement plans. We discuss funding buyouts further in Chapter 5.

Tying It All Together

It is your job (along with your co-owners) to decide which of these provisions you want to include in your buyout agreement. After reading the first part of this book, which explains the various buyout options mentioned above and how they can be used, you and your co-owners will choose the buyout provisions you think are suitable for your company and your situation. You'll select provisions for your agreement depending on several factors, including how long you expect to own your business, whether you want to keep your company very small and private, and who you expect to succeed you when you die.

When Should You Create a Buyout Agreement?

Procrastination is a vice most of us share, and that includes many small business owners, no matter how shrewd they may be. Unfortunately, in the area of business planning, it can lead to financial undoing. Many owners of successful businesses put off creating a buyout agreement—because they don't have time, or they think nothing's going to change—until it's too late. In short, no matter what stage you're at in the business game, the time to create a buyout agreement is now.

When you're forming a new business, by the time you have the notion that you need to talk about "What happens if …," fatigue has probably set in. Often little energy is left over for hashing out the provisions of a buyout agreement. But creating your buy-sell agreement need not be an arduous ordeal. For instance, there's no need to spend a lot of time on complex valuation formulas (for example, the capitalization-of-earnings method) when you're just starting out. In fact, you couldn't use one of the more complicated formulas early on even if you wanted to—they require that you have a few years of earnings history. Later, as the worth of your company grows, and as you develop an earnings record, you can refine your valuation formula to reflect changes in the company's assets and earnings.

The key to a buyout agreement is that all owners agree to a reasonable plan early on, before anyone knows who will be most affected by it. Think of it this way: At the outset, each owner's concerns are roughly the same, because no owner knows who will be the first to leave. Or put another way, it's only when no one wants to sell out that everyone has the same interest in creating an evenhanded buyout agreement that's fair to all owners.

Not coincidentally, the best time to discuss these issues is during the formation stage of your company, when you're already discussing other potentially sensitive issues—such as the amount each owner will invest, the salaries or draws each owner-employee will take home, and the policies that will guide your company.

New owners sometimes worry that focusing on problems surrounding an owner's leaving casts a shadow over their new business. Just the opposite is true: Facing the fact that problems can arise and that negative things do happen can be healthy for your business relationship. Airing concerns, and perhaps a little dirty laundry, often helps you to head potential problems off or, if that's impossible, to be sure they will be handled smoothly, without putting your business's survival at risk. Knowing that possible changes are covered and planned for can act as a reality check and a stabilizing force and can increase your trust in what the future will be like.

No one may want to bring up the awkward issue of what happens if the owners stop getting along or if someone wants out of the business before the others do. But making decisions together with your co-owners from the start can make a world of difference in the future of your company because it requires you to discuss major questions that affect your future. Begin by being frank with your co-owners now.

Does Everyone Need a Buy-Sell Agreement?

Almost every business should have a buyout agreement. In only a few situations, a buyout agreement may not be necessary:

- **One owner.** If you own 100% of a company, you probably do not need a buy-sell agreement, unless you plan on selling the business to an employee who is willing and able to take over (see "Employee Buyouts" in Chapter 5).

- **Married owners.** If you and your spouse (with whom divorce is highly unlikely) own 100% of a company, there normally is little reason to bother creating a buy-sell agreement. It's unlikely that either of you will want to get out of the company unless you both do, and if one of you dies while you still own the business, the other person will probably inherit the ownership interest.

- **Parent/child owners.** If you co-own your small business with your son or daughter (alone) and you plan to leave your share of the business to them at your death, you may want to forgo a buy-sell agreement and just put your wishes in a will or trust (unless your estate may owe estate taxes—see "Estate Tax Issues" in Chapter 9). But even here there is always the possibility that your child will die, divorce, or want to leave the business before you do, so an agreement still makes sense.

In short, there may be some situations where it is unlikely you'll need the protection of a buyout agreement, but you usually take some sort of risk by not having one.

How to Create Your Agreement

Throughout the first part of this book, we present and explain various buyout provisions you can use to handle ownership transition issues, from deciding which potential problems may affect you and your company to choosing how you'd prefer to handle these dilemmas.

We provide a lot of the legal and tax information you need to make informed choices about the future of your company, including the following major issues that will help you decide on the terms of your buyout agreement:

- how to put limits on whom an owner can transfer his interest to (Chapter 2)
- how to provide for forced buyouts in certain circumstances (Chapter 3)
- how the procedure works for buyouts in the future (Chapter 4)
- how to fund future buyouts (Chapter 5)
- how to set the price that will be paid for ownership interests (Chapter 6)
- how to set the terms of payment (such as an installment plan) (Chapter 7), and
- how buy-sell agreements can affect ordinary income and capital gains taxes and estate taxes (Chapter 9).

Throughout the book, after introducing you to these concepts, we help you choose the provisions that are right for your company. This book will be your companion in making these decisions with your co-owners, providing practical and supportive information along the way.

To keep track of the options that interest you and any related thoughts you may have, we provide you with a worksheet that follows the order of the chapters and the issues we discuss. Before you start reading Chapter 2, print out the buyout worksheet from Nolo.com or refer to the form in Appendix B in the back of the book. The text will prompt you to check various options and jot down any relevant notes on your worksheet.

Finally, when you've gone through the book, you'll simply transfer your choices from your worksheet to our blank buyout agreement by filling in the blanks. The agreement is available on this book's companion page on Nolo.com (see Appendix A for the link).

After you're done choosing your provisions, you'll print out your agreement and have all owners sign it. Later on, during an ownership transition, the provisions you choose will remind you and your co-owners how you agreed to handle a potential buyout situation.

One practical suggestion: Take it easy. As you read through the book for the first time, you may feel a bit discombobulated by the numerous possibilities that can be covered in a buy-sell agreement. Expect to feel a bit overwhelmed. Not every company needs to cover every contingency. And there's no need to grasp every detail the first time through. Start by reading the entire book to get a rough understanding of what's involved and making a few observations on your worksheet about what situations or provisions might be particularly applicable to you.

Then spend time considering what you want to happen to your business when you are no longer in charge. Creating a buy-sell agreement has important, long-term consequences for you and your family, and your finances. Allow plenty of time for discussions with your co-owners—talk, argue, and speculate. Perhaps give each owner a worksheet of their own to fill out. When you're ready, go back, focus on the areas of most concern and begin to pin down exactly what you want in your agreement.

After you select the appropriate buyout options and you all sign your buyout agreement, it will then probably sit quietly in a dusty file folder until one of you wants to part with your ownership interest or until an event happens that causes the company or co-owners to want to buy out an owner. When one of these circumstances occurs, the buyout agreement will kick in to protect your investment.

When to Seek a Lawyer's Advice

While we provide a lot of information in this book to help you create your buy-sell agreement, we cannot provide the depth of advice, especially in the tax and estate planning realms, that a buy-sell or financial planner or a tax expert can provide. Since we don't know you and your particular business, we can't customize an agreement for you that exactly suits your company's and each owner's individual needs, though we do make every attempt to provide different alternatives and tips on customizing your own agreement.

So, in general, we recommend you bring your draft buyout agreement to a small business tax or legal adviser before putting your finalized agreement into action. Consultations of this sort are invaluable to make sure that you have considered all the relevant tax angles and the contingencies that apply to your particular business and to make sure you base your agreement on the very latest tax information and strategies. In addition, a lawyer can make sure that your new buyout provisions don't conflict with existing provisions of your business's organizational documents—your articles or bylaws or partnership agreement or LLC operating agreement. (For more information, see "Finalizing Your Buyout Agreement" in Chapter 8.)

Some situations may even merit a conversation with a lawyer or tax planner before you create your buy-sell agreement:

- **Family business owners.** If you own a family business and your plan is to have children or other relatives succeed you, you may need some extra help with succession planning—issues of inheritance and estate taxes can be complicated for family businesses. And although some family members may not want to consider the chance that there may be disagreements in the future, the truth is that serious disputes can and often do arise in family businesses—just as they do in families themselves. We discuss issues that apply to passing the family business from one generation to the next in "Family Succession Agreements," in Chapter 3, but families with high-value businesses or those with complex succession plans may need to bring in advisers (tax experts or estate planners) to help them mesh their buy-sell provisions with their estate planning needs.

- **Minority/majority owners.** If you will own a small minority or a large majority of a business, or you are a silent investor in a company, you may want to seek legal advice that's tailored to your circumstance. You may have some extra concerns that we don't fully address in this book. This book is geared toward companies with two or more owners who are unrelated, who own roughly equal shares of the business, and who actively participate in the day-to-day management or operations of the business.

- **Owners with different situations.** If the needs or circumstances of the owners are substantially different, and the owners' initial capital contributions will be quite high, each owner may wish to check out the tax and estate planning repercussions with his or her individual tax adviser or financial planner.

- **Older owners.** If you are in your fifties or sixties and are forming a new company with others and contributing a lot of cash or property, you may want to consult an estate planner before you adopt your agreement. In particular, choosing the right valuation formula early on can have a minimizing effect on estate taxes when you or a co-owner dies. We discuss estate taxes as they relate to buy-sell agreements in Chapter 9.

If you decide to have an expert prepare your buyout agreement rather than do it yourself, you'll benefit greatly by understanding the critical issues and your options, and by having thought about your expectations for the future of the company. You may want to create a draft of a buyout agreement—or at least fill out the worksheet in the appendix—and bring it with you to your first meeting with a lawyer, along with any questions you have. It will help your planner immensely in knowing where you're at and what you want out of an agreement, and may save you time and money.

In Chapter 10, we discuss how to find an attorney, or legal "coach"— a helpful professional who will review your buy-sell agreement for you. ●

Limiting the Transfer of Ownership Interests

n an age when many people change jobs or even careers a number of times during their adult life, and when businesses are opened and closed with head-spinning speed, it's a risky bet that you and all of your co-owners will be doing the same thing even five years from now. At some point during the life of your business, you or one of your business's co-owners will probably want to sell your interest in the business and move on to do something else. For that reason, the most common event that can disrupt a small business involves owners wanting to sell or transfer their interests in the company.

Transfers of Ownership Interests

One way owners might try to transfer their interests is to sell them to outside buyers (anyone not a current owner)—assuming they're lucky enough to find one. Another, probably more likely, scenario is for the company to buy back an owner's interest or for one or more of the co-owners to purchase the share. Or, for estate planning purposes, an older owner may want to transfer all or part of their ownership interest to a trust or give it to their children.

To help you and your co-owners maintain control of your company, it's essential to create, in advance, an impartial method for reviewing potential ownership transfers and blocking any undesirable ones. The best way to do this is to adopt a buyout provision that gives the company or co-owners the right to buy an owner's interest before it's sold, given away, or otherwise transferred (this is called a "right of first refusal"). This provision covers all of the scenarios discussed above; essentially, it covers any attempt by an owner to transfer an ownership interest in the company by sale or gift or to a trust.

The provisions in this chapter apply only to voluntary, lifetime transfers of owners' interests by sale or gift or to a trust. They don't apply to court-ordered transfers to bankruptcy trustees or to ex-spouses as part of a divorce, to transfers to an owner's estate or beneficiaries upon death, or to other *involuntary* transfers. Other buyout provisions in our buyout agreement, discussed in Chapter 3, cover these additional types of involuntary transfers.

Using a Right of First Refusal

To avoid the possibility that an unwanted person might buy (or otherwise be transferred) an interest in your business, most buyout agreements sensibly contain a Right-of-First-Refusal provision. This type of provision requires owners to first offer their interests for sale to the company and co-owners before selling them or transferring them to anyone else. Depending on the needs of your company, you may want this type of restriction to apply only when owners consider transferring their interests to outsiders. But there can also be reasons why you might want this type of restriction to apply when owners are considering transferring their interests to insiders—current owners.

Selling an Interest to an Outside Buyer

Should co-owners have the unconditional right to transfer their interests in the business to someone who is not already an owner of the company? Although at first thought you might be tempted to say, "Why shouldn't owners be able to do whatever they want with their interest?"—think again.

The Problem

Consider that, if you happen to be one of the continuing owners in the company, you might be horrified if a co-owner were to sell out to an un-qualified or unlikable new owner, who—even if they purchased only a minority share—would have the power to make your life miserable. And, of course, things would be far worse if an outsider stood to gain a majority interest in your company, since this would give them an opportunity to all but take your company away from you.

> EXAMPLE: Brothers Nigel and Aidan, along with Aidan's wife, Monica, open a boutique computer store and service business. They create a corporation with each relative owning a one-third stock interest and each serving as a board member. No buyout agreement is prepared. A few years later, after the service part of the business has become successful, they receive a favorable buyout offer from a competitor—an owner of a chain of inexpensive computer stores.

Nigel has no interest in selling his shares—he wants to keep the business in the family and eventually have his daughter Emilia succeed him. Aidan and Monica, on the other hand, have been looking forward to early retirement and jump at what they see as a golden opportunity to cash out. Since neither the corporate law in their state nor the corporation's bylaws require all owners to approve a transfer of an owner's shares in the corporation, Aidan and Monica sign a contract to sell their two-thirds ownership in the company to the chain operator. The new owner quickly votes her newly acquired, two-thirds controlling interest to elect herself and her husband to fill the two recently vacated board seats. Nigel is left with a one-third interest in a business that he can no longer run independently.

> 💡 **TIP**
>
> **An outside buyer might be a boon to the company.** Not every new owner would make things worse, especially an owner who buys an equal or minority interest. In the real world, the continuing owners may think highly of a person who wants to buy the departing owner's share. And, of course, there can be a real incentive for the continuing owners to allow a new owner to buy in, since it means they won't have to reach into their own pockets to pay the departing owner or ask their company to pony up the cash. Or, sometimes a change in ownership is just what's needed to pep up a sleepy or flagging business. If it looks like it may work out that everyone is happy with the new ownership situation, invoking a buyout restriction won't even be needed.

The key point here is that you won't know what the situation will be—or what new owner will come along—until it happens. In case things aren't so rosy, it's good to have an agreement in place to allow the continuing owners of the company—not the departing owner—to make the decision about who should take part in the company's ownership and future.

It's best for all owners to adopt buyout rules for forced buyouts well in advance of the need to use them. When the business is being formed, or in its early days, no owner knows how circumstances will change—so it's usually not difficult to do this. Since each owner could be the first or last to leave, all are motivated at that time to adopt an evenhanded agreement.

The Solution

A Right-of-First-Refusal provision gives the company, and usually the continuing owners individually, the choice to buy a co-owner's interest before an outsider is allowed to make a purchase (or otherwise receive an interest in the company). If the continuing owners decide they do not want to work with a prospective new owner, the company or the owners individually can exercise their right to buy the transferring owner's interest. On the other hand, if the owners approve of the potential new owner, they can elect not to buy the co-owner's interest—essentially approving the sale (or other transfer).

Here are the details of how our Right-of-First-Refusal provision works with respect to a potential sale of an interest by an owner to an outsider. (We discuss how our clause covers sales to insiders and gifts of interests— two other common types of transfers—later in this chapter.) When an owner receives an offer from an outsider to buy their ownership interest, a Right-of-First-Refusal provision requires that owner (let's call them the "transferring owner") to submit written notice to the company of their intent to sell their interest (a "Notice of Intent to Transfer"). The Notice of Intent to Transfer must include the price and payment terms of the proposed sale and the name and address of the proposed buyer. A copy of the offer from the proposed buyer must be attached.

The company and the continuing owners then have an option to buy the interest (either at the same price and payment terms as that offered by the outsider or at a different price and payment terms, depending on which price option is checked in the buyout agreement—also discussed below).

If the company and the continuing owners decline to purchase all of the transferring owner's interest, the transferring owner is free to sell their interest to the outsider. The transferring owner must, however, transfer their interest to the outsider within 60 days, at the same price and terms stated in their written notice, or they must start the whole process over again before transferring their interest. For example, if the transferring owner wishes to lower the price to be paid by the outsider for their interest, or wishes to change other terms of the sale to the outsider to make them more favorable (for example, a lower interest rate on installment payments or a longer payment term), the transferring owner must submit to the company a new notice—essentially starting the process over again for the transfer of the interest under the new terms. On the other hand, if the company and/or the continuing owners decide they do want to purchase the entire ownership interest, the outsider is out of luck. The company and/or the continuing owners then buy the interest from the transferring owner within a certain period of time. The Right-of-First-Refusal clause included in our buy-sell agreement is shown below.

WORKSHEET

Turn to your worksheet. If you want to have the right of first refusal before owners can transfer their interests, check Option 1 on your worksheet now. (Section II, Option 1.)

Section II: Limiting the Transfer of Ownership Interests

☐ **Option 1:   Right of First Refusal**

(a) No owner ("transferring owner") shall have the right to sell, transfer, or dispose of in any way any or all of his or her ownership interest, for consideration or otherwise, unless he or she delivers to the company written Notice of Intent to Transfer the interest stating the name and the address of the proposed transferee and the terms and conditions of the proposed transfer. Delivery of this notice shall be deemed an offer by the transferring owner to sell to the company and the continuing owners the interest proposed to be transferred.

If the proposed transfer is a sale of the owner's interest, these terms shall include the price to be paid for the interest by the proposed transferee, and a copy of the offer to purchase the interest on these terms, dated and signed by the proposed transferee, shall be attached to the notice.

(b) The company and the nontransferring owners then have an option, but not an obligation (unless otherwise stated in this agreement), to purchase the interest proposed for transfer, and may do so within the time and according to the procedure in Section IV, Provision 1 of this agreement.

If the company and the nontransferring owners do not elect to purchase all of the interest stated in the notice, the transferring owner may then transfer his or her interest to the proposed transferee stated in the notice within 60 days after the end of the nontransferring owners' purchase option, according to the procedure in Section IV, Provision 1 of this agreement.

EXAMPLE: Jason, Tim, Chris, and Bart are four equal shareholders and directors of a small adventure travel corporation called Run-a-Muck. Jason wants to sell his shares to an outsider, Austin. According to the Right-of-First-Refusal provision in the corporation's buy-sell agreement, Jason must first get a signed written offer from Austin, then notify the corporation of his intent to sell his shares to Austin. The price and payment terms of the proposed sale must be included in the notice to the corporation, with a copy of Austin's offer attached. Jason's Notice of Intent to Transfer is simple, and it reads as follows:

Notice of Intent to Transfer

I, Jason Thomas, propose to sell 250 shares in Run-a-Muck to Austin Johnson within 60 days of the date of this notice for $2,500.00 cash ($10.00 per share). Payment of the purchase price by Austin Johnson is to be made in cash on the date of the transfer. A copy of the offer to purchase these shares on these terms, signed by Austin Johnson, is attached to this notice.

Run-a-Muck's Right-of-First-Refusal provision states that the corporation and the continuing shareholders have 60 days from receipt of the notice to purchase all of Jason's shares. If they don't elect to purchase the shares, Jason is free to sell them to Austin according to the terms of Austin's offer. Faced with Jason's notice of a proposed sale, Tim, Chris, and Bart promptly meet as board members and decide that Run-a-Muck, Inc. itself will purchase Jason's shares, shutting Austin out of the company. Run-a-Muck then buys and cancels Jason's shares.

Price to Be Paid for the Ownership Interest

What about price? How much should transferring owners be paid for their shares? Often a Right-of-First-Refusal provision gives the company and the nontransferring owners the right to purchase a transferring owner's interest at the price the proposed buyer is willing to pay (assuming the interest is being sold, not gifted). In other words, the company and the other owners have to match this price or allow the sale to take place.

One potential problem with this approach is that a disaffected owner may be tempted to solicit a phony outside bid, perhaps from a good friend or relative, to prod their co-owners into buying their ownership interest at an inflated price. To help cope with this possibility, our Right-of-First-Refusal provision requires that a written offer for the purchase of an ownership interest, signed by the proposed buyer, be attached to the transferring owner's Notice of Intent to Transfer. Of course, this is no real guarantee that the offer is genuine, but at least it makes the purported buyer sign a commitment to buy the interest—most people will not want to sign such a statement unless they truly intend to buy the interest.

TIP

You can also require a down payment. Some owners may want to go even further and require that the proposed buyer tender a significant down payment to the transferring owner as evidence of good faith, and that the transferring owner present evidence of this payment (check or money order) with the copy of the signed, written offer presented to the company.

You can avoid this problem altogether by having your agreement provide that the company or continuing owners buy an owner's interest under a Right of First Refusal at a set price (called the "Agreement Price"), predetermined in the buyout agreement itself. In this case, even if the transferring owner receives a higher offer from the outsider, the transferring owner must sell to the company or the continuing owners at the Agreement Price, if they choose. This alternative has the virtue of protecting the continuing owners from being forced into business with an outsider who is willing to pay an inflated price—one that the continuing owners can't afford or aren't willing to match. Of course, this provision is weighted heavily toward the interests of the continuing owners and is less favorable to a transferring owner, who could end up selling their interest for less than it's really worth. Setting an agreement price is covered in Chapter 6.

TIP

Using the Agreement Price may help avoid estate taxes. In a limited number of circumstances, there is an additional reason to require the transferring owner to sell at the agreement's predetermined buyout price, rather than requiring the company or continuing owners to match an outsider's price. By requiring any and all departing owners to sell out at the Agreement Price, you take a big step toward establishing a reasonable value for the company for estate tax purposes. (Estate taxes are the taxes that may be owed to the government upon a person's death.) For more on this, see "How Buyout Agreements Affect Estate Taxes" in Chapter 9.

The options in our agreement that cover the price to be paid under a Right of First Refusal are shown below.

WORKSHEET

Turn to your worksheet. If you checked Option 1, "Right of First Refusal," in Section II, also:

- check Option 1a if you want your Right-of-First-Refusal clause to require the company and the nontransferring owners to match any amount offered by a buyer, or
- check Option 1b if you want your Right-of-First-Refusal clause to require the company and the nontransferring owners to pay only the buyout price set forth in the agreement and not be bound to match any amount offered by a buyer.

(c) Price and terms

☐ **Option 1a: Price and terms in offer**

If the proposed transfer is a sale of the owner's interest, the company and the nontransferring owners shall have the right to purchase the interest of the transferring owner only at the purchase price and payment terms stated in the Notice of Intent to Transfer submitted to the company by the transferring owner. The price and terms in this notice override the general Agreement Price selected in Section VI of this agreement and the agreement terms selected in Section VII.

If the proposed transfer is a gift of the owner's interest, the company and the nontransferring owners shall have the right to purchase the interest of the transferring owner at the Agreement Price selected in Section VI and according to the manner of payments and other terms of the purchase as established in Section VII of this agreement.

☐ **Option 1b: Price and terms in agreement**

The company and the nontransferring owners shall have the right to purchase the interest of the transferring owner at the Agreement Price selected in Section VI and according to the manner of payments and other terms of the purchase as established in Section VII of this agreement.

Company vs. Co-Owners as Buyers

Our Right-of-First-Refusal clause provides that either the company or the continuing owners can buy an owner's interest to stop the transfer of that interest.

In the case of a corporation, if the corporate entity, rather than the continuing owners, buys an owner's shares, it "cancels" them, which means that the remaining owners' percentages of ownership in the company increase accordingly. Similarly, in the case of partnerships and LLCs, if the company buys the departing owner's interest, that interest is "liquidated," and the continuing partners' or members' ownership percentages increase.

Compare this to the situation where the remaining shareholders, partners, or LLC members decide to individually buy the transferring owner's interest. When this happens, the transferring owner's interest is not canceled or liquidated, but is reallocated among the remaining owners.

> **EXAMPLE:** Kate, Carmen, and Raisa own and operate a highly successful small, member-managed LLC as equal one-third owners. Kate decides she wants to leave the LLC and, because the company is so lucrative, finds a willing buyer who signs a written offer to buy her LLC interest for cash. If the LLC, under the Right of First Refusal, buys back Kate's interest, Carmen and Raisa become equal one-half owners of the business after the purchase. The same percentage result occurs if Carmen and Raisa both decide to individually buy back one-half of Kate's interest.

In Chapter 4, we discuss the procedure and issues (mainly tax advantages and disadvantages) relating to who the buyer will be—the company or the continuing owners. For now, just understand that it's best to use a procedure that allows for either approach (ours does), leaving the determination as to who should be the buyer to be made at the time of a buyout.

What a Right of First Refusal Doesn't Do

If you think you may become interested in selling your interest later on, it's important to understand that a Right-of-First-Refusal provision alone does not guarantee you'll be able to sell your interest—either to an outsider or to your co-owners. You may find it impossible to find a buyer who will make a legitimate offer for your interest at anything but a flea market price, especially if you own a minority interest. And if you can't get an offer, you can't trigger the Right-of-First-Refusal provision that allows the company or the nontransferring owners to buy your interest. If you want a guarantee that you'll be able to cash out your interest, you'll need to include a Right-to-Force-Sale clause in your buy-sell agreement as well (discussed in Chapter 3).

The flip side of the coin is that a Right-of-First-Refusal provision may not always be able to fulfill its main purpose—to give all owners the ability to control the ownership of their company. Because of a lack of company or personal funds, owners armed only with a Right-of-First-Refusal provision may not be able to prevent a majority owner from selling to a proposed buyer.

> **SEE AN EXPERT**
>
> **Check with your attorney.** This is a good example of why minority owners should check with a small business attorney to investigate the pros and cons of any Right-of-First-Refusal provision before signing a buyout agreement. Again, most of our advice is tailored to small businesses where the owners own largely equal shares of the company. If you are a minority owner, you'd be wise to have an attorney look over your agreement. We cover finding expert help in Chapter 10.

Selling an Interest to a Current Owner

Many companies allow co-owners to transfer their interests among themselves freely—without being subject to a Right-of-First-Refusal or other buyout provision. After all, a transfer to a current owner would not bring a stranger into the ownership ranks—the current owners already share management duties with each other.

The Problem

In situations where there are more than two owners, there's another reason to establish rules governing interowner transfers: Without rules, there is no mechanism to prevent one or two co-owners from grabbing control of the business by snapping up a transferring owner's share. Here's how this can happen:

EXAMPLE: Serena, Petra, and Alexei start a small corporation that sells mailing lists, with each owning 333 shares of the 999 shares that were initially released. They do not create a buyout agreement. After suffering through several management quarrels with Petra and deciding that the work is not personally meaningful to him, Alexei decides he wants to cash out his interest and go to cooking school. Needing a large chunk of change for tuition, he secretly negotiates a deal with Serena, who agrees to buy his shares without telling Petra, for whom Alexei and Serena have developed a general distaste. The result is that Serena is able to purchase all of Alexei's interest without Petra's knowing and ends up with a total of 666 shares—and control of the company. Poor Petra no longer has a say in managing the company.

The Solution

To avoid situations where an equal owner suddenly and surprisingly becomes a majority owner, you can have your Right-of-First-Refusal clause apply to sales to current owners as well as outsiders. In other words, whenever an owner's interest is offered for sale to a current owner, *all* co-owners are given the opportunity to buy it first. The language that covers this choice in the agreement is shown below.

(d) Potential transferees

☐ **Option 1c: Right of first refusal applies to sales to current owners**

The Right-of-First-Refusal clause in this agreement shall apply to all potential transferees, whether they are current owners of any interests in the company or not.

☐ **Option 1d: Right of first refusal does not apply to sales to current owners**

The Right-of-First-Refusal clause in this agreement shall only apply to those potential transferees who are not current owners of any interests in the company.

WORKSHEET

Turn to your worksheet. If you checked Option 1, "Right of First Refusal," in Section II, also:

- check Option 1c if you want your Right of First Refusal to apply to sales to outsiders and current owners alike, or
- check Option 1d if you want your Right-of-First-Refusal clause to apply only to sales to outsiders.

Transferring an Interest to a Trust

Gifting ownership interests and transferring them to trusts can be subject to your buyout agreement, or not: You can make gifts of ownership interests and/or transfers to trusts subject to the same Right-of-First-Refusal provision that sales are subject to, or you can exempt these types of transfers, essentially giving owners free rein to give away their ownership interests.

Let's first take a brief look at why allowing owners the flexibility to transfer their ownership interests freely may be an important part of estate planning to you and your co-owners.

The Problem

One aspect of estate planning is avoiding probate. Probate is a costly and time-consuming court process during which a deceased person's will is proved authentic, all property subject to the will is inventoried and appraised, and relatives and creditors are notified. Finally, the property is distributed to the people entitled to inherit it. Probate can take months or even years and can cost as much as 5% of the value of the probated property.

If the family members or business partners of a deceased owner have to wait one or more years to gain title to their ownership interests from a probate court, business can grind to a halt. For this reason, keeping ownership interests (and the voting power and management of the company) o' probate is essential to ensure the smooth transition of the busine

Putting your ownership interest into a probate-avoidance l' can avoid the hassles and costs of probate. Here's how livi' probate: When business owners are at an age where esta. becomes necessary, they sign their ownership interests over

called a trust. The business owners are the trustees of the trust and have control over the ownership interests, just as if they owned the interests in their own names. Upon their deaths, the ownership interests are transferred directly to the beneficiaries of the trust—usually the owner's spouse and/or children—without having to go through probate.

Another aspect of estate planning for high-value estates is reducing or eliminating federal estate taxes. The federal estate tax is a form of inheritance tax that is taken from an estate after death. Whatever property you leave behind, including an ownership interest in a small business, might be subject to federal estate taxes when you die. However, only estates worth more than a specified exclusion amount (currently over $12 million) are subject to the federal estate tax. This threshold amount is referred to as the estate and gift tax exemption.

Buyout agreements may be able to lower estate taxes in limited circumstances. We discuss estate taxes more fully, including whose estate may incur them and several common methods of eliminating or lowering them, in "Estate Tax Issues" in Chapter 9.

The Solution

Because putting ownership interests in living trusts usually doesn't threaten the company or the continuing owners with an actual change of ownership— it's really just a paper transfer—many companies exempt from the Right of First Refusal owners' transfers of their interests to a trust, as long as the following conditions are met:

- The power to revoke (cancel) the trust remains with the owner of the business interest.
- The owner of the business interest is a trustee of the trust.

If the owner ceases to be a trustee of the trust (for example, a new trustee takes over because the owner becomes mentally incompetent), the new trustee would control the owner's interest and be able to vote on the management of the company. Therefore, this change would be considered an ownership transfer that causes the Right-of-First-Refusal clause to kick in, giving the company and the other owners' the right to buy the interest back.

Our Right of First Refusal covers transfers to trusts in Subsection (e) of Option 1. It is shown below.

WORKSHEET

Turn to your worksheet. If you want transfers to trusts to be *exempt* from the Right of First Refusal, you do not have to do anything. If you want transfers to trusts to be *subject* to the Right of First Refusal, you can simply remove Subsection (e) from your word processing file. (Section II, Option 1.) If you would like them to be subject to the Right of First Refusal, make a note to do this on your worksheet.

(e) This Right-of-First-Refusal clause shall not apply to an owner's transfer of an ownership interest to a trust as long as the following conditions are met:

(i) the power to revoke the trust remains with the grantor (the owner of the interest), and

(ii) the grantor (the owner of the interest) is a trustee of the trust.

If either of the above conditions ceases to be true, this change will subject the ownership interest to this Right-of-First-Refusal.

Making Gifts of Ownership Interests

The provision discussed just above, allowing transfers to living trusts, does not address the matter of gifts—giving ownership interests to relatives or long-term employees, usually to reduce eventual taxes at death.

Making partial gifts of an ownership interest over time can be an integral part of reducing estate taxes and avoiding probate. Giving away partial interests to family members in $16,000 chunks each year is one method of reducing estate taxes and taking an ownership interest out of probate. In 2022, you can make an unlimited number of $16,000 gifts (to different recipients) of cash or other property each calendar year, completely free of the estate or gift tax. This amount increases every few years.

EXAMPLE: Each year for the rest of your life, you can give your son and your daughter each $16,000 (or something worth $16,000), without incurring estate or gift taxes or eating into your personal estate and gift tax exemption. Your spouse can also give $16,000 per year to each child tax-free. (This would allow you to give away up to $64,000 per year.) On top of that, both of you can also make tax-exempt gifts to your children's spouses and their children. This could allow you to gift another $64,000 (two spouses, but no grandchildren) or even another $192,000 per year (two spouses and four grandchildren).

SEE AN EXPERT

The $16,000 annual exclusion amount for gifts is subject to change. Check Nolo's website or ask your tax adviser for the latest information.

The Problem

Most owners do not want their co-owners to be able to transfer their interest to outsiders without any kind of oversight or approval process—even if the outsiders in this case are children or other relatives. The reasons for this are the same as for restricting any transfer—mainly so that continuing owners don't have to work with and share control of the company with a new, untested owner.

The Solution

Our buyout agreement does not exempt gifts of ownership interests from the Right-of-First-Refusal provision. Instead, the buyout agreement gives the company and the continuing owners—those whose livelihood could be affected by ownership changes—the discretion to allow or disallow gifts of ownership interests. (If you and your co-owners have a different perspective and wish to allow unrestricted gifts of ownership interests, see "Allowing Unrestricted Gifts of Ownership Interests," below.)

Our Right-of-First-Refusal clause works with respect to proposed gifts in almost the same way as it does for proposed sales. Before giving part or all of an interest away, the owner who is considering gifting an interest (the transferring owner) must give written notice to the company of the proposed transfer, including the proposed recipient's name and address. (However, the gifts provision says that in this case the price and terms at which the company or the nontransferring owners can purchase the interest are the standard Agreement Price and payment terms established elsewhere in the buyout agreement.)

If the company and the other owners decline to purchase the ownership interest, the transferring owner is free to give away the interest. But if the company or other owners decide they don't want the transfer to go through, they must pay the owner for the interest according to the price and terms in the agreement. Keep in mind that if the company or the nontransferring owners buy the interest, the transferring owner will have cash available from the sale proceeds that can be given away to relatives for estate planning purposes.

SEE AN EXPERT

Older business owners may want the ability to freely plan their estates. Owners with estate planning concerns may need more freedom to avoid probate and estate taxes by gifting partial ownership interests. They should be aware of how a buyout agreement can hinder an owner's individual estate plan. (As discussed above, giving away part of your ownership interest to family members in $16,000 chunks each year is one method of reducing estate taxes and taking the ownership interest out of probate. To allow this type of gifting, see "Allowing Unrestricted Gifts of Ownership Interests," below.) If you are of an age where estate planning is high up on your to-do list, you should have your estate planner look over your buyout agreement before you sign it, to make sure it won't conflict with your estate planning goals.

WORKSHEET

Turn to your worksheet. If you want gifts of ownership interests to be subject to the Right of First Refusal discussed above, you don't need to check anything on your worksheet or change anything in the buyout agreement.

Allowing Unrestricted Gifts of Ownership Interests

You and your co-owners may want the unlimited right to give away your interests to whomever you please. If you and your company choose not to place restrictions on the transfer of owners' interests to their family members, you can simply check a box in your agreement so that the Right-of-First-Refusal provision does not apply to gift giving. Of course, remember that in allowing the unchecked gifting of ownership interests, owners give up some of their collective control over the ownership of the company. The option from our agreement is shown below.

☐ **Option 2: Transfers to Relatives Can Be Made Without Restriction or Approval Notwithstanding Any Other Provision in This Agreement**

WORKSHEET

Turn to your worksheet. If you are interested in allowing owners to give away their ownership interests to their relatives freely, not subject to a Right of First Refusal, check this option on your worksheet now. (Section II, Option 2.)

Using Absolute Transfer Restrictions

Just saying "no" to the possibility of all ownership transfers, including gifts and sales to outsiders and current owners, is another way that owners can keep control of company ownership. But we don't recommend this all-or-nothing approach. Not only is it inflexible, but it also doesn't reasonably balance the needs of an individual owner who wants or needs to transfer ownership with those of the continuing owners who want to stay.

A complete ban on the transfer of ownership interests would prevent all owners from selling, gifting, or otherwise transferring their interests (unless, of course, their co-owners agree to change or ignore the ban later).

A similar clause that can have the same effect—called No Transfers Without Consent—would require an owner to get the approval of the other co-owners before selling any interest to an outsider, gifting it to relatives, or making other transfers. No question, either of these provisions gives a lot of power to the other owners; they really can "just say no" to the owner who wants to sell, without even having to buy the interest. (At least with the Right-of-First-Refusal clause, discussed above, the continuing owners have to fork out some cash to stop a transfer, meaning it's less likely they'll disallow a sale on a whim.) One nasty result of a No-Transfers-Without-Consent clause may be that the majority owners withhold their consent to a sale and then pressure a minority owner to sell their ownership interest to the company or to them at an unfairly low price.

Here's an example of what such a clause would look like.

☐ **No Transfers Without Consent**

No owner shall sell, transfer, or in any way dispose of any of his or her ownership interest or any right or interest in the company without obtaining prior written consent of the company and of all other owners.

A restriction that provides a little more flexibility is a clause that provides for Transfers to Qualified Buyers Only. Here, transfers to certain qualified buyers are allowed, and you and your co-owners have the opportunity to define the term "qualified buyer" in advance in your buyout agreement. For example, your agreement could require a potential buyer to hold a license for a particular profession or have a certain number of years of experience in your particular field.

While this restriction protects the nontransferring owners from having to share management with an obviously unqualified person, most business owners feel that it doesn't offer them adequate protection because it doesn't give them a way to stop a sale to a new owner for other reasons.

Here's an example of what such a clause would look like.

☐ **Transfers to Qualified Buyers Only**

No owner shall sell, transfer, or in any way dispose of any of his or her ownership interest or any right or interest in the company except to a buyer or other proposed transferee who has [*insert qualifications, such as "five years' full-time experience in selling real estate"*].

The opposite of this restriction is a No-Transfers-to-Certain-Persons clause. Typical uses of this type of provision would be to prohibit a sale to a competitor, to any existing owner who would then own a greater-than-50% ownership interest, or to any buyer whose purchase would jeopardize a key tax election or violate state law. For example, if your company is an S corporation, you may prohibit a sale to a non-U.S. citizen, a corporation, an LLC, or a partnership, all of whose ownership would terminate S corporation tax treatment. This type of restriction is normally legal as long as you do not prohibit transfers to outsiders based on discriminatory criteria such as a buyer's race or sex.

Here's an example of what such a clause would look like.

☐ **No Transfers to Certain Persons**

No owner shall sell, transfer, or in any way dispose of any of his or her ownership interest or any right or interest in the company to a buyer or other proposed transferee who is [*insert restricted class, such as "an existing owner who would, after such transfer, own 50% or more of the company"*].

CAUTION

These transfer restrictions are not included in our buyout agreement. Since we remain unconvinced that these clauses provide flexible and intelligent solutions for controlling the ownership of small companies, we do not include the three transfer restrictions discussed above in our agreement. (We believe the Right-of-First-Refusal clause does a balanced job of restricting ownership in most cases.) In addition, in at least some states, courts have refused to enforce such strict prohibitions on the sale of ownership interests. If you are nevertheless interested in using one of the clauses, get the advice of a small business lawyer or other expert before you do so. We cover finding expert help in Chapter 10. ●

Providing the Right to Force Buyouts

Over the course of its business life, your company will probably experience a few bumps in the road, and maybe even a pothole or two. Many of the unwelcome jounces will involve the business itself, such as problems with sales, employees, or product quality. But often the most troublesome shocks will occur when an owner's personal situation changes. In this chapter we look at some of the common life changes that can upset any business, and we discuss ways your buyout agreement can be structured to cope with such predictable upheaval.

Changes in an Owner's Circumstances

In Chapter 2, we discussed how a buyout agreement can control or prevent an owner from selling, giving away, or otherwise transferring an ownership interest. In this chapter, we discuss how a buyout agreement can regulate the transfer of ownership when certain events occur that can upset the functioning of a closely managed company. These events typically include the retirement, disability, divorce, bankruptcy, or death of an owner.

The Problem

Changes in one owner's circumstances will affect the business as a whole. For example, what will happen if an owner becomes disabled or loses his needed vocational license? Or, what if the owner retires from active work or simply wants to leave the company? The fortunes of all owners of the company will no doubt be affected.

Other events, like an owner's divorce, death, or personal bankruptcy, can cause the owner's business interest to be transferred to an outsider. These events can be traumatic, for both the affected owner and the company as a whole. For instance, if an owner gets divorced, the ex-spouse might receive half of an ownership interest as part of the divorce settlement, or, if an owner files for bankruptcy, the bankruptcy trustee might take over the ownership interest.

Or, if you are the owner who wants to leave the company or can no longer actively work in the company, you'll no doubt want a way to convert your ownership interest to cash.

Sometimes these changes or buyouts are handled in a collegial fashion even without a buyout agreement, with the company or continuing co-owners simply agreeing to buy out the share of the departing owner (or his estate), and the departing owner (or his estate) agreeing to sell out at a fair price. But it's more common that co-owners, or the company and a deceased co-owner's family members, don't see eye to eye. For example, a retiring owner, an inheriting son, or an ex-spouse who receives a partial ownership interest during divorce may demand a price for the ownership interest that is much higher than its market value.

Bickering over the terms of a buyout, or even whether one should occur, can use up a lot of the company's important time and, should lawyers become involved, money. Such disputes can also weaken bonds between ongoing owners and even lead to the failure of a company. In these cases and others like them, a lot of grief can be avoided if the owners can simply turn to their buyout agreement to force a buyout at a preestablished price.

The Solution

When a disruption occurs, the company or the continuing co-owners usually want to readjust the ownership of the company to restore it to something closer to what it was before the change in circumstances upset the status quo. For instance, in the case where an ownership interest is transferred to an ex-spouse or a bankruptcy trustee, the company or co-owners will no doubt want the right to buy back that interest, to be able to restore control to the original owners of the company.

Similarly, should an owner no longer be able to work, perhaps because he has become disabled, lost his license, or retired early, the company or continuing co-owners will probably want the right to buy out his interest, to keep control of the company in the hands of active owners.

In these situations, your buyout agreement can allow the company and continuing owners to force a departing owner to sell out. This option, called an "Option to Purchase an Owner's Interest," gives your company and its owners the right to purchase an ownership interest from an owner or her estate or her family members. Here, the company and the continuing owners have the right, but not the obligation, to purchase all or part of a departing owner's interest within a certain time period, at the price and terms that are preestablished in the buyout agreement.

On the other hand, if you are the owner who wants to leave the company or can no longer actively work in the company, you will probably want to be able to force the company or your co-owners to buy you out. (We look at the pros and cons of this for each circumstance—retirement, death, divorce, disability—below.) In any of these cases, your buyout agreement can allow a departing owner to force a buyout by the company or the continuing owners—called a "Right to Force a Sale." This option *requires* the company or its owners to buy out an ownership interest from an owner or her family members, if the departing owner or her family members make the request. When the departing owner demands that the company or the continuing owners buy his ownership interest, within a certain time period the company or the continuing owners must purchase the departing owner's interest, at the price and terms that are preestablished in the agreement.

Our forced buyout provisions provide that, in any potential buyout situation, either the company or the continuing owners may buy a departing owner's interest. In Chapter 4, we discuss the procedure for deciding who the buyer will be: the company or the continuing owners. We also discuss the pros and cons—mainly tax advantages and disadvantages—that will affect that decision. For now, just understand that it's a determination that will be made at the time of a buyout by the company and the continuing owners.

Common Scenarios

While all sorts of specific events can trigger or call for a change in the ownership of a company, a few broad scenarios are most likely to affect small businesses. In the rest of this chapter, we consider the most common types of business-disrupting events, discuss the various ownership transition issues that arise with each one, and present the ways to provide for forced buyouts.

Of course, as you read this material, you'll want to think about the ownership transition problems that are most likely to occur in your company. Then, as you prepare your buyout agreement, you'll want to be sure you address not only the several types of ownership transition problems likely to be faced by lots of small businesses, but also the specific issues that concern you. Remember, you can include any or all of our clauses and options as is or custom tailor them to fit your situation. Now let's jump into the scenarios that can cause business disruptions and discuss possible solutions for each.

Advice for Majority Owners

Most of our advice is aimed at companies that were started by several people owning roughly equal percentages. But when a majority owner runs the business along with one or more small minority owners, things change a bit. A majority owner may not want to be subject to the same restrictions that the minority owners are subject to. And, indeed, there is no rule that says all owners must be treated alike in a buyout agreement (except when used to minimize estate taxes—we discuss special requirements of buyout agreements regarding estate taxes in "Estate Tax Issues" in Chapter 9).

For instance, a majority owner may want her children, but not the minority owners' children, to be able to take over the business after her death. In that case, she wouldn't want the company or the remaining owners to be able to force her children to sell their interest subject to an Option-to-Purchase provision. (We discuss this scenario in "If an Owner Dies," below.)

If you are a majority owner and don't want to be restricted under a certain provision, you can add a sentence at the end of any forced buyout provision saying: "This section applies only to owners of less than 50% of the interests in the company." (Note that if you do this, your agreement cannot set the value of the ownership interests for estate tax purposes. We discuss setting the value for estate tax purposes in "Estate Tax Issues" in Chapter 9.)

As a majority owner, you might also want to consult a small business lawyer before signing a buy-sell agreement to ensure that you don't give up important elements of control unintentionally and unnecessarily.

If an Owner Retires or Stops Working

At a time when some people hope to retire early and others want to work well past middle age but will change fields several times over their lifetime, it's common for an owner to retire, move on, or simply stop working for your company. A buyout agreement can both protect the continuity of the company and advance the departing owner's exit strategy.

Option to Purchase a Departing Owner's Interest

Most, but not all, of the time, an owner who wants to leave will also want to take his marbles (cash) with him—usually by having the company or the continuing owners buy out his interest.

The Problem

Sometimes an active owner (as opposed to a passive investor) who wants to retire or stop working for the company will want to retain all or part of his ownership stake. In some situations this may be just what the continuing owners want, since this allows them to keep the departing owner's capital in the business; they don't have to come up with money for a buyout. But in other situations, the remaining owners may not like this arrangement, reasoning that they don't want a passive investor to reap the benefits of their continuing hard work to increase the value of the company.

Consider what might happen if a departing owner stops working for your business under less-than-amicable circumstances and is poised to make trouble for management. Even if circumstances are initially friendly, tensions may eventually arise between the active owners, who may be working long hours to build up the company, and an inactive owner, who may still want to have a say in things and retain her right to a share of the profits.

> **EXAMPLE:** Andromache and Eddie leave their management positions at a large software company to form a small custom-programming shop (Scripts Are Us). They convince a programmer, Mark, to work with them by offering him a minority

interest in the new company. After two years, during which Scripts Are Us is modestly successful, Mark and the majority owners no longer see eye to eye on product development issues. As a result, Mark quits to follow his own dreams.

In the absence of a buyout agreement, Mark can—and does—refuse to sell his minority interest to Andromache and Eddie, apparently believing that even though they are not as farsighted as he is, Scripts Are Us is likely to enjoy a profitable future. Unfortunately, Mark doesn't go quietly into the night. Instead, Mark's continual kibitzing becomes a constant annoyance to Andromache and Eddie, who particularly resent his periodic demands to inspect the company's books. Finally, after several nasty spats at shareholders meetings over the reinvestment of profits, Mark brings a lawsuit against Andromache and Eddie, claiming they have breached their "fiduciary duty to him as a minority shareholder."

No question that Andromache, Eddie, and Mark would have been far better off if, at the time their business was formed, they'd adopted a buyout agreement covering the eventuality that one of them might cease to be active in the business.

One thing is sure: It's hard to know how one owner's deciding to retire or quit will be viewed in the future. A lot will probably depend on whether the departing owner and the remaining owners are on good personal terms. But just because you can't predict the future doesn't mean you shouldn't prepare for it by providing options in the buyout agreement.

The Solution

On balance it's usually best to provide that when an owner quits her active duties, whether as an officer or employee, the company and the continuing owners have the *option* to purchase that owner's interest—in other words, to force the departing owner to sell them the ownership interest. Such a provision doesn't *obligate* the company or the continuing owners to purchase the departing owner's interest, but it gives them the option to decide what to do in the future. Our agreement allows the company and continuing owners to buy any or all of the departing owner's interest. For example, if the company and continuing owners can afford to buy only half of the departing owner's interest, they can do so.

We include a clause that provides for this in our buyout agreement. It's called an "Option to Purchase" clause, and it is shown below.

WORKSHEET

Turn to your worksheet. If you are interested in giving the company and the continuing owners the option to buy a departing owner's interest, check Option 1 on your worksheet now. (Section III, Scenario 1.)

Section III: Providing the Right to Force Buyouts

Scenario 1.   When an Active Owner Retires or
**   Quits the Company's Employ**

You may check Option 1 and/or Option 2 (or neither) below.

Check Option 1, below, if you want the company and continuing owners to have the option to buy a retiring owner's interest.

☐   **Option 1:   Option of Company and Continuing Owners to**
**   Purchase a Retiring Owner's Interest**

(a)   When an owner voluntarily retires or quits the company's employ, he or she is deemed to have offered his or her ownership interest to the company and the continuing owners for sale. The company and the continuing owners shall then have an option, but not an obligation (unless otherwise stated in this agreement), to purchase all or part of the ownership interest within the time and according to the procedure in Section IV, Provision 1 of this agreement. The price to be paid, the manner of payments and other terms of the purchase shall be according to Sections VI and VII of this agreement. An owner who stops working for the company is referred to as a "retiring owner" below.

CAUTION

Not for silent investors. If your company is owned by both inactive, "silent" investors and actively participating owners, this buyout option may not suit your needs. (If an investor was not working in the first place, retirement should not change his situation with regard to the company.) Since most of our advice is tailored to small businesses where the owners are active in the business, we don't deal in detail with the special needs (or problems) of "silent" investors. If you face this situation, be sure to have an attorney look over your agreement. We cover finding expert help in Chapter 10.

Right of Departing Owner to Force a Sale

Rather than having trouble forcing a departing owner to sell out, it's far more likely that, when a co-owner decides to leave a business, she'll be anxious to sell her interest, either to an outsider or back to the company or the continuing owners. Assuming she has no luck finding an outsider to buy her interest, she'll probably approach the company and the continuing owners.

In this situation, the question often becomes: Can departing owners force the continuing owners to purchase their share of the business? As you've probably guessed, the answer is: not unless there is an agreement requiring it.

In the absence of an agreement, sometimes the company or the continuing owners will be happy to buy the departing owner out—perhaps the company is now quite profitable and the remaining owners will be pleased to increase their shares. Or, perhaps the departing owner is leaving precisely because she wasn't getting along with the other owners and they're glad to see her go, even if it means they have to pay her for her share of the company. In these and other workable circumstances, an ownership buyout is normally a fairly straightforward situation. Once the deal is done, it's business as usual with one less owner.

The Problem

It's not always so simple. What if the remaining owners don't want to, or can't afford to, buy a departing partner out? Before you adopt a buyout provision that will deal with this situation, you and your co-owners should ask yourselves a simple question: Do you want an owner (who, after all, could be any of you) to be able to force the company and the continuing owners to buy her interest if she decides to leave?

Especially if you're a minority owner, your answer is likely to be yes. It can be hard enough to sell a majority interest in a small business, but it can be next to impossible to sell a minority stake—or even a 50% share.

EXAMPLE: Luis and Marta are equal partners in a successful burrito shop that caters to the business lunch crowd. After a few years of long hours and hard work, Marta decides she wants to sell her interest to Luis and get a job where she can work shorter hours and spend more time with her kids. Luis, who feels personally abandoned, is reluctant to further stretch his already tight finances and is worried about competition from a new deli that is about to open in the area. He shrugs and says he's not interested in buying Marta's interest. Since she and Luis didn't sign a buyout agreement, Marta has to search for an outside buyer. She hires a business broker and spends money advertising, but finds out that no one wants to buy only half of a burrito shop. Potential buyers want the whole enchilada or nothing. After looking for a buyer for months, Marta finally ends up selling her share to Luis's cousin for far less than it was worth.

To avoid this, departing owners can be allowed to force a buyback of their interests. But this does give owners full leeway in deciding if and when to leave the business. Personal flexibility may not necessarily be a good thing for your company or for the owners who are left behind when one owner quits. Leaving aside the fact that it may weaken all owners' commitment to their company, it creates the real possibility that one or more owners will demand to be cashed out precisely at a time when the company is doing poorly or needs every bit of its cash for another purpose, such as expansion.

Recognizing that a forced buyout may be highly problematic, you may decide to head in the opposite direction and say that a departing owner can never force the company or other owners to buy him out. But, of course, that brings you right back to the worry you started with: the possibility of getting stuck forever owning a share of a business you no longer want, or selling your share at a huge discount because you're so desperate to get out. This prospect is so unattractive—and potentially unfair—that it can lead to horrendous results.

EXAMPLE: Dakon and Jed each contribute $20,000 of their savings to open a climbing gear store in Colorado. To purchase inventory and cover other start-up costs, they also take out a bank loan. From the start, they are successful enough to pay the bills and eke out small salaries, but not much else. Near the end of the first year, Dakon tells Jed he wants out of the business and would like his $20,000 back—running a business, it turns out, doesn't give him enough time to hit the peaks. Jed can't figure out a way to give Dakon his investment back without selling off badly needed inventory at fire sale prices (and perhaps having to close the shop). Refusing to do this, he tells Dakon that he can't take his money out of the business so soon and on such short notice. This angers Dakon—after all, he has worked hard at low pay for almost a year! So one night Dakon grabs what he guesses is $20,000 worth of climbing gear from the store, loads it into his Jeep, and takes off. On the counter he leaves a note saying that the store now belongs 100% to Jed. Left with inadequate inventory, Jed can't pay the store's debts and has to file for bankruptcy. Of course, Jed may have a claim against Dakon, but with Dakon off climbing mountains in Chile, Jed is unlikely to collect anything.

The Solution

One way to deal with this situation is to include a buyout provision that requires either the company or its remaining owners to buy out an owner who wants to leave. This type of clause—we call it a "Right-to-Force-a-Sale" clause—can protect a departing co-owner (who, after all, might be leaving as the result of personal or financial distress) by guaranteeing a buyer for his ownership interest.

The financial effects of a required buyout on the company can be buffered by providing disincentives to leaving early, by requiring advance notice of a departure, and by using installment plans. This way an owner who leaves prematurely can get back at least some of his investment, without bankrupting the company.

Financial disincentives. Your Right-to-Force-a-Sale clause can require the company to buy out an owner at full price only when he has been an active owner in the company two or three years or more. If the owner leaves before the expiration of the required time period, the company will be required to buy him out only at a discounted price (say, 50% of the business's appraised value). This makes it clear to the owners that, by going into business, they are making a financial commitment to stick it out until the business becomes profitable—if they don't, they may lose all or part of their investment.

EXAMPLE: Let's rewind our cameras and give Jed and Dakon a legal framework designed to cope with change. Knowing that Dakon is highly susceptible to the call of the wild, early on Jed raises the subject of what would happen if one of them becomes unhappy with the business and wants out. They jointly decide that to get the business past its start-up pains, each must make a minimum two-year commitment. To enforce this point, they adopt a buyout provision stating that if one of them decides to leave during the first year, the other will buy him out at a price that is 40% of the standard buyout price set in the agreement (the "Agreement Price," discussed in Chapter 6). If one of them leaves during year two, he will get 60% of the Agreement Price. Only if a co-owner stays with the business into the third year is he eligible to force a purchase at 100% of the full Agreement Price.

The good news is that Dakon, realizing he is committed, hangs in for almost three years, at which point Jed has no trouble borrowing part of the money to buy Dakon's share for 100% of the Agreement Price; the rest he pays Dakon in installments over three years.

TIP

Choosing the required time period. The length of time you require for a departing owner to receive 100% of the Agreement Price can vary with your type of business. For example, if yours is the type of business that requires a high initial investment and is likely to take four or more years to fully establish, you may want to pay a departing owner 100% of her interest's value only after four years.

There are, of course, times when an owner really needs to leave and be cashed out, as opposed to simply wanting to bail out to do something else. For example, an owner with a sick child may need to move closer to a particular medical center, or an owner whose own health is declining may be advised to quit working. In situations like these, should the departing owner be subject to the same penalty discounts that would apply to an owner who leaves his spouse and runs off to the Cayman Islands? If your answer is no, you can provide that an owner who leaves for a short list of personal or family reasons is entitled to a better deal than an owner who leaves on a whim.

> **EXAMPLE:** Let's rewind one more time. Dakon and Jed are running their climbing gear business with a solid buyout agreement in place that outlines what will happen if one of them leaves the business. Dakon learns that his elderly mother has severe multiple sclerosis. He decides he has to move back east to help out his parents. Even though he and Jed have only been in business less than a year, Dakon points out that in case of a serious illness of a co-owner's spouse, child, or parent, their agreement provides that a departing owner is entitled to 100% of the Agreement Price for his interest.

The "Right-to-Force-a-Sale" clause included in our buy-sell agreement is shown below. Note that our Right-to-Force-a-Sale provision does not allow a departing owner to require the company and the continuing owners to buy just a portion of her interest. A departing owner can request only that the company and continuing owners buy all of her interest or none of it.

☐ **Option 2: Right of Retiring Owner to Force a Sale**

(a) When an owner voluntarily retires or quits the company's employ, he or she can require the company and the continuing owners to buy all, but not less than all, of his or her ownership interest by delivering to the company at least 60 days before his or her departure a notice of intention to force a sale ("Notice of Intent to Force a Sale"). The notice shall include the date of departure, the name and address of the owner, a description and amount of the owner's interest in the company and a statement that the owner wishes to force a sale due to the owner's retirement as provided in this provision. The procedure for purchase of the ownership interest shall be according to Section IV, Provision 2 of this agreement. The price to be paid, the manner of payments and other terms of the purchase shall be according to this section and Sections VI and VII of this agreement. An owner who requests that his interest be purchased is referred to as a "retiring owner" below.

WORKSHEET

Turn to your worksheet. If you are interested in giving a departing owner the power to force a sale of her interest to the company and the continuing owners, check Option 2 on your worksheet now. (Section III, Scenario 1.) You can include both Option 1 and Option 2 for departing owners in your agreement. It's possible, and perfectly valid, to include both Option 1—the option for the company and continuing owners to buy out a departing owner—and Option 2—a departing owner's right to force a sale—in your agreement.

The language included in our buyout agreement that gives you a choice of disincentive options, one with an illness/injury release and one without, is shown below.

(b) Disincentive option

☐ **Option 2a: Disincentive period, with illness/injury exception**

If a retiring owner gives notice that he or she wishes his or her ownership interest to be bought before the end of [*insert number of months, such as "24"*] months of ownership of the company, he or she is entitled to receive only [*insert percentage, such as "50"*]% of the Agreement Price for the sale of ownership interests in this company under this agreement, unless he or she is required to leave because of serious personal illness or injury or the serious illness or injury of a spouse, parent or child, in which case he or she is entitled to 100% of the Agreement Price.

☐ **Option 2b: Disincentive period, without illness/injury exception**

If a retiring owner gives notice that he or she wishes his or her ownership interest to be bought before the end of [*insert number of months, such as "24"*] months of ownership of the company, he or she is entitled to receive only [*insert percentage, such as "50"*] of the Agreement Price for the sale of ownership interests in this company under this agreement.

WORKSHEET

Turn to your worksheet. If you want a departing owner to receive a discounted price if he leaves within a certain time period for any reason, check Option 2a on your worksheet. (Section III, Scenario 1, Option 2.) If you want a departing owner to receive a discounted price if he leaves within a certain time period, *unless he is leaving because of a personal or family illness or injury,* check Option 2b on your worksheet. If you check one of these options, also:

- Insert the amount of time an owner must be with the company before being able to sell out for the full Agreement Price, usually at least one or two years, maybe more.

- Insert the amount of the discount to be taken off the Agreement Price if an owner leaves before the end of the required time period.

Payment plans. Allowing a flexible payment plan, such as an installment plan, is another way to allow the company (or the continuing owners) to buy out a departing owner without threatening the survival of the company. In fact, a lengthy payment can even allow the company to pay a departing owner a higher price. You may be wondering how Jed could afford to pay Dakon 100% of the Agreement Price after being in business less than a year. The best way to accomplish a sudden buyout without bankrupting the business is to pay a departing owner in installments over several years. We cover payment plan options in Chapter 7.

When a death or disability is involved, planning to fund a buyout with insurance is also an option. We cover insurance funding in Chapter 5.

> **CAUTION**
>
> **Get released from personally guaranteed loans.** When an owner leaves the company, he should attempt to get released from loans that he has personally guaranteed. However, it may not be easy to get a bank to release the owner from a loan. In that case, the owner should insist the loan be paid off and a new loan taken out by the continuing owners, if necessary.

Advance notice. Another smart way to ease the burden of a forced buyout is to require an owner who wants to quit or retire to give the company advance notice of her intention to leave (except in the case of death or sudden illness or disability, of course). In some companies, requiring as much as a six- to 12-month advance notice is often considered reasonable. Our agreement requires a 60-day notice. This hopefully will give the remaining owners some time to take a collective deep breath and devise a plan to buy out the owner and continue the business. Of course, if you and your business partners think you'll need more notice, you can change the agreement to reflect this.

Be Ready to Customize Standard Clauses to Fit Your Situation

Throughout this book we provide options and technical language to solve common buyout situations. But because every situation contains its own nuances, you may want to tinker with our clauses and clause options to be sure your agreement fits like a custom-made glove, not a one-size-fits-all handcuff. For instance, as noted in the text, a well-drawn buyout agreement will balance the desire to protect each owner in case of personal problems with the need to protect the financial integrity of the business. We've talked about several ways to approach this balance. But only you and your co-owners know what's best for your company.

If you want to provide a market for a departing owner without overburdening the company and aren't satisfied with the options we suggest, such as requiring advance notice, financial disincentives, and a payment plan, you can create your own contractual language. For example, a customized Right-to-Force-a-Sale provision might state that the departing owner must first try to find an outside buyer who is acceptable to the other owners. Assuming no buyer comes forward after six months, your agreement could then provide that the company or the continuing owners must purchase the departing owner's interest at 40% of the full Agreement Price. This discount gives the departing owner some incentive to find an outside buyer first and lessens the immediate financial burden on the company and remaining owners.

WORKSHEET

Turn to your worksheet. If you are interested in providing for a longer notice period, make a notation on your worksheet to change this time period. (Section III, Scenario 1, Option 2, Paragraph (a).)

If an Owner Becomes Disabled

The next business-disrupting event we help you plan for is the possibility that an owner becomes disabled. Disability, of course, includes physical injuries and illnesses, but also can be caused by mental illness, such as clinical depression, Alzheimer's disease, and other forms of dementia or incapacity.

> **TIP**
>
> **Look at disability and retirement buyout clauses together.** If an owner feels he cannot work and wants to be bought out, but does not fit under a doctor's or the disability insurance company's definition of disability, arguments can arise. These conflicts can often be defused in advance if you have also adopted a clause allowing an owner to force a sale due to retirement (discussed above in "If an Owner Retires or Stops Working").

Option to Purchase a Disabled Owner's Interest

Have you considered what would happen if an owner were to develop a chronic illness, become injured, or otherwise be unable to participate in company affairs for an extended period of time? If the owner is an investor and was never involved in the day-to-day operations of the business, the answer may appropriately be "nothing"—after all, it probably makes little difference to the company whether an inactive, silent investor is or isn't disabled. But for our purposes, let's assume the owner has been active in the business and takes a salary or regular draws from it.

The Problem

There are obvious reasons why co-owners might sooner or later want to replace a disabled owner who can no longer work but takes money out of the company. Of course, after a decent interval the co-owners could stop the salary of the disabled owner (who, after all, is no longer earning it), but allow him to continue to own his share of the business. (For partnerships or LLCs, where the owner automatically draws a percentage of profits from the company, this may entail a change to the partnership agreement or LLC operating agreement, which the disabled owner might have to agree to.)

However, the co-owners of a small company may not want to share future successes and management decisions with an owner who is no longer adding anything to the company. In this situation, the co-owners might want the right to buy out the disabled owner.

Absent this right, there can be highly emotional disagreements when a disabled owner does not want to be bought out (he may even disagree as to whether he is unable to perform his duties). It is because of the debilitating nature of these disputes that you need to have a disability-triggered buyout provision in place.

EXAMPLE: George has been a partner in a printing company for ten years, along with his longtime friends Faiza and Ali. Now in his 80s, he frequently experiences significant lapses of memory. More than once his forgetfulness has led to an unfinished job, and unhappy clients have begun to whisper to Faiza and Ali that they no longer want to work with George. George admits he is sometimes forgetful, but he insists that he is fit to continue working. But when they almost lose their biggest client, Ali and Faiza face the truth that George is not mentally up to continuing to work. Since George is a general partner entitled to an annual share of the company profits, the only sensible way to stop him from receiving one-third of the company's profits is to ask him to sell out. But when confronted by Ali and Faiza, George refuses, threatening to get a lawyer. Faiza and Ali rue the day, ten years before, when they didn't, as a condition of starting the business, insist on a buy-sell agreement dealing with disability.

The Solution

Your agreement can include a clause that allows the company and the other owners to require a disabled owner (or the owner's conservator, guardian, or other legal representative) to sell the ownership interest back to the company or to the other owners on demand. This protects the continuing owners of the company from having to share management with someone who can't handle the requirements of the job, or simply from having to support that person.

Before you decide to adopt a disability provision, you'll want to ask two questions:

- Will the continuing owners be able to come up with the money to fund the buyout?
- Who will determine whether the owner is truly disabled?

Funding. Most small to midsized businesses need every penny they can scare up to maintain or expand their business—they don't have a ready store of cash to fund a buyout. One way to cope with this problem is to call for a long-term installment plan, allowing the company or continuing owners to make partial payments to a disabled owner over a number of years.

But for larger companies, especially, there is a better way to cope with this issue that doesn't make the disabled owner wait many years to be paid off for her interest. Your buy-sell agreement can require the purchase of disability insurance for all co-owners. This way, if a disability occurs, the insurance policy proceeds will provide a source of funds to allow the company or the co-owners to buy back the interest of a disabled owner without diminishing company or personal cash reserves.

If desired, additional financial benefits such as a wage continuation plan for the disabled owner can also be funded by disability policy proceeds. (We discuss using insurance to fund your agreement in more detail in Chapter 5.)

Defining disabled. A big issue you'll have to face is: When is an owner truly disabled? Does the owner decide when she can no longer work? Does the owner have to be unable to work for a few weeks? A few months? What if the owner gets better?

Our agreement specifies that the owner must be "permanently and totally disabled"—that is, unable to perform most or all of his duties for the foreseeable future. Our agreement also includes a procedure to determine when an owner is considered disabled—by using the opinion of the owner's doctor. Note: If you intend to fund a future disability buyout with disability insurance (discussed in Chapter 5), our agreement provides that the insurance company will be the arbiter of whether the co-owner really is disabled. (An added bonus of going that route is that the other owners will be relieved of the burden of supervising the disability claim and asking the disabled owner for medical evidence of a disability.)

There are several additional issues you should consider to ensure that your disability clause has the maximum chance of working well:

- **Waiting period.** You should agree on a period of time—a waiting period (or, in insurance lingo, an elimination period)—over which an owner's disability must persist before a buyout can occur. This allows for the fact that the owner might recover. We recommend that your waiting period be at least six months, or perhaps as long as a year. A buyout attempted before it's really clear that the owner probably won't recover can result in bitterness and wasted time and money if the former owner recovers in a short period of time.

  Our agreement also provides that time spent off work by an owner with a series of illnesses with the same or related causes can be added up to fulfill the waiting period requirement. Otherwise, requiring a period of *continuous* inability to work might discourage an injured or ill individual from returning to work if he's feeling better (perhaps to test whether going back to work would be feasible). Of course, if your agreement will require the purchase of a disability insurance policy to fund the agreement, your waiting period should coincide with the elimination period in the disability insurance policy.

- **Date of valuation.** You should decide when the value of the company will be determined for the purpose of a disability buyout. Your agreement specifies how the buyout price will be determined—the value of the disabled owner's interest is determined using the standard buyout price; this follows the same formula used if the co-owner quits, dies, or retires (this set price or formula is called the "Agreement Price," discussed in Chapter 6). However, "when" the price is determined is usually addressed as a separate issue in the disability provision. Here's why: There may be a significant difference in the worth of the company in between the date the owner became unable to work and the date the disability waiting period is over. Most companies use the date the owner stopped working as the date to value the business—since that is the date the owner stopped contributing to the company. This way, any changes in the worth of the company can be attributed to the remaining owners.

The disability provision included in our buy-sell agreement, which allows you to insert a waiting period and choose the date that disability is established, is shown below.

WORKSHEET

Turn to your worksheet. If you are interested in giving the company and the continuing owners the option to buy a disabled owner's interest, check Option 1 on your worksheet now (Section III, Scenario 2), and insert the amount of time an owner must be disabled before the company has the option of buying out his interest, at least six months to one year. If you check Option 1, either check Option 1a to establish the Agreement Price when the disabled owner first stops working or check Option 1b to establish the Agreement Price as of the date of the buyout.

Scenario 2. When an Owner Becomes Disabled

☐ **Option 1:   Option of Company and Continuing Owners to Purchase a Disabled Owner's Interest**

(a) When an owner becomes permanently and totally disabled, and such disability lasts at least [*insert number of months, such as "six"*] months (the "waiting period"), either consecutively or cumulatively, he or she is deemed to have offered his or her ownership interest to the company and the continuing owners for sale. The company and the continuing owners shall then have an option, but not an obligation (unless otherwise stated in this agreement), to purchase all or part of the ownership interest within the time and according to the procedure in Section IV, Provision 1 of this agreement. The price to be paid, the manner of payments and other terms of the purchase shall be according to this section and Sections V and VI of this agreement.

An owner is considered disabled when he or she is unable to perform his or her regular duties. If disability insurance is used to fund a buyout under this provision, the insurance company shall establish whether an owner is disabled; without disability insurance, the owner's doctor will establish whether an owner is disabled. An owner who becomes disabled according to this section is referred to as a "disabled owner" below.

(b) Price

☐ **Option 1a: Date disabled owner stops working**

The Agreement Price as selected in Section VI of this agreement shall be established as of the date the disabled owner first stopped working.

☐ **Option 1b: Date of buyout**

The Agreement Price as selected in Section VI of this agreement shall be established as of the date of the proposed buyout of the disabled owner's interest.

Right of Disabled Owner to Force a Sale

You may have noticed that we haven't mentioned the needs of the disabled owner himself.

The Problem

It's possible that a situation may arise where an owner becomes unable to work but the other owners don't jump to buy out the disabled owner, most likely because they don't have the necessary funds. In this situation, a disabled owner whose salary is discontinued and who does not automatically draw a percentage of profits from the company will probably be anxious to be bought out. (And even if the disabled owner remains entitled to a percentage of profits after she stops working, that draw will no doubt decrease, as the profits of a small company will likely drop soon after one of the owners stops working for it.)

> EXAMPLE: Steve is a 10% owner and employee of FastShip, Inc., a small, family-run freight-forwarding corporation, where the owners participate in the heavy lifting. After he injures his back lifting boxes, Steve's doctor says he can no longer work, so he stops getting a paycheck. (Steve, as an owner, does not have workers' compensation insurance, and FastShip, like many corporations, doesn't pay stock dividends. With the exception of a small monthly disability payment, Steve's income is now zero.) Short of cash, Steve asks his co-owners to buy him out. While sympathetic, the other owners had just made a personal loan to the business (which has been struggling) to purchase new timesaving electrical lifting equipment. They tell Steve that neither they nor the company itself can afford to buy Steve out for at least two years. Steve can't find an outside buyer for his shares and is stuck keeping an interest in a company that produces no dividends and that he can no longer work for.

To avoid being locked into a business in whose profits they can no longer participate or depend on, many owners want an exit strategy: a buyout provision that guarantees a buyer for their ownership interest in case they become disabled.

The Solution

Steve, from the above example, would have been much better off if he and the other owners had created a buyout agreement at the outset that required the company or co-owners to buy out a disabled owner, using policy proceeds from mandatory disability insurance. Fortunately, your buyout agreement can do this with a "Right to Force a Sale" clause that's very similar to the "Option to Purchase a Disabled Owner's Interest" clause we just discussed above. This provision provides some security for a disabled owner who no longer works for the company.

The Right-to-Force-a-Sale disability provision in our buyout agreement is shown below. Note that this provision does not allow a disabled owner to require the company or the continuing owners to buy just a portion of his ownership interest. A disabled owner can request only that the company and continuing owners buy all of her interest.

WORKSHEET

Turn to your worksheet. If you would like to give a disabled owner the right to force the company or continuing owners to buy her interest, check Option 2 on your worksheet now (Section III, Scenario 2), and insert the amount of time an owner must be disabled before the owner can force a sale. If you check Option 2, either check Option 2a to establish the Agreement Price when the disabled owner first stops working or check Option 2b to establish the Agreement Price as of the date of the buyout.

CAUTION

Not for silent investors. If your company is owned by both inactive, silent investors and actively participating owners, this buyout option may not suit your needs. (If an investor was not working in the first place, disability should not necessarily give him the right to force a buyout of his interest.) Again, since most of our advice is tailored to small businesses where the owners are active in the business, we don't deal in detail with the special needs of investors. If you face this situation, be sure to have an attorney look over your agreement. We cover finding expert help in Chapter 10.

Scenario 2. When an Owner Becomes Disabled

☐ **Option 2: Right of Disabled Owner to Force a Sale**

(a) When an owner becomes permanently and totally disabled, and such disability lasts at least [*insert number of months, such as "six"*] months (the "waiting period"), either consecutively or cumulatively, he or she can require the company and the continuing owners to buy all, but not less than all, of his or her ownership interest by delivering to the company within 30 days of the expiration of the waiting period, a notice of intention to force a sale ("Notice of Intent to Force a Sale") in writing. The notice shall include the name and address of the owner, a description and amount of the owner's interest in the company, and a statement that the owner wishes to force a sale due to disability as provided in this provision. The procedure for purchase of the ownership interest shall be according to Section IV, Provision 2 of this agreement. The price to be paid, the manner of payments, and other terms of the purchase shall be according to this section and Sections VI and VII of this agreement.

An owner is considered disabled when he or she is unable to perform his or her regular duties. If disability insurance is used to fund a buyout under this provision, the insurance company shall establish whether an owner is disabled; without disability insurance, the owner's doctor will establish whether an owner is disabled. An owner who becomes disabled according to this section is referred to as a "disabled owner" below.

(b) Price

☐ **Option 2a: Date disabled owner stops working**

The Agreement Price as selected in Section VI of this agreement shall be established as of the date the disabled owner first stopped working.

☐ **Option 2b: Date of buyout**

The Agreement Price as selected in Section VI of this agreement shall be established as of the date of the proposed buyout of the disabled owner's interest.

For a discussion of how disability is defined, how the waiting period before a buyout will be triggered, the valuing of the ownership interest, and the funding of a disability buyout, see the discussion under "Option to Purchase a Disabled Owner's Interest," above.

> **TIP**
>
> **Possible overlap between clauses is not a problem.** A disabled owner may, of course, decide to retire. Thus, there could be situations where, if you include in your buy-sell agreement a Right-to-Force-a-Sale clause for both departing owners and disabled owners, a disabled owner could use either provision. Which one would he use? Undoubtedly, whichever clause has more generous terms. It follows that if you decide to include one or more buyout clauses, you'll want to be sure they fit well together. For instance, many companies choose to give the company and continuing owners an option to purchase a departing owner's interest, give a disabled owner the right to force a sale, and allow a departing owner to force a sale only if the owner has worked for the company for a minimum number of years.

If an Owner Dies

Do not skip this section. Even if you and your co-owners are all young and in radiant health, it's crucial to deal with the possibility that one of you will die. What happens in case of an owner's death may be the most important scenario you can include in your buyout agreement.

The death of a co-owner, especially one who is an active manager or worker, is sure to be extremely traumatic for your business, both emotionally and economically. First, you will lose the services of a central player and worker (and probably a friend). And if the owner was someone your customers highly regarded (common in a service business), you'll face the real possibility of a business meltdown. And, even if you keep your business together, you'll need to cope with the fundamental fact that someone else will have control over your former co-owner's interest after her death.

This raises a key question: Who will own the deceased owner's share? Right after an owner's death, her interest will be part of her estate (along with all other property she owned at death). If the deceased co-owner left her business interest to an inheritor under the terms of a will, a personal representative or executor (named by the will or by the court) will manage the estate through a lengthy probate process before it is eventually transferred to the inheritor. If the owner put the interest into a probate-avoiding living trust before she died, the interest will be promptly transferred to whoever is named to receive it in the trust (absent a buy-sell agreement).

RELATED TOPIC

Interested in trusts? Probate-avoidance living trusts are discussed in "Transferring an Interest to a Trust" in Chapter 2.

Business succession. Whether an owner of a small business leaves her interest by will or is wise enough to use a probate-avoiding living trust, the end result is that the surviving owners are faced with the specter of sharing management duties and profits of the company with new owners—the inheritors of the deceased owner's interest. If the deceased owner was married or had children, the inheritors would likely be his spouse and children. If not, the inheritors would likely be his parents or possibly a domestic partner. These people may be inexperienced, uninterested, immature, or even destructive—or they may be a perfect fit for the company.

Surviving owners who find themselves in this situation have several options. They can:

- welcome the deceased owner's inheritors into the company and share the work, control, and profits with them
- accept the inheritors as silent, nonworking owners—potentially giving them a free ride if the business prospers
- negotiate with the inheritors to convince them to sell their interest
- negotiate with the inheritors to convince them to buy the rest of the company, or
- liquidate the business.

If these options haven't been discussed—and a clear plan enshrined in a buyout agreement—beforehand, tensions can arise as the new owners and the old owners discuss the future of the company. If arguments turn nasty, resulting in business owners' losing focus on continuing operations, the company's business and reputation can suffer, sometimes even causing the business to fail.

Family businesses. If yours is truly a family business, your first thought may be, "Well, of course my family will inherit and hold on to my share of the business." Not so fast. This is an issue you should discuss in depth with your co-owners and your family. Co-owners should frankly talk about whose kids, if anyone's, will be welcome to work in the business when one of you retires or dies. You may well conclude that unless one of your kids already works in the business and has been fully accepted by your co-owners, it's best to provide that no owners' kids are guaranteed a spot.

As part of having this discussion, here are some key questions you and each of your co-owners will want to answer:

- Do your adult children want to take over your position in the company? Have they shown any interest in the company? Do they have any knowledge of the business?
- Who do you want to have most control and management of the company? The existing owners? Your inheritors?
- If you want your inheritors to retain their interest in the company and succeed you, will they really be able to do the work you now do? When? If not now, who will run the company in the meantime, until your inheritors have the maturity and skills to take over?
- Do you want your business partners' inheritors to be able to fill their shoes? Do you want the right to say "yes, they can" or "no, they can't" or "only under these conditions"?

EXAMPLE: Mike and his co-owners informally discuss their company's future when Mike is 45 years old. Mike gets his co-owners to agree that his son, Josh, will eventually take over his ownership interest and his management duties when he retires at age 55. But Mike dies suddenly of a heart attack at age 50, when Josh has just started college. Josh and his father's surviving co-owners agree that he is not ready to take over the business. But Josh wants to hold on to his interest until he graduates, at which point he'll join the company. The surviving owners, however, don't want to have to share profits with Josh while he finishes his education, and they aren't so sure they want him to take over his father's role with no real-life business experience. To try to head off the problem, they offer Josh a generous lump-sum payment to sell out. Josh says, "No way. I want to join the company." Without a buy-sell agreement, the surviving owners can't *force* Josh to sell. Eventually relations between Josh and the other owners deteriorate to the point where they decide to liquidate the company and go their separate ways.

Luckily, it's possible to use your buy-sell agreement to create appropriate tools to manage what happens when an owner dies. Any owner who wants to give his business a decent chance to succeed after he dies should work with his co-owners to create and fund a sensible succession strategy. Decisions that are well thought out, made beforehand, and recorded in a buyout agreement can really help avoid delays, financial problems, and conflicts.

There are two sides to what your buyout agreement can provide for after the death of an owner: (1) If one owner should die, and the owners hadn't previously agreed that the deceased owner's children or other relatives would succeed him, then the continuing owners are likely to want to be able to buy the deceased owner's interest from his estate; (2) If you were to die unexpectedly, undoubtedly you would want your spouse or children (technically, your estate) to be able to ask and expect the continuing owners to buy your share from them. Let's look at both sides of the equation.

Option to Purchase a Deceased Owner's Interest

Whether yours is a family business or not, it's sometimes not easy to decide who will continue the company when you or a co-owner dies: the surviving co-owners or the deceased owner's inheritors or a combination of both.

The Problem

Conflicts are almost inevitable during business ownership transitions. When an inheritor steps into a deceased owner's shoes, especially if she doesn't plan to take an active part in the company, it's likely that her view of the business will differ from that of the other owners.

New owners' needs. The new owner(s) may want to:

- receive cash to pay for estate or state inheritance taxes and administrative expenses
- not work due to lack of experience, age, ability, or desire
- influence decision making to protect or further their interests
- maximize the profits allocated to them as owner, and/or
- sell their interests to outsiders for cash.

Surviving owners' needs. The surviving owners may want to:

- keep control of the company to themselves
- share ownership only with those who actively work in the business
- maintain or increase their salaries, and/or
- reinvest earnings and profits in the company rather than distributing them to the new owners.

In addition to these potential problem areas, there is also the possibility that an inheritor and one or more of the surviving owners simply won't like each other.

Or, even if both sides like each other fine and have unselfish interests, there just may not be enough money to go around. Let's take a look at how problems can arise even in relatively amicable circumstances.

EXAMPLE: Jack and Chris, brothers and good friends, went into the sporting goods business years ago as partners of a retail store, sharing the profits equally. They put in long hours both in the store and behind the scenes, buying inventory and keeping the books. Jack married his high school sweetheart and had three kids, while Chris never married.

One night as he is locking up, Jack suffers a stroke and dies. Luckily, Jack had some life insurance. But it's not even close to enough to support his family indefinitely. Jack's wife, Pat, imagines continuing to own Jack's share of the shop and tells Chris how much she'll need to draw against her share of the profits to take care of herself and her kids. Since this amount is almost as much as Jack was receiving in salary, Pat is essentially proposing that she receive close to 50% of the company's profits without doing any work. Chris, who is very close to his sister-in-law and nieces and nephew and wants to do right by them, nevertheless knows the company can't operate along the lines Pat proposes, given the fact that Chris will have to hire someone to take Jack's place.

Family Succession Agreements

Let's expend a little ink looking at the special problems that the transition of family businesses often brings up. Although it happens less and less these days, some readers of this book may be interested in having their inheritors continue as owners. (In fact, while about half of family business owners plan on a family member continuing the business, this only works out a small percentage of the time.)

First, if you really want your children to succeed you, you need to plan for the smooth transition of your ownership interest—in writing. Unfortunately, family members are often touchy about making formal agreements with each other—some families wrongly believe that a written agreement is a badge of dysfunction. As a result, family businesses are often run on the basis of oral promises and informal understandings that have never been formalized. But when the tension produced by the death of a key person arises, this is almost always a recipe for disaster!

Second, it is crucial that you select inheritors who are willing, and able, to succeed you. If there's any doubt that an inheritor won't be able to take over for you right away, you might want to choose an interim successor, such as a long-term employee or a trustee, who can keep the business running smoothly until your inheritor can take over.

Third, if you have more than one child, it's important not to confuse your desire to split up your estate fairly with the fact that only one of them may be equipped to run the business. Here's one possible approach: If you want to leave equal inheritances for your children, but not all of them are interested in working in and running the business, consider leaving the business to the children who are active in it and buying life insurance of equal value for the others. (You should buy insurance for this purpose early, rather than waiting until you are in your 60s or 70s, when it might be too expensive.) Alternatively, your buyout agreement can provide for the business-minded child to buy the ownership interests from your other inheritors after your death—but for this to be enforceable, all of your inheritors must sign the agreement.

Without a formal legal structure for business succession, co-owners, successors, and siblings have been known to get into battles over money and control.

The idea is to have a plan in place that allows the surviving owners of the company to make sensible decisions fair to all at the time of an owner's death, because when an owner dies, the surviving owners of the company—not the inheritors—are probably best equipped to make a decision about the company's future.

The Solution

For the reasons mentioned above, most savvy business owners have their buyout agreement provide the company and the surviving co-owners with the option to buy a deceased owner's interest from his estate or trust. Normally, such a provision states that when an owner dies, the company and the surviving owners have the right to buy the interest from the executor of the estate (or the trustee of a trust) that holds the ownership interest. This clause is referred to as an "Option to Purchase a Deceased Owner's Interest." Of course, under this type of provision, the surviving owners have the discretion to decide not to buy the interest, if they feel they can work well with any inheritors who evince an interest in participating in the business.

> **EXAMPLE:** Remember Jack and Chris, the two brothers who co-owned a sporting goods store before Jack died suddenly, leaving a wife, Pat, and their children behind? Let's keep the facts the same, except that this time Jack and Chris had the wisdom to adopt a buyout agreement. When Jack dies, Pat says she needs an income to support herself and her kids. Chris—who realizes the company can't survive if it has to pay half the profits to a nonworking owner—invokes their buyout agreement, which provides that he can buy out Pat's interest by paying her $100,000 over three years. Combined with the payoff from a life insurance policy Jack had purchased, this is enough money to give Pat the time she needs to freshen up her skills as a paralegal and go back to work. And it allows Chris to search for a new partner to share work and profits with.

Understand that this provision, which allows surviving owners to buy out the interests of the owner who dies first, often results in the owner who remains alive the longest ending up with the whole business. This is probably a reasonable outcome, since the last owner to die managed and/or worked for the company for the longest amount of time. Nevertheless, you should understand how it can work against your survivors in some circumstances. Suppose your son works for the company and wants to succeed you as one of the owners, but you die before the other owners. If you've included an Option-to-Purchase clause and the company or the surviving owners force your son to sell out, his career could be over before it started.

However, a reasonable buyout price can protect your inheritors. You may not be crazy about the idea of giving the company and surviving owners the absolute right to buy your share from your estate, rather than letting it go to your inheritors. But as long as your agreement ensures that the price paid to your estate for your share is fair—and you can take pains to make sure that it will be—then at least you know your inheritors will be justly compensated. We discuss how to set a fair price in Chapter 6.

> **TIP**
>
> **Look at the situation from both sides.** You usually have no way of knowing which owner will die first. You could be a surviving owner faced with the possibility of a deceased co-owner's unqualified son wanting to join the company. Or, you could be the first co-owner to become critically ill and die, hoping the others will accept your capable daughter as a fully participating co-owner. So, in drafting your agreement, try to balance the future needs of the owner whose circumstances will have changed against the interests of the company and the other owners as a whole.

The death buyout provision in our agreement is shown below.

> **WORKSHEET**
>
> **Turn to your worksheet.** If you are interested in giving the company and the continuing owners the option to buy a deceased owner's interest from his estate representative or trustee upon notice of death, check Option 1 on your worksheet now. (Section III, Scenario 3.)

RELATED TOPIC

Buyout provisions affect estate taxes. Note that you should include this option if you want to use your agreement to try to set the value of the ownership interests for estate tax purposes. We discuss setting the value for estate tax purposes in "Estate Tax Issues" in Chapter 9.

Scenario 3. When an Owner Dies

☐ **Option 1: Option of Company and Continuing Owners to Purchase a Deceased Owner's Interest**

(a) When an owner dies, he or she, and the executor or administrator of his or her estate or the trustee of a trust holding his or her ownership interest, are deemed to have offered the deceased owner's ownership interest to the company and the continuing owners for sale as of the date of the notice of death received orally or in writing by the company. The company and the continuing owners shall then have an option, but not an obligation (unless otherwise stated in this agreement), to purchase all or part of the ownership interest within the time and according to the procedure in Section IV, Provision 1 of this agreement. The price to be paid, the manner of payments, and other terms of the purchase shall be according to Sections VI and VII of this agreement. An owner who has died is referred to as a "deceased owner" below.

CAUTION

Majority owners beware. Majority owners may want to change their agreement so that this provision doesn't apply to them, particularly if it's a family business and they expect a son or daughter to succeed them. To avoid being restricted under any provision of a buyout agreement, a majority owner simply needs to add a sentence at the end of the provision, such as: "This section applies only to owners of less than 50% of the interests in the company." Note that if you do this, however, the Agreement Price will not set the value of the ownership interests for estate tax purposes. This is another example of why a majority owner should consult a small business expert before signing a buyout agreement.

Right of Estate, Trust, or Inheritors to Force a Sale

Up until now, we've talked about situations where the company or surviving owners *want* to buy out a deceased owner's interest from her estate. But what happens to a deceased owner's inheritors if the company or the surviving owners do not choose to buy the deceased owner's interest (for instance, because the company is short of funds)?

The Problem

There are many reasons inheritors might want to promptly sell their interest—for instance, they're not interested in working in the company; they're too young, too old, or unqualified; or they may simply have other places to spend or invest the proceeds they could get from selling their interests. And, as we discussed in Chapter 1, it can be difficult to impossible to find an outside buyer for a partial interest in a small business.

> EXAMPLE: Juan, Anna, and Diane buy a parking garage downtown. Juan dies suddenly in a car accident soon afterward. His wife, Angelina, inherits his interest in the garage. Unable to survive on her salary alone, Angelina asks Anna and Diane to buy out her share of the garage. Anna and Diane, however, with no surplus funds to buy her out, say "not right now." Juan's wife looks for an outside buyer, but no one wants to purchase a minority interest in the business, since the business will continue to be controlled by Anna and Diane. Angelina and her kids are stuck. She is eventually all but forced to sign over her share in the company to pay her bills, getting credit for far less than her share of the business was really worth.

Probate Fees and Estate Taxes

If you are planning for your heirs to take over your position in the company, you should address the issue of debt and taxes before you die. On the personal side, your estate may have to pay probate costs, funeral expenses, and final illness bills. On the business side, the estate may owe estate taxes because of the value of your company, assuming there is an estate tax when you die (if the value of the estate exceeds the current exemption amount). Where will this money come from? Without advance planning, your heirs could have to take working capital from the company or even sell the business to pay for these expenses.

EXAMPLE: Hillary and her brother Mike run a bed and breakfast on the edge of town, which provides them with a satisfying and fairly profitable living. They have a steady, seasonal clientele, who keep returning because of Hillary's gracious hospitality and Mike's gourmet cooking.

Mike dies unexpectedly and leaves his share of the business to his daughter Miriam, using a probate-avoiding living trust. Hillary welcomes Miriam to the B&B, since she and Miriam get along fine. So far, so good, but to pay state inheritance taxes, funeral expenses, and several big debts that her father had left behind, Miriam must take out a mortgage on the building that houses the bed and breakfast. On top of the financial strain the mortgage causes, Miriam doesn't know how to cook, so they have to hire a third person to replace Mike. And, still depressed by her brother's death, Hillary is in no mood to play the happy hostess much of the time. Eventually, when word spreads that the quality of the food and hospitality at the bed and breakfast has declined, bookings drop off. Before long, Miriam can't make her loan payments, and Hillary doesn't have the cash to buy her out. They end up hurriedly selling their B&B for less than its real value.

Although planning ahead won't deal with the sadness that accompanies the loss of a loved one, you can protect your heirs from a financial squeeze by planning ahead for money problems. One way to do this is by purchasing enough life insurance to be paid to your inheritors upon your death, so that they can pay any debts, taxes, and bills your estate may owe without having to take it out of the business you worked so long to build up. Another way is to plan ahead to lower your eventual estate taxes. We discuss estate taxes in detail in Chapter 9.

The Solution

To deal with this potential problem, you may want your agreement to contain a Right-to-Force-a-Sale clause that requires the company or the surviving owners to buy back the interest of a deceased owner if the estate representative, trustee, or inheritors want to sell it. For instance, if an owner dies and leaves his ownership interest to his wife and children, and they need cash for their expenses (to pay bills or to fund tuition), they have the power to force the company to buy back the interest.

The purpose of this clause is to guard against the possibility that neither the company nor the surviving owners want to buy the deceased owner's share from the deceased owner's estate, trust, or inheritors.

Of course, making sure funds will be available to pay for a buyout is a key part of making sure a buyout after the death of an owner does not bankrupt the company. One way to do this is for the company to take out an appropriate amount of life insurance on the life of each owner. The company pays the premiums on each policy and receives the benefits from them when an owner dies. The insurance policy payoff is then available to buy the interest of the deceased owner. (We discuss using insurance to fund buyout agreements in more detail in Chapter 5.)

EXAMPLE: Let's give Juan's wife and kids a better outcome with a buyout agreement. Remember that Juan, Anna, and Diane owned a downtown parking garage when Juan died suddenly in a car accident. His wife, Angelina, inherited his interest in the garage. Needing cash to pay for living expenses for herself and her children, Angelina invokes the Right-to-Force-a-Sale clause in the company's buy-sell agreement to require Anna and Diane to buy out her share of the garage. Since their agreement required the purchase of life insurance policies on each owner, Anna and Diane have no problem buying out Angelina at the price in their agreement with the proceeds from the life insurance policies. Now Angelina, Diane, and Anna can part on good terms, since all of them feel fairly treated.

The Right-to-Force-a-Sale clause in our buyout agreement is shown below. Note that this provision does not allow the holder of a deceased owner's interest to require the company and the continuing owners to buy just a portion of the deceased owner's interest. They must offer all or nothing.

☐ **Option 2: Right of Estate, Trust, or Inheritors to Force a Sale**

(a) When an owner dies, the executor or administrator of the deceased owner's estate, or the trustee of a trust holding the deceased owner's ownership interest, or the deceased owner's inheritors can require the company and the continuing owners to buy all, but not less than all, of the deceased owner's ownership interest by delivering to the company within 60 days a notice of intention to force a sale ("Notice of Intent to Force a Sale") in writing. The notice shall include the name and address of the deceased owner, the date of death, a description and amount of the owner's interest in the company, the name and address of the person exercising the right to force the sale, and a statement that this person wishes to force a sale of the interest due to the owner's death as provided in this provision. The procedure for purchase of the ownership interest shall be according to Section IV, Provision 2 of this agreement. The price to be paid, the manner of payments and other terms of the purchase shall be according to Sections VI and VII of this agreement. An owner who has died is referred to as a "deceased owner" below.

WORKSHEET

Turn to your worksheet. If you are interested in giving a deceased owner's estate, trust, or inheritors the right to force the company or the remaining owners to buy the deceased owner's interest, check Option 2 on your worksheet now. (Section III, Scenario 3.)

You Can Customize Any Buyout Option to Make It Mandatory

Another way to plan ahead for the death of a co-owner is to adopt a buyout agreement that *requires* the company or the remaining owners to buy the interest of the deceased owner from his estate. In other words, after an owner dies, the company or the surviving owners would have no choice but to buy the deceased owner's share. This clause, however—often called a mandatory purchase provision—takes away much of the surviving owners' discretion and doesn't provide much flexibility for either side.

We believe it should be used only in limited circumstances, and only after consultation with a small business lawyer. If you do decide to *require* the company or the continuing owners to purchase a deceased owner's interest, in Subsection (a) of Option 1, simply cross out the words "an option, but not an obligation (unless otherwise stated in this agreement)" and write in "an obligation."

In fact, any of the Options to Purchase in our buy-sell agreement can be made mandatory in this way—but we don't see the need for this in most cases. We think it's better to let the parties decide at the time of the business-changing event, when they have more information than the drafters of the buyout agreement do today.

If an Owner Divorces

If you don't cover the possibility of divorce in your buyout agreement, you'll have to face the possibility that if a co-owner gets divorced, the owner's ex could become your new business partner! The co-owner who is getting a divorce may have no power to stop this in a situation where, under state law, a judge has the power to divide marital property. And we hope you don't need us to tell you that, at a time when one in two marriages ends in divorce, it's just plain silly to overlook this possibility.

The Problem

Absent a bulletproof premarital agreement (an oxymoron if there ever was one), in which spouses agree to keep their property separate, chances are good that your business partner's spouse has a legal interest in your company. This is certainly true in community property states (Arizona, California, Idaho, Nevada, New Mexico, Texas, Washington, and Wisconsin), where each spouse owns one-half of all the couple's community property. (Community property includes most property earned or accumulated after the wedding.) And, practically speaking, it's likely to be true in most other states as well, where "equitable distribution" laws require that marital property be divided fairly during divorce. (Not to mention inheritance laws, which normally require that a surviving spouse receive at least one-third to one-half of a deceased spouse's estate.)

An inexperienced or mistrustful ex-spouse may not have the company's best interests at heart. For instance, ex-spouses sometimes want to get as much money as they can out of the company in the short term, even at the risk of damaging the company's long-term prospects.

Perhaps the most troublesome prospect of becoming co-owner with an owner's ex-spouse involves a situation where the owner who gets a divorce is still involved in the business.

EXAMPLE: Mike and Marti, friends from college, start a medical supply company while Mike is married to Betsy. A few years later, Mike and Betsy file for divorce. Betsy's lawyer demands half of Mike's interest in the company. Mike, having few other assets, has no choice but to sign it over as part of a property settlement agreement. Mike and Marti dread being in business with Betsy, who has a dozen reasons to be mad at Mike and, by extension, his friend Marti. Betsy insists on being involved in the day-to-day decisions of running the business, and the three owners argue all the time and can't agree on a direction for the business. Without a buy-sell agreement, Mike and Marti have no way to force Betsy to sell her interest and, as a result, they eventually disband the company.

The Solution

A "contemplation of divorce" buyout provision protects the owners of the company from having to work with potentially undesirable ex-spouses. Under such a provision, the company and the other owners can buy the ownership interest received by a former spouse if they choose, at the price in the agreement. However, and this is a big however, ex-spouses cannot be required to sell back their interest if they did not sign the original buyout agreement.

To avoid this prospect, all married owners should have their spouses read and sign the buyout agreement. By signing, the spouse agrees to sell any interest received in a divorce settlement back to the company or to the other owners at the standard buyout price set in the agreement (the Agreement Price, discussed in Chapter 6), if the owners so request.

If the company and the other owners decide not to buy back the interest from the ex-spouse (meaning the ex-spouse becomes a bona fide owner), the spouse agrees to abide by the terms of the buyout agreement that are applicable to all owners. Again, remember, contractual provisions contained in a buyout agreement don't have to be binding if none of the parties want them to be when a change of circumstance occurs. Owners have buyout agreements to protect and define their rights, not to freeze them in legal straitjackets. For example, suppose that, despite a forced buyout provision, the remaining owners actually like the ex-spouse—perhaps even better than they ever liked their old business partner—and want her to join the business. As long as she agrees, this is no problem, since, when all parties agree, any agreement can be changed.

TIP
The buyout agreement should mesh with any prenuptial agreement. If any couples also prepare prenuptial agreements defining their property ownership, they should contain the same provisions regarding business ownership as the buyout agreement.

The language of the "contemplation of divorce" clause contained in our buyout agreement, which includes the options mentioned above, is shown below. Note that it gives the divorced owner the first chance to buy back the interest awarded by a court to his former spouse, and then gives the company and all owners (including the divorced owner) a chance to buy the interest. We think this makes sense—it allows divorced owners to return to their status quo ownership position in the company by buying the interest back from their former spouses—if they can afford it.

WORKSHEET

Turn to your worksheet. If you are interested in giving the company and the continuing owners the option to buy a former spouse's ownership interest, check Option 1 on your worksheet now. (Section III, Scenario 4.)

Spouses Need to Understand the Agreement

When the owners ask their spouses to sign the agreement, they need to make sure the spouses understand what they're signing. In at least one case, the court refused to enforce a provision in a buyout agreement requiring an ex-spouse to sell back an interest received as part of a divorce, even though the ex-spouse had signed the agreement. The ex-spouse, who didn't work in the business or have a financial background, successfully argued that she never understood the agreement (and that she wasn't represented by a lawyer). To avoid the possibility of this happening, in our agreement, the spouses who sign the agreement agree that they understand the agreement and have had opportunity to hire a lawyer of their own ("independent counsel") to advise them. You could also have the spouses sign and attach an acknowledgment that they have received a copy of your company's financial report and fully expect the agreement to be binding in case of divorce.

Scenario 4. When an Owner's Interest Is Transferred to His or Her Former Spouse

☐ **Option 1: Option of Company and Continuing Owners to Purchase Former Spouse's Interest**

(a) If, in connection with the divorce or dissolution of the marriage of an owner, a court issues a decree or order that transfers, confirms, or awards part or all of an ownership interest to a divorced owner's former spouse, the former spouse is deemed to have offered his or her newly acquired ownership interest to the divorced owner for purchase on the date of the court award or settlement, according to the terms of this agreement. If the divorced owner does not elect to make such purchase within 30 days of the date of the court award or settlement, the former spouse of the divorced owner is deemed to have offered his or her newly acquired ownership interest to the company and the co-owners (including the divorced owner) for purchase, according to the terms of this agreement. The divorced owner must send notice to the company, in writing, that his or her former spouse now owns an ownership interest in the company. The notice shall state the name and address of the owner, the name and address of the divorced owner's former spouse, a description and amount of the interest awarded to the former spouse, and the date of the court award. If no notice is received by the company from the divorced owner, an offer to the company and the co-owners is deemed to have occurred when the company actually receives notice orally or in writing of the court award or settlement transferring the divorced owner's interest to the owner's former spouse. The company and the co-owners (including the divorced owner) shall then have an option, but not an obligation (unless otherwise stated in this agreement), to purchase all or part of the ownership interest within the time and according to the procedure in Section IV, Provision 1 of this agreement. The price to be paid, the manner of payments and other terms of the purchase shall be according to Sections VI and VII of this agreement.

(b) A former spouse who sells his or her ownership interest back to the company or continuing owners agrees to be responsible for any taxes owed on his or her sales proceeds.

If an Owner Loses a License

So far we have covered the most common scenarios that happen to the owners of small businesses. In the rest of this chapter, we deal with a few less likely scenarios: the loss of a professional license, the personal bankruptcy of an owner, a default on a personal loan, and the expulsion of an owner. First, let's look at what happens if an owner loses his professional or vocational license.

The Problem

When an owner loses a license that he needs to do the job, the owner can be prevented from working. For example, a veterinarian cannot legally treat animals without a veterinarian's license. What will happen to your business if your co-owner loses his professional or vocational license, keeping him from doing his job for a year or more?

Does the owner have to offer his interest for sale back to the company or to the still-licensed owners? Even absent a buyout agreement, the laws of many states prevent some professionals from owning part of a partnership or corporation without a license. Regardless of what your state says on the issue, it's good to address this situation in your buyout agreement to deal with the issues of how much the departing owner's interest is worth and what kind of payment method should be required.

EXAMPLE: Betty and Zach start a professional corporation to engage in the practice of architecture. After he starts to drink heavily, Zach begins improperly using a client's funds. After a hearing, the state board revokes his license. Because Zach is no longer able to work, Betty demands that he sell his interest in the firm to her. When Betty refuses to pay Zach's asking price for his ownership share, she has to sue him, claiming he deserves very little for his share because his own wrongdoing greatly harmed the firm's reputation. While the outcome is hard to call, it is certain that both parties will rack up attorneys' fees.

The Solution

If you find this little scenario sobering, it's likely you'll want to include loss of license in your buyback scenarios. Your buyout agreement can require a co-owner who has his license suspended or revoked to relinquish his duties and sell his ownership interest back to the company or to the other owners. This protects the owners of the company from having to share profits with someone who can no longer practice and may be in disrepute.

In addition, you may want to provide that the company or the continuing owners can pay less than full value for the interest of an owner who has lost his license. For instance, your agreement can allow the company or the remaining owners to purchase the owner's share at 40% to 50% of the full agreement price—to allow for the possibility that the conduct that caused the co-owner to lose his license may have hurt the reputation of your business or lost the company clients. Or, you may simply want to provide for a new appraisal of the company's value to establish its current worth given what has happened. (We discuss appraisals in Chapter 6.)

The language of the loss-of-license provision in our agreement, with the price options we discussed, is shown below.

WORKSHEET

Turn to your worksheet. If you are interested in giving the company and the continuing owners the option to buy the interest of an owner who has lost a required professional license, check Option 1 on your worksheet now. (Section III, Scenario 5.) If you check Option 1, also check:

- Option 1a to use the regular Agreement Price as the price for the departing owner's ownership interest, or

- Option 1b to call for an appraisal of the departing owner's ownership interest, or

- Option 1c to use a discounted Agreement Price as the price for the departing owner's ownership interest. If you check Option 1c, also fill in the percentage amount of the discount to be taken off the Agreement Price, such as 50%.

Scenario 5. When an Owner Loses His or Her Professional License

☐ **Option 1:** **Option of Company and Continuing Owners to Purchase Interest of an Owner Who Has Lost His or Her Professional License**

(a) If an owner suffers the surrender, revocation, or suspension, which will stand for at least three months, of his or her license to perform services essential to the business purposes of the company, that surrender, revocation, or suspension of the license shall be deemed to constitute an offer by the owner to sell his or her interest to the company or the other owners. The owner shall notify the company in writing of such surrender, revocation, or suspension. The notice shall include the name and address of the owner, a description and amount of the owner's interest in the company, and a description and effective date of the decision that resulted in the surrender, revocation, or suspension of the owner's license. If no notice is received by the company, an offer is deemed to have occurred when the company actually learns of the decision to surrender, revoke, or suspend the owner's license. The company and the continuing owners shall then have an option, but not an obligation (unless otherwise stated in this agreement), to purchase all or part of the ownership interest within the time and according to the procedure in Section IV, Provision 1 of this agreement. The price to be paid shall be as specified in this section; if not so specified, then according to Section VI of this agreement. The manner of payments and other terms of the purchase shall be according to Section VII of this agreement.

(b) If an owner's license is surrendered, revoked, or suspended, the price that the company and/or the continuing owners will pay for the expelled owner's ownership interest will be:

☐ **Option 1a:** **The full Agreement Price according to Section VI of this agreement**

☐ **Option 1b:** **Decided by an independent appraisal, according to the Appraised Value Method in Section VI of this agreement**

☐ **Option 1c:** **The Agreement Price as established in Section VI of this agreement, decreased by** [*insert percentage, such as "50"*]**%.**

If an Owner Files for Personal Bankruptcy

When an owner can't pay his bills and files for bankruptcy protection, it affects not only *his* future, but the company's as well.

The Problem

When a business owner files for personal bankruptcy, a bankruptcy trustee (a clerk of the bankruptcy court) has the right to gather and sell all of the debtor's nonexempt property, including her stake in a co-owned business, to pay off creditors.

Depending on state law and on how your business is organized, there can be three ways a bankruptcy trustee could use a bankrupt owner's ownership interest to pay off creditors, including:

- selling the ownership interest
- selling a proportional share of the business's assets, such as business equipment and inventory, or
- forcing the entire company to be liquidated.

In reality, however, even if the bankruptcy trustee does take hold of the ownership interest, circumstances rarely require the trustee to take drastic measures (in fact, in many situations, the trustee is allowed to try to sell only the ownership interest as is, not any equipment or inventory of the business). As long as the company or the co-owners are willing to pay the trustee a reasonable amount of money for the ownership interest in question, the bankruptcy trustee will usually be willing to sell it back to them. The trustee should be glad to have the cash to pay off the bankrupt owner's creditors.

But while the bankruptcy trustee is trying to sort things out, your company can end up in legal and ownership limbo while the trustee holds the ownership interest—a situation banks and other creditors would not take kindly to.

The Solution

It follows that the company and the remaining owners will want the means to prevent a bankruptcy trustee or others from selling a bankrupt owner's ownership interest. No question, it pays to plan to keep the bankruptcy trustee from taking an ownership interest in the first place, to avoid any possibility that an ownership interest gets tied up in bankruptcy court or, in a worst-case scenario, that your company might be liquidated.

To do this, your agreement can require an owner to give the company 30 or 60 days' notice before filing for bankruptcy, to give the company time to structure a purchase. Our agreement also states that this notice of an imminent bankruptcy filing is considered an automatic offer to sell the bankrupt owner's interest back to the company or to the other owners immediately, at which point the company and the co-owners can purchase it if they choose to.

> **CAUTION**
>
> **Pay a fair price for a bankrupt owner's shares.** Even if a co-owner sells his interest back to the company or continuing owners before filing for bankruptcy, a bankruptcy trustee has the power to disallow and reverse the transaction (and may well do so if it looks like a phony or underpriced transaction). To reduce the likelihood of this happening, you should pay the standard buyout price set in the agreement (the Agreement Price, discussed in Chapter 6) for the bankrupt owner's interest.

Of course, people don't always follow their buy-sell agreement, especially when they have little to lose. To be safe, if an owner violates the buyout agreement by filing for bankruptcy without first giving notice to his co-owners (in which case the company can't buy out the ownership interest before the bankruptcy filing takes place), our agreement provides that an owner who obtains or becomes subject to a bankruptcy order is automatically subject to the buyback provisions contained in your buy-sell agreement.

SEE AN EXPERT

Consult with a bankruptcy attorney. Should a co-owner get into serious financial problems, step one should be for everyone involved to consult with an experienced bankruptcy lawyer.

The clause in our agreement that contains the bankruptcy filing scenario we discussed is shown below.

Scenario 6. When an Owner Files for Personal Bankruptcy

☐ **Option 1:** **Option of Company and Continuing Owners to Purchase Interest of an Owner Who Has Filed for Bankruptcy**

(a) When an owner is planning to file for bankruptcy, he or she must give notice to the company, in writing, [*insert number of days, such as "30" or "60"*] days before he or she files for bankruptcy. The notice shall state the name and address of the owner, a description and amount of the owner's interest and the expected date of filing by the owner for bankruptcy. This notice shall be deemed to constitute an offer by the owner to sell his or her interest to the company or the other owners. If an owner files for bankruptcy without giving notice, the date when the company learns of the filing for bankruptcy will be deemed to be the date of this notice. The company and the continuing owners shall then have an option, but not an obligation (unless otherwise stated in this agreement), to purchase all or part of the ownership interest within the time and according to the procedure in Section IV, Provision 1 of this agreement. The price to be paid, the manner of payments and other terms of the purchase shall be according to Sections VI and VII of this agreement. An owner who has filed for bankruptcy is referred to as a "bankrupt owner" below.

WORKSHEET

Turn to your worksheet. If you are interested in giving the company and the continuing owners the option to buy a bankrupt owner's interest, check Option 1 on your worksheet now. (Section III, Scenario 6.) If you check Option 1, also insert the number of days' notice an owner must give to the company before filing for bankruptcy.

If an Owner Defaults on a Personal Loan

After reading this section, you and your co-owners will have to decide whether owners will have the right to offer their ownership interests as collateral for personal loans—called "encumbering their interest." Buyout provisions can restrict owners from using their ownership interest in this way.

The Problem

If an owner defaults on the loan for which his ownership interest was pledged as collateral, the creditor can foreclose and take title to the ownership interest.

> **EXAMPLE:** Chris and Lisa run a medical supply corporation together. They have a buy-sell agreement with a foreclosure clause. Chris comes up with an idea for reducing inflammation for patients with arm or elbow injuries. It consists of a sleeve filled with a gelatinous substance that can be cooled in the freezer and then pulled over the arm, icing the whole arm at once. Lisa doesn't want any part of funding the development and sale of this new product, because she doesn't think the product will sell.
>
> Undaunted by Lisa's lack of enthusiasm, Chris sets up a separate sole proprietorship and applies for a patent. Then, to finance development costs, he gets a loan from the bank by offering his one-half interest in the medical supply company as collateral. Due to a manufacturing problem, Chris has no product to sell and misses his first three loan payments, with the result that the bank starts to foreclose on his share of the medical supply company.

The Solution

Our buyout agreement provides two options: one that prohibits encumbering an ownership interest, and another that allows encumbrances with added provisions in case of default.

Prohibiting encumbrances. To avoid the problem entirely, some owners choose to prohibit owners' shares from being used as collateral for personal loans. The provision in our agreement that forbids owners from pledging their ownership interests for loans is shown below.

Scenario 7. Encumbrance of Interest

Option 2: No Encumbrance Allowed

No owner may encumber any or all of his ownership interest in the company in connection with any debt, guarantee, or other personal undertaking.

WORKSHEET

Turn to your worksheet. If you do not want to allow the owners of your company to be able to use their ownership interests as collateral for personal loans, check Option 2 on your worksheet now. (Section III, Scenario 7.)

Allowing encumbrances. After reflection, you, like many business owners, may decide not to prohibit owners from using their interest in the company as collateral for borrowing money, since to do so would mean you and your business partners might have a greatly reduced ability to qualify for personal loans. Especially for owners who have most of their net worth tied up in the business, it can be overly harsh to prevent owners from borrowing against the business. It could even result in their being unable to reinvest their profits in the company because of a personal shortage of cash.

If encumbrances are allowed, your buyout agreement will include a provision to handle the situation where an owner defaults on a personal loan and a creditor seeks foreclosure of the ownership interest. If an owner defaults on the loan and the creditor threatens to foreclose and take title to the interest, the company (and/or the other owners) have the ability to "cure" the default—that is, pay off the loan and take back the interest from the defaulting owner or the creditor.

> **EXAMPLE:** Let's go back to Chris and Lisa's company. When Lisa gets wind that the bank is preparing to foreclose on Chris's share of the company, she reads their buy-sell agreement and discovers she can pay off Chris's loan to the bank and, in exchange, take control of Chris's shares. Fortunately, Lisa is able to quickly gather financing and savings to repay Chris's debt. The creditor accepts Lisa's payment for the interest and stops foreclosure proceedings, because the bank is happy just to close out the loan.

TIP

Keep tabs on any personal pledges of ownership interests to secure loans. If you learn of a default by an owner on a loan secured by an ownership interest, notify the creditor immediately of the company's and the co-owners' buyback rights under your agreement.

This buyout provision can help prevent an outside creditor (or the person or entity to whom the creditor sells the interest) from gaining a share of the company and possibly a say in management—the main predicament your buyout agreement is meant to avoid.

Of course, the amount that the company or nondefaulting owners (whoever buys the ownership interest of the defaulting owner) pay to the creditor to pay off the loan is likely to be higher or lower than the standard buyout price set in the agreement (the Agreement Price, discussed in Chapter 6). If the amount that the company or nondefaulting owners pay to the creditor is less than the Agreement Price, they are required to pay the remainder of the Agreement Price to the defaulting owner. If the amount that the company or nondefaulting owners pay to the creditor is more than the Agreement Price, the defaulting owner owes them the difference.

The language in our buyout agreement that allows encumbrances and includes this buyback option is shown below.

Option 1: Encumbrances Allowed Subject to Option of Company and Continuing Owners to Purchase Interest

(a) Any owner may encumber any or all of his ownership interest in the company in connection with any debt, but any such encumbrance is subject to the following conditions:

(b) If an owner defaults on a debt secured by his or her ownership interest, he or she must promptly give notice in writing to the company. The notice shall include the name and address of the owner, a description and amount of the owner's interest in the company, the date and description of the encumbrance on the owner's interest, and the date and description of any action taken by creditors as a result of the default. If no notice is provided by the owner, notice shall be considered given to the company on the date the company learns of the owner's default or of any action by a creditor as a result of the default. (An owner who defaults on a debt secured by his or her ownership interest is referred to as a "defaulting owner" below.) The company and the continuing owners shall then have an option, but not an obligation (unless otherwise stated in this agreement), to pay off the debt and to take title to the interest.

(c) If the amount paid to the creditor (debt plus any interest) is less than the Agreement Price selected in Section VI of this agreement, the remainder of the Agreement Price shall be paid to the defaulting owner by the buyer of his or her ownership interest. If the amount paid to the creditor (debt plus any interest) is more than the Agreement Price selected in Section VI of this agreement, the defaulting owner shall owe the difference to the buyer of his or her ownership interest.

(d) If the company and/or the other owners do not cure the default as provided in Subsection (b) above, the creditor may pursue any and all legal and equitable remedies.

Ownership Interests and Charging Orders

The above section offers a payoff solution that may be acceptable to a creditor who has loaned money to a defaulting owner. However, this is just one scenario in which an outsider can claim an interest in a business. An ownership interest, whether it's shares of a corporation or a percentage interest in a partnership or LLC, is a personal asset of an owner, and, as such, it may be subject to seizure by a creditor who obtains a legal judgment against the owner. What does this mean? Quite simply, that if one of the business owners loses a lawsuit, whether based upon a defaulted loan, a personal injury lawsuit, or other legal action, the creditor may have a right under state law to take legal possession of the shares of stock or ownership interest in the partnership or LLC. When this happens, depending on state law, a creditor may be able to:

- obtain the economic benefits belonging to the ownership interest (such as stock dividends or a percentage of the ongoing partnership or LLC profits)
- vote the shares or ownership interest (have a voice in business management), or
- force a liquidation of the business in order to cash out the ownership interest (in some states and under some circumstances).

The legal mechanism that is used to seize an ownership interest is known as a "charging order," and it represents one of the ways that outsiders become silent (or not so silent) in a privately held business. Protecting your business from charging orders is a complex area that is subject to state-by-state variation, and is beyond the scope of this book. Make sure to discuss this issue with a business lawyer if you want to learn more about your state's rules and how you can help protect yourself and your business from charging orders made against ownership interests in your business.

WORKSHEET

Turn to your worksheet. If you want to allow the owners of your company to use their ownership interests as collateral for personal loans, but want to give the company and the remaining owners the ability to "cure" a default by buying an owner's interest, check Option 1 on your worksheet now. (Section III, Scenario 7.)

TIP

Place a legend on any stock certificates. If you allow owners to encumber their ownership interests, you should place a legend on any certificates of ownership (which usually only exist for stock in a corporation) to give notice to others who lend money based on ownership interests that the interest cannot be freely transferred and is subject to transfer restrictions under the terms of your buyout agreement. We show you how to do this in "Placing a Legend on Your Certificates" in Chapter 8.

If an Owner Needs to Be Expelled

Expelling a co-owner from your business can be a wrenching experience, one you surely hope you never have to encounter. Certainly many new business owners find it very difficult to even consider this possibility. But putting your head in the sand and pretending you'll never have to deal with a co-owner who fails to adequately perform her job-related duties— or breaks the law—is a serious mistake. When bad things happen to the owners of good companies, you need to be able to deal with them.

Here is a short list of some of the unhappy possibilities you may have to cope with:

- An owner becomes seriously alcohol or drug dependent and jeopardizes the company's welfare.
- An owner exhibits disturbing personal behavior patterns such as extreme anger or depression.
- An owner loses interest in the business and endangers its profitability.
- An owner steals from the business or is otherwise dishonest.
- An owner engages in unacceptable conduct at work, such as harassing coworkers.

To cope with an owner who is irresponsible, untrustworthy, or just not performing up to the company's standards, it can make sense to include in your buyout agreement a provision that requires such an owner to relinquish his duties and sell his ownership interest to the company or the other owners. Sounds good, but actually implementing such a clause can be tricky.

Cause for expulsion. Whether an owner really is underperforming or acting badly is usually a matter of opinion. That's why, if you want your agreement to cover this scenario, it's a good idea to put reasons for expelling an owner explicitly into your agreement. Then an owner who signs the agreement can't later claim that it's unfair.

Our agreement allows you to define adequate cause as criminal conduct against the company and/or a serious breach of duty or of company policy. It also allows you to write in your own reasons. Consider including a list of specific grounds that constitute "adequate cause" for expulsion, such as "alcohol or drug abuse that jeopardizes the welfare of the company." In real life, people can and do challenge "adequate cause" in wrongful termination suits, but at least if you've set out some standards to measure against, you'll be ahead of the game. If you don't check any of the adequate clause options in our agreement or write in any reasons for expulsion, adequate cause will be determined at the time of expulsion.

Full vs. discounted price. If the co-owner's failure to meet her obligations is objective and clear, your agreement can provide a method for discounting the buyout price according to possible impairment of your company's reputation. For instance, your agreement can allow the company or the remaining owners to purchase the share of an expelled owner at 50% of the standard buyout price set in the agreement (the Agreement Price, discussed in Chapter 6)—to allow for the possibility that the co-owner's conduct has hurt the business's economic future. Or, you may simply want to provide for a new appraisal of the company to establish its current worth. (We discuss the procedure for getting an appraisal in Chapter 6.) However, in order to avoid more bitterness than is already likely to surround any expulsion, you may want to provide that the company or the continuing owners will repurchase an expelled owner's interest at the full Agreement Price, not at a discounted price.

CAUTION

Expulsion may be one area where you do not want to allow binding arbitration. Arbitration (discussed in Chapter 8) is a method of settling a conflict where a neutral third party makes a decision rather than a judge. For many people, it's a better choice than going to court, but in this situation, an arbitrator might decide that you can't expel a partner or other co-owner when you think it is absolutely necessary for your business's survival. So you may not want the arbitration required by the agreement to apply to expulsion. To accomplish this, at the end of your expulsion clause, add a declaration that "any expulsion decision is absolutely final and is not subject to arbitration or other review, including review by any court." (This will make the arbitration clause not apply, since the arbitration clause in our agreement starts with the phrase, "Except as otherwise provided in this agreement.")

The expulsion clause included in our buyout agreement is shown below.

WORKSHEET

Turn to your worksheet. If you are interested in giving the company and the continuing owners the option to buy an expelled owner's interest, check Option 1 on your worksheet now. (Section III, Scenario 8.)

If you check Option 1, you can choose to define adequate cause. You may do one or all of the following by checking:

- Option 1a to include criminal conduct as an instance of adequate cause
- Option 1b to include breach of duties as an instance of adequate cause, and/or
- Option 1c to list your own reasons for expulsion for adequate cause.

If you do not check any of these options, adequate cause will be determined at the time of expulsion.

If you checked Option 1a, 1b, or 1c, you must choose the price to be paid for the expelled owner's interest by checking:

- Option 1d to use the regular Agreement Price
- Option 1e to call for an appraisal of the expelled owner's ownership interest, or
- Option 1f to use a discounted Agreement Price. If you check Option 1f, also fill in the percentage amount of the discount to be taken off the Agreement Price, such as 50%.

Scenario 8. Expulsion of Owner

☐ **Option 1: Option of Company and Continuing Owners to Purchase an Expelled Owner's Interest**

(a) At a time when the company has three or more owners, situations may arise in which a group of owners wish to expel another owner. An owner may be expelled upon a unanimous vote of all other owners for adequate cause. Upon such expulsion, the expelled owner is deemed to have offered to sell all of his or her interest to the company and the continuing owners. The company and the continuing owners shall then have an option, but not an obligation (unless otherwise stated in this agreement), to purchase all or part of the ownership interest within the time and according to the procedure in Section IV, Provision 1 of this agreement. The price to be paid shall be as specified in this section; if not so specified, then according to Section VI of this agreement. The manner of payments and other terms of the purchase shall be according to Section VII of this agreement. An owner who has been expelled is referred to as an "expelled owner" below.

(b) Adequate cause includes, but is not limited to:

☐ **Option 1a: Any criminal conduct against the company (such as embezzlement)**

☐ **Option 1b: A serious breach of the owner's duties or of any written policy of the company**

☐ **Option 1c:** _____ *[insert reasons]* _____

(c) If an owner is expelled for a reason listed in Subsection (b), the price that the company and/or the continuing owners will pay for the expelled owner's ownership interest will be:

☐ **Option 1d: The full Agreement Price according to Section VI of this agreement**

☐ **Option 1e: Decided by an independent appraisal, according to the Appraised Value Method in Section VI of this agreement**

☐ **Option 1f: The Agreement Price as established in Section VI of this agreement, decreased by** *[insert percentage, such as "50"]***%.**

Expulsion Provisions for Two-Owner Companies

Our expulsion provision applies only to businesses with more than two owners. If you own your business with one other person, you will not be able to expel that person. This means that if your co-owner is acting badly or not working up to par, unless you convince her to sell out, your only other option might be to disband the company.

If your company has only two owners, you may want to ask a small business attorney with expertise in buy-sell agreements to fashion a buyout provision that provides for this situation. There is a commonly used provision for two-owner companies where one owner names a buyout price and the other owner has the option to either buy the other owner's interest at that price or to sell his own interest at that price. This is sometimes called a "Texas shootout" or "Russian roulette" provision. However, you'll need to hire a lawyer to draft this provision for you to take into account both owners' strategic and financial positions.

Structuring Buyouts

I n Chapters 2 and 3, we discussed how you can use buyout provisions—including the Right of First Refusal, the Option to Purchase an Owner's Interest, and the Right to Force a Sale—to control who owns your company and to give departing owners a mechanism to cash out. If you include any of these provisions in your buyout agreement, at some point during your company's life, the company or the continuing owners will probably purchase a departing owner's interest. To ensure that all buyout situations are handled smoothly, your buyout agreement also provides *how* a future buyout will be carried out.

Our agreement's buyout procedure includes the following details:

- how and when the company and the continuing owners decide who will buy the ownership interest of the selling, departing, or deceased owner (we'll call that owner the "transferring" owner, and the ownership interest at stake the "available interest"). In other words, our agreement provides a framework for deciding whether the company itself or the owners who will remain in the company (we'll call them the "continuing owners") will buy the available interest.

- how and when the company and continuing owners must notify the transferring owner that they will purchase the available interest.

We explain how our buyout agreement handles these items below. The only choices you'll have to make in this chapter involve the number of days for decisions, notices, and the like.

Company Versus Co-Owners as Buyers

There are three common approaches to implementing a buyout. The main difference among these methods involves who will buy the transferring owner's interest—the company, the continuing owners, or a combination of the two. For the reasons explained below, our agreement allows a combination of buyers, using a "Wait and See" approach.

Company as Buyer

This first type of buyback procedure is called an "entity purchase buyback," or a redemption buyback for corporations. When an owner retires, dies, or wants to sell out, only the company (the "entity") has the option, or sometimes the obligation—depending on what clauses are included in the buyout agreement—to buy the transferring owner's interest in the company.

If the company itself buys the available interest, here is what happens. In a corporation, the company simply cancels the redeemed shares after a buyback, and the continuing shareholders' ownership percentages in the company increase accordingly (though the number of shares they own will not change).

In a partnership or an LLC, after the company buys an owner's interest, the interest is liquidated and the continuing partners' or members' ownership percentages increase.

The entity purchase method is popular because it allows company funds rather than personal funds or personal loans to complete a buyout. But the main advantage of this method is its simplicity. By deciding who will buy the transferring owner's interest far in advance of the actual buyback, this method eliminates the need to decide who will make the buyback at the time of the buyout.

However, because this method is so simple, it lacks flexibility. For example, it doesn't give one or more continuing owners the option of buying the ownership interest themselves, an approach that can sometimes result in significant income and capital gains tax advantages to both the continuing owners and the transferring owner. In short, since changing tax laws as well as constant changes in companies' and owners' situations make it impossible to know years in advance whether it would be best have the company or the continuing owners buy the interest in question, it makes sense to allow an informed decision to be made at the time of the buyout.

RELATED TOPIC

Read about the tax issues. We discuss the income tax disadvantages of company-sponsored buyouts briefly in "Income Tax Issues" in Chapter 9. Note, however, that this is a complicated and changing area, and you will no doubt want to get a tax expert's opinion before having your company or the continuing owners buy out an owner's interest.

CAUTION

Corporations and LLCs can't always buy out a departing owner.
To buy back the interest of a departing owner, a company is required to be in
good financial shape—in other words, to have sufficient surplus funds available.
(See "Financial Solvency Tests," just below.)

Financial Solvency Tests

As a rule, state corporation and LLC laws prevent a corporation or an LLC from
buying back an owner's interest if specific financial solvency tests cannot be
met. Generally, state law requires that, after a buyback, the company's assets
must exceed its liabilities (sometimes by a specified amount). For example, a
state may say that a company's assets must be at least one and one-half times
its liabilities after the buyback. And, almost as a universal rule, to participate in
a buyback the corporation or LLC must be able to pay its debts as they become
due after the buyback (that is, the company must remain solvent after the
purchase of the owner's interest).

Rather than worry too much about these restrictions now, just realize
that in the future, if your corporation or LLC would have to use most or all
of its cash reserves to buy back a departing owner's interest, it might not be
lawful to go forward with the deal. In this case, you might want one or more
co-owners to be able to individually buy back an owner's interest. Which, of
course, is another way of saying that it's important to have a buyout agreement procedure in place that lets you decide at the time of the buyout who
should buy the shares of a transferring owner.

Co-Owners as Buyers

The second common type of buyback procedure is called a "cross-purchase
buyback." Under this approach, when an owner retires, dies, or wants to sell
out, only the continuing owners—not the business itself—have an option
(or sometimes an obligation, depending on what clauses are included in the
agreement) to purchase that owner's interest.

Usually, this method allows each continuing owner to purchase a share of the departing owner's interest in proportion to his or her current holdings (for instance, a 10% owner—that is, a person holding 10% of the total interests held by all continuing owners—can purchase 10% of the ownership interest in question). Since the company itself is not a party to this type of agreement, it cannot purchase the transferring owner's interest itself.

Two problems with co-owners' individually buying out a departing owner is that when a company has more than two or three owners, this method can get complicated in terms of notice requirements, and insurance funding becomes harder to deal with (see "Buying Insurance" in Chapter 5). And, like the entity purchase buyback, this procedure does not allow the flexibility of deciding at the time of the buyout who should buy the ownership interest: the company or the continuing owners. When you're forming your buyout agreement, you may not have the necessary information you need to make the best decision—taxwise and financially—as to who should buy a departing owner's interest.

RELATED TOPIC

We discuss the advantages and disadvantages of owner-sponsored buyouts briefly in "Income Tax Issues" in Chapter 9. Note, however, that this is a complicated area. In the future, before deciding to buy out an owner's interest, you should get a tax expert's opinion.

"Wait and See" Approach

This third type of buyback procedure (a combination of the entity purchase and cross-purchase buyback) usually works best for most buyout situations. That's because it affords both the company and the continuing owners an option to purchase an owner's interest when a buyout situation presents itself. Usually, the company gets the first opportunity to purchase the interest in question, and then the continuing owners are allowed to purchase any of the transferring owner's interest that has not been purchased by the company, usually in proportion to their current holdings.

Probably the biggest advantage of this method is its flexibility. It allows the company and the continuing owners to make no decisions until a buyout situation comes up, at which point they can decide—considering tax consequences and the company's and owners' financial circumstances—who will buy a transferring owner's interest.

For these reasons, in our agreement we use this third "wait and see" approach. We believe it is best to allow the company and the continuing owners to decide at the time of the buyout—and not when the buyout agreement is drafted—who will buy a departing owner's interest.

 SEE AN EXPERT

See a lawyer if you are interested in using a different procedure. Though we see few situations in which they are preferable, if you think a straight entity purchase procedure or cross-purchase procedure would best suit your company, see a lawyer for help in changing our agreement. We discuss finding and working with lawyers in Chapter 10.

While the "wait and see" buyback procedure works similarly for all three types of buyout provisions discussed in Chapters 2 and 3 (the Right of First Refusal, the Option to Purchase, and the Right to Force a Sale), a few different steps must be followed to implement it in each situation. Let's take a brief look at each type of buyout situation.

How the "Wait and See" Approach Works

By choosing the buyout provisions discussed in Chapters 2 and 3, you've already handled the details of *when* a buyout right or obligation is triggered. As a short review, this happens:

- upon receipt of written notice that an owner intends to sell or transfer an interest (in a Right-of-First-Refusal buyout situation)
- upon the happening of an event that triggers a buyout right, such as an owner's retirement, disability, death, divorce, bankruptcy, loss of license, or loan default (in an Option to Purchase an Owner's Interest), or

- upon receipt of a written notice to force a sale (in a Right-to-Force-a-Sale situation).

You still need to learn about what happens *after* the buyout right or obligation is triggered. Let's look at each type of buyout situation to see what the next steps are.

How the Option to Purchase Works

The procedure for the Option to Purchase an Owner's Interest (Section IV, (1) in our agreement) is triggered whenever notice is received by the company of an option to purchase, whether it's by a Notice of Intent to Transfer according to a Right of First Refusal (Chapter 2) or notice of a business-disrupting event such as the retirement, divorce, disability, or death of an owner (Chapter 3).

Of course, in a small company, informal notice of departure or death happens almost automatically and immediately, but notice of a divorce or bankruptcy may not occur until the ex-spouse of an owner or the bankruptcy trustee gets hold of an ownership interest. But no matter how informally notice may be given, it's important to understand that the amount of time that the company has to decide whether to purchase (the "option period") starts to tick only after the company knows that the triggering event has occurred. (For example, if the company does not receive formal notice that an owner has filed for bankruptcy, only when the company becomes aware of the bankruptcy does the buyback right get triggered, and the option period starts to run.)

Company's Option to Purchase

After the company receives notice, the company's owners (or, in a corporation, its board of directors and shareholders) should meet with their tax advisers and each other to decide if it's in their best interest for the company itself to buy the available interest.

It is up to you to decide on what a fair amount of time is for the company to make its decision, but we think 30 or 60 days is reasonable. (Remember, the continuing owners of the company then have another period to decide individually whether they want to purchase the available interest.) Of course, you can insert a longer time limit for the company to decide to buy back the interest.

CAUTION

Allow adequate time for a buyback decision. For a high-stakes buyout, less than 30 or 60 days can be too short a time for a company to make an informed decision with the help of a tax adviser.

The language taken from the Option-to-Purchase provision in our buyout agreement that covers this part of the procedure is shown below (see Section IV, (1) of the agreement).

Section IV: Buyout Procedure

(1)   Option of Company and Continuing Owners to Purchase an Interest

    (a) This provision is triggered upon receipt of notice by the company according to Section II or the notification of any of the events checked in Section III where the company and/or the continuing owners have an option, but not an obligation (unless otherwise stated in this agreement), to purchase the interest that is the subject of the notice (called the "available interest").

    (b) The company shall have an option to purchase any or all of the available interest within [*insert number of days, such as "30"*] days after the date on which the company receives notice or becomes aware of the event triggering the Option to Purchase.

If the owners or directors decide that the company should buy all of the available interest, the company must exercise its option by delivering a written Notice of Intent to Purchase to the transferring owner (or the current holder of the interest) within the designated time period. (In other words, the Notice of Intent to Purchase is sent to the transferring, retiring, disabled, expelled, bankrupt, or defaulting owner if the interest is still in the owner's hands, or to the person who now has ownership or control of the interest, such as a creditor, a bankruptcy trustee, an estate representative, or the ex-spouse of an owner.) The contents of the Notice of Intent to Purchase are covered just below.

WORKSHEET

Turn to your worksheet. Add to your worksheet the number of days that you want your company to have—after receiving notice or becoming aware of the event triggering the Option to Purchase—to make its buyback decision under an Option to Purchase. (Section IV, (1), (b).)

Contents of Notice of Intent to Purchase

Now, let's look at the last few details of the buyback procedure contained in the buyout agreement.

If the company or any of the continuing owners exercise their option to buy the available interest, the company sends out a collective notice to the transferring owner, or the current holder of the interest, regarding the company's and/or continuing owners' intent to purchase a part or all the available interest (called a Notice of Intent to Purchase).

Generally, the Notice of Intent to Purchase should be sent to the person who provided the original notice to the company of a proposed transfer or the occurrence of any of the triggering events that give rise to a buyback (the death, disability, or expulsion of an owner, and the like). For example, the Notice of Intent to Purchase the interest of a deceased owner will go to the representative of the deceased owner's estate.

The Notice of Intent to Purchase should include the following information:

- the name and address of the company and the name and title of the officer or employee who can be contacted at the company regarding the Notice of Intent to Purchase
- a description and the amount of ownership interest to be purchased by the company and/or each of the continuing owners and the name and address of each such continuing owner
- the total amount of the available interest to be purchased by the company and the continuing owners

- the terms of the purchase according to the buyout agreement
- a copy of the buyout agreement, and
- if the interest to be purchased is represented by certificates, such as share certificates, a request for the surrender of the share certificates to the company.

Here's an example of a straightforward Notice of Intent to Purchase, in letter format.

Notice of Intent to Purchase

June 25, 20xx

Babak Pakroo
1500 West Covina Ave.
Covina Cove, CA 94560

Dear Babak,

ADC Data Corp has decided to exercise its right to purchase 500 shares of Class A voting stock owned by you for $5,000.00, as provided in the buyout agreement dated April 15, 20xx and on file with the company. A copy of the agreement is attached. Terms for payment shall be according to Section VII of the buyout agreement. The first payment, according to these terms, will be mailed to you on or by Juy 30, 20xx. Please surrender the share certificates representing these shares to me at the address listed below, prior to this date. If you have any additional questions, please contact me at the address or telephone number shown below.

Sincerely,

Ali Hayward

Ali Hayward, Secretary
ADC Data Corp
28 Narragansett Bay Ave.
Warwick Neck, CT
Telephone: 555-555-5555

Continuing Owners' Option to Purchase

If the company decides not to purchase all of the available interest, the company must immediately let each of the continuing owners know that some or all of the interest is available for purchase by them (any part of the interest not purchased by the company). The continuing owners are given another time period (usually 30 or 60 days) following the expiration of the company's option period to decide individually whether they want to purchase any of the interest not purchased by the company. Again, it is up to you and your co-owners to decide on what you think is a fair amount of time for the continuing owners to reach their decisions.

The language that covers this part of the procedure is shown below. It is taken from the Option-to-Purchase provision in our buyout agreement. (Section IV, (1).)

(c) If the company does not decide to purchase all of the available interest within the time allowed, it shall immediately and, in all cases, no later than the date of expiration of the company's right to exercise its purchase option of the available interest, notify the continuing owners of their right to purchase the available interest not purchased by the company. This notice by the company to the continuing owners shall state:

1) the amount and description of the interest available for purchase by the continuing owners

2) the date by which the continuing owner must respond in writing to the company that he or she wishes to purchase any or all of the available interest, which date shall be [*insert number of days, such as "30"*] days after the date of the expiration of the company's purchase option, and

3) that any purchase by a continuing owner must be according to the terms of this buyout agreement.

A copy of this buyout agreement shall be immediately furnished to any continuing owner who requests a copy.

Turn to your worksheet. Add to your worksheet the number of days that you want the continuing owners to have to make their individual buyback decisions under an Option to Purchase. (Section IV, (1), (c).)

Within this second time period, each individual owner who wishes to purchase any of the available interest must submit to the company a notice of how much of the interest he wants to buy.

The language that covers this part of the procedure is shown below. It is taken from the Option-to-Purchase provision in our buyout agreement. (Section IV, (1).)

(d)   Each continuing owner may exercise his or her option to purchase any or all of the available interest in writing by delivering or mailing to the company an individual Notice of Intent to Purchase. This notice shall be sent to the secretary or equivalent officer of the company, and shall show the name and address of the continuing owner who wishes to purchase part or all of the available interest and the amount and a description of the interest that the continuing owner wishes to purchase.

Splitting the Interest Among the Owners

If only one continuing owner wants to individually purchase the available interest, it's simple—that owner simply purchases the interest in its entirety.

The purchasing procedure can become a bit more involved if more than one of the continuing owners want to buy the available interest. Problems develop when two or more continuing owners together wish to buy an amount larger than the available interest being offered to the continuing owners. When this occurs, the available interest must be split up according to the terms set out in the buyout agreement. Usually, the owner who currently owns the largest percentage of the company gets to buy the lion's share of the available interest.

Our agreement allows the owners who wish to purchase the available interest to buy in an amount relative to their ownership percentages within the group of owners who elect to buy the interest (let's call them "the purchasing group"). In other words, an owner who wishes to purchase some of the available interest can buy as much of the interest as the percentage she owns of the total amount currently owned by the purchasing group. Note that this purchasing group excludes the transferring owner's interest or the interests of any owners who don't want to buy the newly available interest. The available interest is then divvied up to the purchasing owners based on those percentages.

Confused by all this legal terminology? Here are a couple of examples that should help. First, here is an example that illustrates the allocation of the available interest among shareholders.

EXAMPLE: In Chapter 2, we introduced you to an adventure travel company called Run-a-Muck, owned by Jason, Tim, Chris, and Bart. You may remember that each of the four owners owns 250 shares of the corporation. Jason (the transferring owner) gives the company notice of his intent to sell the shares to an outsider (Austin). The company itself declines to exercise its buyback option. Out of the three continuing owners of the company, only Tim and Chris decide to purchase Jason's shares as individual owners. Together Tim and Chris (whose interests are pooled in computing the total interest owned by the purchasing group) already own 500 shares. Since each of them owns half (250) of the total shares (500) owned by the purchasing group, each is entitled to purchase half of Jason's shares, or 125 shares apiece. (Note that before purchasing Jason's shares, Tim and Chris were both 25% owners of the company—but they nevertheless each were able to purchase 50% of Jason's shares.)

Second, here is an example that illustrates the allocation of the available interest among the owners of an LLC or a partnership.

EXAMPLE: Janet, Spencer, Patti, and Stephen own a limited liability company called Megasoft. Patti owns 45% of the company, Janet owns 25%, Spencer owns 15%, and Stephen owns 15%. Patti gets an offer from an outsider to buy her 45% of the company, and she notifies the company of her intention to sell, attaching a copy of the offer to her notice. The directors of the corporation decide the corporation itself isn't interested, but Janet and Spencer, using their Right of First Refusal, want to buy as much of Patti's interest as they are allowed; Stephen, who needs every penny to put his son through medical school, opts not to buy any.

Here's how Janet and Spencer divide up the interest: Together, Janet and Spencer (the purchasing group) own 40% (25% + 15%) of the company. Janet determines her ownership percentage of that total by dividing her individual ownership percentage (25%) by the total owned by the group (40%) to arrive at a percentage of 62.5%. Spencer divides his individual ownership percentage (15%) by the total (40%) to arrive at 37.5%. Therefore, Janet will get 62.5% of Patti's interest, and Spencer will get 37.5%. (If you're interested, after the buyout Janet ends up owning 53.125% of the company, Spencer 31.875%, and Stephen 15%.)

The language that covers this part of the procedure is shown below. It is taken from the Option-to-Purchase provision in our buyout agreement. (Section IV, (1).)

(e)   If the total amount of interest specified in the notices by the continuing owners to the company exceeds the amount of the interest available for purchase by them, each continuing owner shall be entitled, up to the amount of interest specified in his or her individual Notice of Intent to Purchase, to purchase a fraction of the available interest, in the same proportion that the amount of the interest he or she currently owns bears to the total amount of the company's interest owned by all continuing owners electing to purchase.

The language of our buyout agreement that covers the Notice of Intent to Purchase is shown below. It is taken from the Option to Purchase procedure. (Section IV, (1).)

(f) If the company or any continuing owner exercises their option to purchase a part or all of the available interest, the company shall deliver or mail to the current owner or, if different, the current holder of the available interest, no later than five business days after the expiration of the period to exercise their option to purchase the available interest, a Notice of Intent to Purchase that includes the following information:

- the name and address of the company, and the name and title of the officer or employee who can be contacted at the company

- a description and the amount of ownership interest to be purchased by the company and/or each of the continuing owners, and the name and address of each such continuing owner

- the total amount of the interest to be purchased by the company and the continuing owners

- the terms of the purchase according to Section VII of this agreement

- a copy of this agreement, and

- if the interest to be purchased is represented by certificates, such as share certificates, a request for the surrender of the share certificates to the company.

After mailing the notice of intent, the company and/or the continuing owners buy back the interest according to the price and payment terms in the agreement.

The language that covers the final part of the procedure is shown below. It is taken from the Option-to-Purchase provision in our buyout agreement. (Section IV, (1).)

(g) The company and the continuing owners shall purchase the portion or all of the available interest each has exercised an option to purchase in the Notice of Intent to Purchase, according to the terms specified in Section VII of this agreement, each making payment for the interest to be purchased and complying with other terms as appropriate. The sale shall be considered final when the company and the continuing owners make payment to the owner or holder of the interest or, if payment is made over time, when all paperwork necessary to the sale has been executed by the company, the continuing owners, and the owner or holder of the interest to be purchased.

How the Right of First Refusal Works

As we discussed in Chapter 2, when an owner whose buyout agreement contains a Right-of-First-Refusal clause receives an offer from an outsider (or, sometimes, a current owner) to buy her ownership interest, the Right-of-First-Refusal clause is triggered. This clause says that, before making a sale or transfer, the owner considering a sale or transfer must offer her interest to the company and to her co-owners for purchase by delivering notice to the company of the terms of the intended transfer (called a Notice of Intent to Transfer).

The Notice of Intent to Transfer must include the price and payment terms of the proposed sale and the name and address of the proposed buyer. A copy of the offer from the proposed buyer must be attached. Here's a sample of a simple notice:

Notice of Intent to Transfer

Jason Thomas proposes to sell 250 shares in Run-a-Muck to Austin Johnson, 113 Pine Glen Drive, West Greenwich, RI, within 60 days of the date of this notice for $2,500.00 cash ($10.00 per share). Payment of the purchase price by Austin Johnson is to be made in cash on the date of the transfer. A copy of the offer to purchase these shares on these terms, signed by Austin Johnson, is attached to this notice.

At that point, the transaction unwinds just as if it arose under an Option-to-Purchase clause—the company and the continuing owners now have an option to purchase the transferring owner's interest if they choose. This part of the buyback procedure is the same under the Right-of-First-Refusal provision as it is under an Option-to-Purchase provision; see "How the Option to Purchase Works," above, for an explanation.

The only significant difference between a regular Option to Purchase and the option to purchase following a Right of First Refusal is in what happens if neither the company nor the continuing owners buy all of the interest at stake. If the company and the continuing owners decline to buy *all* of the transferring owner's interest, the transferring owner is then free to sell her entire interest to the outsider or current owner (or give her interest to a relative, if that's what she was after) within 60 days, at the same price and terms in her Notice of Intent to Transfer. On the other hand, if the company or the continuing owners buy *all* of the transferring owner's interest, the outsider or potential transferee is essentially shut out of the company.

How a Right to Force a Sale Works

The procedural details and agreement clauses that apply to a Right-to-Force-a-Sale scenario, where the company and continuing owners are *required* to buy back an owner's interest upon request (discussed in Chapter 3), are almost entirely the same as those discussed above for the

Option-to-Purchase procedure by the company and continuing owners. We won't explain each clause individually here; we'll just point out the few differences between the two procedures and the portions of the agreement that need to be completed. Reread "How the Option to Purchase Works," above, if you have any additional questions about the forced sale procedure or agreement language.

First, forced sales may occur only in a few instances under our agreement: in the case of the retirement, disability, or death of an owner. In these instances, the retiring or disabled owner or, if an owner has died, his or her family member, estate representative, or trustee can force a buyout of the owner's interest by submitting a Notice of Intent to Force a Sale. The contents of this notice under Section III of the agreement vary, depending on the nature of the forced sale event (death, disability, or retirement), but here's a sample notice based upon an owner's retirement.

Notice of Intent to Force a Sale

Niall Carnahan requests that Olympic Parking, LLC, purchase all of his 50% capital interest in Olympic Parking, LLC, due to his retirement from the company, effective October 10, 20xx. Price and terms for payment shall be according to the buyout agreement dated April 15, 20xx, and on file with the company, a copy of which is attached.

A copy of the buyout agreement should be attached to the notice.

Company's Option to Purchase

Once this notice is received by the company, first the company has a chance to buy the interest of the retiring, disabled, or deceased owner under the same procedure as that discussed in "How the Option to Purchase Works," above.

You must decide how much time to give the company to make its buyback decision. We think 30 or 60 days is reasonable.

The language that covers the first part of the procedure is shown below. It is taken from the Right-to-Force-a-Sale procedure in our buyout agreement. (Section IV, (2).)

---

(2) Right to Force a Sale

(a) This provision is triggered upon receipt by the company of a Notice of Intent to Force a Sale according to Section III, where the company and the continuing owners have an obligation to purchase the interest that is the subject of the notice (called the "available interest").

(b) The company shall have an option to purchase any or all of the available interest within [*insert number of days, such as "30"*] days after the date on which the company receives the Notice of Intent to Force a Sale.

WORKSHEET

Turn to your worksheet. Insert in your worksheet the number of days that you want your company to have—after receipt of a Notice of Intent to Force a Sale—to make its buyback decision under a Right to Force a Sale. (Section IV, (2), (b).)

Continuing Owners' Option to Purchase

If the company does not decide to buy all of the interest, the continuing owners get a chance to buy any part of the interest not bought by the company. As in the Option-to-Purchase procedure, a continuing owner who wants to purchase any or all of the available interest must submit a Notice of Intent to Purchase the interest within a specified time period (see "How the Option to Purchase Works," above, for details). Again, you must specify the period the continuing owners have to make their buyback decision.

The language in our agreement that covers this part of the procedure is shown below. It is taken from the Right-to-Force-a-Sale procedure in our buy-sell agreement. (Section IV, (2).)

(c) If the company does not decide to purchase all of the available interest within the time allowed, it shall immediately and, in all cases, no later than the date of expiration of the company's right to exercise its purchase option of the available interest, notify the continuing owners of their right to purchase the available interest not purchased by the company. This notice by the company to the continuing owners shall state:

1) the amount and description of the interest available for purchase by the continuing owners

2) the date by which the continuing owner must respond in writing to the company that he or she wishes to purchase any or all of the available interest, which date shall be [*insert number of days, such as "30"*] days after the date of the expiration of the company's purchase option, and

3) that any purchase by a continuing owner must be according to the terms of this agreement.

A copy of this agreement shall be immediately furnished to any continuing owner who requests a copy.

WORKSHEET

Turn to your worksheet. Add to your worksheet the number of days that you want the continuing owners to have (immediately after the expiration of the company's period for making its purchase decision) to make their individual buyback decisions under a Right to Force a Sale. (Section IV, (2).)

Splitting the Interest Among Owners

If more than one continuing owner is interested in purchasing the available interest, the continuing owners get to purchase the available interest in proportion to their current ownership holdings (see "How the Option to Purchase Works," above, for the mechanics of how this allocation works among the continuing owners). If the continuing owners do not buy all of the remaining interest available for purchase by them, the Right-to-Force-a-Sale procedure requires one very important extra step. In this case, the company itself *must* purchase 100% of the available interest not bought by the continuing owners, according to the price and payment terms in the agreement. Remember, in any forced sale scenario under Section III of the agreement, the company or the remaining owners are *required* to buy all of the retiring, disabled, or deceased owner's interest if a forced sale is requested.

The language that covers this last part of the procedure is shown below. It is taken from the Right-to-Force-a-Sale provision in our buyout agreement. (Section IV, (2).)

(f) If the continuing owners decline to purchase all of the available interest that remains, the company *shall* purchase the amount of available interest not purchased by the continuing owners.

SEE AN EXPERT

Don't change the purchasing order of this procedure without a tax expert's help. The order of the purchasing options is important for tax purposes—first the company has an option to purchase the transferring owner's interest and then the continuing owners do. If the total interest has not been purchased or subscribed to at that point, the company must buy whatever remains to be purchased.

The company must then send out a consolidated Notice of Intent to Purchase the interest to the owner or the owner's estate, inheritors, guardian, or whoever is forcing the sale. The entire interest is then purchased by the company and/or the continuing owners according to the terms in Section VII of the agreement. ●

Funding Buyouts

n Chapter 4, we discussed how a buyout will play out in the future. Now you'll need to adopt a sensible plan to provide the company or continuing owners with funds to carry out a future buyout. If you don't think about funding now, your buy-sell provisions may not be able to help you later on (for example, if your company or co-owners can't come up with the money to buy out an owner's estate after he has died, his inheritors will be able to keep their ownership interest in the company and may start to interfere).

It is key to plan to fund a future buyout now, since some types of funding require long-term planning and accrual. In this chapter we briefly discuss several common ways to fund a buyback under your buy-sell agreement.

Funding With Cash

The most obvious way to pay for a buyout is with cash. Funding with cash is simple and has no immediate expense (unlike paying up-front premiums for life insurance, which we discuss in "Buying Insurance," below). But unless your company or its owners are solidly solvent, planning to buy back an owner's interest with cash has a big downside. It requires that your company or the continuing owners keep a large cash reserve available at all times. And, of course, this ties up money (or the ability to borrow it) that could better be used for other purposes.

If neither the company nor the continuing owners have adequate cash reserves when the time comes to buy out an owner or his family members, the capital, or current income, of the company or the continuing owners' personal savings could be seriously depleted. Or, in the worst-case scenario, the buyback might not even happen.

> **CAUTION**
>
> **Corporations: Watch out for the accumulated earnings tax.** For corporations, it's even possible that holding a large cash reserve to fund a future buyout could trigger an accumulated earnings tax penalty. This tax is assessed when corporations hold on to earnings and profits that the IRS decides are not needed for normal business expansion or growth purposes (although most corporations get an automatic allowance to accumulate $250,000). Ask your tax adviser for more information.

WORKSHEET

Turn to your worksheet. If you plan on funding a future buyout with cash only, you do not need to check anything in Section V on your worksheet or in the buyout agreement.

Borrowing Money

Borrowing money to fund a buyout is also fairly simple and does not require an immediate outlay of cash, but this method has its obvious problems. At the time of a buyout, the company or continuing owners might have trouble getting a loan, especially if a co-owner has just died (since the business has probably just lost an important asset).

There are other problems with borrowing. The company may have already exhausted its ability to borrow, or high interest rates may make getting a loan unaffordable.

WORKSHEET

Turn to your worksheet. If you plan on funding a future buyout through company or personal loans, you do not need to check anything in Section V on your worksheet or in the buyout agreement.

Buying Insurance

Life insurance and disability insurance can play a big part in funding buyouts. Not only can they fund buyouts in situations of the death or disability of an owner, but in some cases they can also provide some monies for the buyout of a retired owner (see "Life Insurance," below).

Here's how insurance funding works: The company or the co-owners take out insurance policies on each owner. When an owner dies or becomes disabled, the insurance payoff is used to buy the departing owner's interest.

Of course, some business owners do not like the idea of paying dollars up front for a need that may be years away. But paying insurance premiums can actually be cheaper than either saving or borrowing money. Plus, having insurance is a guarantee that cash will be available to purchase an owner's interest.

Insurance, however, cannot be used to fund a buyout that is triggered when an owner gets divorced, files for personal bankruptcy, loses a professional license, or defaults on a personal loan. For those buyout scenarios, cash, loans or other types of funding must be used.

Who Pays the Insurance Premiums?

There are two alternatives here: The company buys and owns policies on each owner or each owner buys and owns policies on each of the co-owners.

Company Pays Premiums

One approach is to have the company pay the premiums on an insurance policy for each owner, with the company being the owner and beneficiary of each policy. When an owner dies or becomes disabled, the company uses the insurance policy payoff to buy the ownership interest of the owner. This type of arrangement is called an "entity-purchase," or "company-purchase" arrangement.

> EXAMPLE: A company has three owners. They adopt a buy-sell agreement calling for the company to buy out the estate of a deceased owner under an entity-purchase arrangement. The company buys three insurance policies, which insure the lives of each of the three owners. The face amount of each policy is enough to add up to the full Agreement Price for the entire company (or at least will come close enough).

This approach is simple and cheap—only one policy is needed on each owner (rather than several, as is necessary when the owners purchase the policies themselves—discussed next).

Owners Pay Premiums

Another approach is for each owner to individually purchase and pay for insurance policies on the lives of each of their co-owners—this type of arrangement is called a "cross-purchase" arrangement. The individual owners pay the premiums, own the policies, and receive the insurance benefits if there's a payout.

In a three-owner company, the face amount of a policy on another owner should be high enough to pay for half of the purchase price of the owner's interest.

EXAMPLE: Jackie, Elizabeth, and Graciela open a photography studio, to be operated as a partnership. They adopt a buy-sell agreement calling for the continuing owners to buy out a disabled owner with disability insurance, under a cross-purchase arrangement. Under the buy-sell agreement, each person's share of the company is worth approximately $100,000. Jackie buys two disability insurance policies: one on Elizabeth for $50,000 and one on Graciela for $50,000. Elizabeth also buys two policies for $50,000: one on Jackie and one on Graciela. And, of course, Graciela buys two policies for the same amount: one on Jackie and one on Elizabeth. Jackie suffers a chronic disability from long-term exposure to developing chemicals, and their disability insurance company rules that she is permanently and totally disabled. After the required six-month waiting period goes by, Elizabeth and Graciela each purchase half of Jackie's interest with the $50,000 disability insurance payout they each receive from the insurance company.

Cross-purchase arrangements require more paperwork and more premiums (more policies) and are more difficult to maintain than a company-purchase insurance arrangement, especially for companies with more than a few owners. Also, paying for several smaller policies (required by a cross-purchase insurance plan) is sometimes more expensive than paying for one larger policy (under an entity-purchase plan). Therefore, in businesses with more than two or three owners, company-purchased insurance may be the way to go.

There are many other factors involved in choosing between company-purchased and owner-purchased insurance, but we can make a few observations here. If you expect your company, not the continuing owners, to exercise buyback rights when it comes time to buy out an owner under your agreement, it makes sense to opt for an entity-purchase option in your agreement. On the other hand, if you expect the continuing owners to buy out ownership interests under your agreement, you would probably be best choosing the cross-purchase option.

Of course, if you don't know whether the company or the continuing owners will buy out a departing owner, or you expect both the company and the continuing owners to effectuate buyouts under your agreement, either type may make sense. But, in this case, we believe it's better to choose the entity-purchase option. Again, having the company purchase one policy on each owner can be simpler and less expensive than having three, four, or more owners purchase a policy on each of their co-owners.

But what happens if the continuing owners want to exercise their option to buy a deceased owner's interest, and your agreement calls for company-purchased insurance? In small businesses where all of the owners participate, the company can always make loans to the continuing owners to purchase the available interest, and then use the cash from its insurance payout to increase the owners' bonuses and salaries to allow them to make their loan payments to the company.

SEE AN EXPERT

Since this is a complicated area of buyout agreements, you should consult your insurance agent or broker as well as a tax expert before deciding on an entity-purchase or cross-purchase arrangement.

The language of the provision in our buyout agreement that calls for company-purchased life insurance (Section V, (1) of the agreement) is shown below.

Section V: Funding

(1) Life Insurance

☐ **Option 1: Company-Purchased Life Insurance**

The company will apply for, own, and be the beneficiary of a life insurance policy on the life of each owner. The company will take any actions necessary to maintain in force all of the insurance policies it is required to maintain under this section, including paying all premiums, and will not cancel them or allow them to lapse. The policy benefits shall be applied to the purchase price in a buyout of a deceased owner.

WORKSHEET

Turn to your worksheet. Check Option 1 for this provision on your worksheet if you wish to provide for company-purchased life insurance. (Section V, (1).)

SEE AN EXPERT

There are disadvantages to entity-purchased life insurance. Since the policies are company assets under this scheme, the cash values of the policies are subject to the claims of business creditors. Also, for corporations, the corporate alternative minimum tax (AMT) may trigger an income tax liability when proceeds are paid out. To avoid tax problems, you should see a tax adviser to discuss these issues before having your company purchase life insurance policies on the owners' lives.

The language calling for owner-purchased life insurance contained in our agreement (Section V, (1)) is shown below.

☐ **Option 2: Owner-Purchased Life Insurance**

Each owner will apply for, own, and be the beneficiary of a life insurance policy on the life of each other owner. Each owner will take any actions necessary to maintain in force all of the insurance policies he or she is required to maintain under this section, including paying all premiums, and will not cancel them or allow them to lapse. The policy benefits shall be applied to the purchase price in a buyout of a deceased owner.

WORKSHEET

Turn to your worksheet. Check Option 2 for this provision on your worksheet if you wish to provide for owner-purchased life insurance; this option is an alternative to Option 1, covered just above (do not check both Options 1 and 2). (Section V, (1).)

> ⓘ **CAUTION**
>
> **There are disadvantages to cross-purchase arrangements.** Younger owners, who are usually in the weakest financial position to pay high life insurance premiums, bear the burden of paying higher premiums for older owners. In addition, cross-purchase arrangements may not be the ideal choice for corporations. If the corporate tax rate is lower than the individual owners' marginal tax rates, it will be cheaper for the company to pay for premiums than for the individual owners to (the after-tax cost will be lower). Investigate these financial issues with your insurance agent and your tax adviser before going ahead with a cross-purchase insurance plan.

Life Insurance

In this section, we touch on a few things you should understand if you're interested in funding your buyout agreement with life insurance. However, most of your planning in this area will be done with an insurance agent or broker (one who must be familiar with buy-sell agreements and small businesses) and/or a qualified financial planner or CPA.

> ⓘ **CAUTION**
>
> **Not everyone can get life insurance.** Life insurance may not be available to owners of advancing years or who have ill health. If this describes you or your co-owners, you'll have to consider other funding methods, such as accumulating cash reserves and/or borrowing money. Also, see "Making Installment Payments," below.

Here are some key points you should know when shopping for life insurance:

Purchase policies now. Ideally, life insurance policies should be purchased at the same time you create a buy-sell agreement. That's because the cost of premiums will only go up as owners get older. You should estimate the amount you'll need for a buyout, and then get life insurance policies for a little more than that amount. Also, the face amounts of life insurance policies should be scheduled to keep up with the value of the owners' interests.

Employee Buyouts

When a sole proprietor dies, her business may die with her unless other steps are taken. If there is a family member who is willing and able to take over, the owner can leave the business to that person as a gift. But often an owner doesn't have the option of giving the business to family members or relatives. In that case, the owner may want to sell the business to a key employee who is willing and able to take over.

To fund an employee buyout of a sole owner, the employee can purchase an insurance policy on the life of the owner. The employee is the owner, the payer of premiums, and the beneficiary of the policy. When the owner dies, the insurance proceeds will be used to buy the business from the owner's estate (and the proceeds will then go to the sole proprietor's inheritors). In case an owner retires (instead of dying), the cash value of the insurance (if a whole life policy is purchased) can be used by the employee to make a down payment toward purchase of the owner's interest.

Increase insurance regularly. After the buyout of another owner, the value of the remaining owners' interests will increase. Unfortunately, increasing the policy amounts at that point could be costly. But with some policies, policy dividends can be applied to purchase additional one-year term insurance. In this way you can automatically keep increasing the amount of life insurance held. Make sure to ask your insurance agent or broker about this type of insurance.

Investigate specialized policies. A variety of alternatives to standard life insurance policies exist that should be discussed with your insurance agent or broker prior to deciding on the best way to fund the buyout of deceased owners. For example, some insurance companies now offer a less-expensive "first to die" life insurance policy that pays when the first of two or more individuals dies. Another alternative is the "adjustable life" policy, whose payoff amount can be increased (with a corresponding increase in premiums) during the life of the policy. As your business becomes more valuable, you can increase the death benefit payable under this type of policy.

Avoid Estate Taxes on Life Insurance Payouts

To ensure that the proceeds of life insurance are not included in a deceased owner's estate for estate tax purposes, make sure that each insured owner has no "incidents of ownership" in the policy on his life and that the policy proceeds will not be directly available to the owner's estate or inheritors to pay taxes or estate debts. (However, the company or continuing owners can buy the interest from the deceased owner's estate or inheritors with the life insurance proceeds, and the estate or inheritors could then use the proceeds to pay taxes or estate debts.)

If the policy provisions or your buy-sell agreement gives the insured owner an option to purchase the policy prior to death (for example, upon termination of the buy-sell agreement or cancellation of the policies by the corporation), the IRS may decide that the owners have been given "incidents of ownership" in the policies. If so, the insurance proceeds may be included in a deceased owner's taxable estate (even if the deceased owner never exercised her option to take title to the policy prior to her death). Our agreement does *not* provide an owner with the option to purchase the insurance policies that the company or owners hold on his life.

There's also a special estate tax trap to watch out for when the owners individually take out policies on the lives of each other. Namely, when an owner dies, if your arrangement requires his estate to transfer the insurance policies he owned on the lives of the surviving owners back to the surviving owners, the IRS might consider this arrangement a "transfer for value" feature of these policies. In this case, life insurance proceeds paid upon an owner's death would be taxable as part of her estate. Our agreement does *not* require an owner's estate to transfer the policies back to the surviving owners.

Without going further into the ins and outs of these special rules (which are subject to change), one bit of advice: You will want your insurance or tax adviser to scrutinize any life insurance arrangement you adopt to make sure that insurance proceeds will not be included in the taxable estate of a deceased owner. See Chapter 9 for more on estate tax issues.

Consider the benefits of whole life insurance. Not only can life insurance policies fund buyouts after the death of an owner, but some types of life insurance can also help to fund a buyout during an owner's lifetime (or at least provide a down payment for a buyout). In this type of arrangement, the company or the owners take out whole life insurance policies in the name of each owner, which build up cash surrender values. If an owner retires or becomes disabled, the company or the continuing owners can cash out the policies they hold on the life of the departing owner and give the cash surrender value of the policies to him in exchange for his ownership interest. If the cash surrender value of the policies is less than the buyback price (which it probably will be), then the company or the owners must pay the difference or sign one or more promissory notes to cover what remains of the purchase price, plus interest, until it is paid off.

Understand the tax consequences. Here are the normal income tax consequences of buyback arrangements funded by life insurance:

- The purchasers of the insurance (the company or the owners) get no income tax deduction for the amount of the premiums paid.

- Premiums paid by the company or co-owners for a policy on the life of an owner will not be taxable to the insured owner.

- Life insurance proceeds paid to the policy owners (the company or the continuing owners) are generally not subject to income tax. The owners or the company does not have to report the funds as income; the funds are simply used to buy the ownership interest back, usually from a deceased owner's estate.

- Life insurance proceeds will not be included in the estate of a deceased owner for estate tax purposes as long as the proceeds are not payable directly to the estate and the deceased owner did not own the policy (see "Avoid Estate Taxes on Life Insurance Payouts," above). Policy proceeds should be payable to the company or the continuing owners, whoever held the policy.

SEE AN EXPERT

Ask your insurance agent or broker about the life insurance alternatives and tax issues. This short section above should serve as an introduction to insurance funding for buy-sell agreements, and not as advice for choosing and buying insurance policies.

CAUTION

Set buyout price independent of insurance. We don't think it's smart to tie the price to be paid for an ownership interest to the payoff value of the insurance taken out. A big reason for this is that the insurance policies may not be updated to reflect increased earnings of the company. In such cases, the buyout price set by the insurance policy will probably be unfairly low. Also, agreements that have an insurance policy fix the buyout price might not establish the value of an ownership interest for estate tax purposes (estate taxes are discussed in Chapter 9).

Our approach is to have the buy-sell agreement set a buyout price independent of the means used to fund the buyout. Of course, your company can still fully fund a buyout with insurance proceeds by updating the policies regularly to reflect any increase in the value of the ownership interest.

Disability Insurance

One way to handle funding the buyout of a disabled owner is to have your buyout agreement require the purchase of disability insurance on all co-owners. This way, if a disability occurs, the insurance policy proceeds can provide a source of funds to allow the company or the continuing co-owners to buy back the interest of a disabled owner—without diminishing company or personal cash reserves or having to borrow.

Some disability policies are designed to fund buyouts under buy-sell agreements. These policies usually pay a lump-sum cash benefit of up to $1 million to fund the buyout of a disabled owner. If desired, additional financial benefits can be funded by policy proceeds, such as a wage continuation plan to the disabled owner (prior to a buyout of ownership interest). Be sure to ask your insurance agent or broker about these special policies.

Disability insurance operates in much the same way that life insurance does to provide funds to buy out a deceased owner's ownership interest. Much of the information we covered in the life insurance discussion above applies here also. In addition, there are several issues specific to disability insurance to be aware of:

- **Definition of disability.** If you choose to purchase disability insurance, our agreement uses your insurance company's definition of "total disability" and provides that the insurance company is the arbiter of whether the co-owner is totally disabled—that is, the insurance company decides whether an owner's disability will trigger a buyout under your buyout agreement. (In the agreement, see Section III, Scenario 2, When an Owner Becomes Disabled).

- **Waiting period.** As covered in Chapter 3, our agreement establishes a period of time—an "elimination period"—that an owner's inability to work for the company must persist before a buyout can occur. The length of this waiting period should be dictated by the insurance policy. (See Section III, Scenario 2.)

- **Date of valuation.** As covered in Chapter 3, you need to specify *when* the buyout price will be determined. Most companies use the date the owner stopped working as the date to value the business—since that is the date the owner stopped contributing to the company. This way, any changes in the worth of the company can be attributed to the remaining owners. (See Section III, Scenario 2.) You can, however, have the buyout price be determined on the date of the buyout.

- **Policy payout.** Your disability insurance policy can provide just a down payment to buy a disabled owner's interest, or it can be set up to provide the entire purchase price. However, the insurance company will likely pay only up to the amount of the buyout—essentially, you'll lose any policy benefit in excess of the buyout price. In addition, your insurance policy can be set up to pay off either a lump-sum payment or a series of payments. Your insurance agent should review your agreement to make sure that it is not in conflict with your insurance policy regarding payment terms, price, and elimination period.

The disability funding clauses we use in our agreement (Section V, (2)) are shown below.

---

(2)   Disability Insurance

☐ **Option 1: Company-Purchased Disability Insurance**

The company will apply for, own, and be the beneficiary of a disability insurance policy for each owner. The company will take any actions necessary to maintain in force all of the insurance policies it is required to maintain under this section, including paying all premiums, and will not cancel them or allow them to lapse. The policy benefits shall be applied to the purchase price in a buyout of a disabled owner.

☐ **Option 2: Owner-Purchased Disability Insurance**

Each owner will apply for, own, and be the beneficiary of a disability insurance policy for each other owner. Each owner will take any actions necessary to maintain in force all of the insurance policies he or she is required to maintain under this section, including paying all premiums, and will not cancel them or allow them to lapse. The policy benefits shall be applied to the purchase price in a buyout of a disabled owner.

TIP

Life insurance can partially fund the buyout of a disabled owner. Some types of life insurance (for example, whole life) can help to fund a buyout of a disabled owner by providing cash surrender values. If an owner becomes disabled, the company or the continuing owners can cash out the policies they hold on the life of the disabled owner and give the cash surrender value of the policies to her (plus some cash—up to the Agreement Price) in exchange for her ownership interest. Ask your insurance agent or broker about this possibility.

WORKSHEET

Turn to your worksheet. Check Option 1 for company-purchased disability insurance, Option 2 for owner-purchased disability insurance, or neither if you are not interested in funding your agreement with disability insurance. (Section V, (2).)

Making Installment Payments

Another way to ease the financial burden of future buyouts is to allow the buyer to pay the purchase price, or at least part of it, over time. Your buyout agreement can provide that payment for an owner's interest will be made by the company or the continuing owners in installments, perhaps over three to five years. This way, the installment payments to the departing owner come from cash flow that is generated after the departing owner leaves the business, which means the company may not have to build up cash reserves or borrow money to fund a company buyout. (Installment plans are discussed in Chapter 7.)

To pay for the installment payments made by the company to the departing owner, the continuing owners could decrease their salaries or distributions. Or, if the continuing owners buy out the departing owner's interest, they might take more of the company's cash flow in salary or distributions to pay for the installment payments (of course, they will owe income taxes on this money). However, when continuing owners (or family members or key employees) buy out a departing owner, often the only cash source available to them—outside of loans—is the future cash flow of the business.

However, receiving payments in dribs and drabs can be inconvenient for the departing owner or his family members, especially if they don't have confidence in the abilities of the remaining owners to successfully continue the business in the meantime. Also, if a company has to pay the entire purchase price in installments, the drain on future cash flow might not allow the continuing owners to maintain their business and salaries or distributions comfortably. For these reasons, if you choose to set up installment payments, you'll also probably want to provide that some portion of the purchase price will be paid up front, with either cash reserves, a loan, or the purchase of insurance (discussed above). ●

How to Set the Buyout Price in Your Agreement

B y now, you should have your eye on the buyout provisions that will best handle prospective ownership changes for your company. Also, after reading Chapters 4 and 5, you should understand how buyout procedures work and how you might fund a future buyout. Now, as explained in this chapter, your next big job is to decide how to establish a fair price for any future buybacks or buyouts that occur. (The standard price for all buyouts is referred to here as "Agreement Price.")

Unfortunately, choosing a price that will be perceived years from now— by all owners and the IRS—as representing the true value of your company is no easy task. After all, as you read this, you can't know if in the years ahead your business will prosper mightily, struggle to make a profit, or fail.

SEE AN EXPERT

Settling on a fair buyout price can be challenging. After reading the following chapter, we recommend you choose a buyout price in consultation with a tax and/or financial adviser.

Why Choose a Price in Advance?

Even with a pile of up-to-date facts, coming up with an accurate price for a small, privately owned business interest is not easy. For one thing, unlike publicly traded corporations, there is no public market for small business interests, so it's hard to establish comparative prices for similar businesses. And even if you are able to find out how much similar businesses are selling for, there's no guarantee yours would fetch a similar price. Depending on the economy and competitive pressures in your industry, as well as the health (or lack thereof) of your business, plus many other more subtle factors, the true value of your company could be much more or much less.

Although it is hard to value an interest in a small business, and even harder to do it years in advance of a sale, it's a job that must be done in order to prepare an adequate buyout agreement. If owners neglect to do this, they might end up arguing over price any time an owner's interest is bought under the buyout agreement. And if the divorce or death of an owner is the reason for a buyout, negotiations would almost surely be burdened by the emotions of the owner's spouse, inheritors, or estate representative, making agreement over price difficult or impossible. Especially when a divorce is involved, such emotion-laden conflict can result in a lawsuit.

Should a co-owner die, her inheritors can find themselves at a truly unfair disadvantage in the absence of an agreement. For instance, a recently widowed spouse who needs cash to pay a child's college tuition may be easily pressured into selling her ownership interest back to the company or the remaining owners at a too-low price (or a spouse may simply not be familiar with the business and, as a result, not know what a fair price for the interest is).

While no price or formula will be perfect, choosing one in advance does have the great advantage of allowing you and your co-owners a chance to think about, discuss, and vote on how a reasonable price for the company should be calculated, at a time when none of you are planning to sell out. Just the fact that a particular method was agreed to by all owners is likely to go a long way toward reducing conflict when you or a co-owner leaves. Even if, at the time of an owner's departure, you all agree to modify the Agreement Price to better reflect current realities, the fact that you start with an agreement—not a vacuum—should make the negotiating process easier. Fortunately, there are some techniques that can help you come up with a fair price. Let's look at how they work.

TIP

It may be easier to establish a price in advance. Think of it this way: When you're creating your buyout agreement, no owner knows who will leave first. So even though it's hard to agree on a future price for a new or growing business, making this decision before any owner leaves has huge advantages.

Your Buyout Agreement and Estate Taxes

One reason to set a price or formula in advance concerns "estate taxes"—taxes collected after your death by the government. Carefully setting a price for estate tax purposes can potentially save your estate a lot of dough—which is important if your heirs want to hang on to the business interest they inherit. Of course, this assumes that your estate, including your small business, is worth more than the estate tax threshold when you die—and that the estate tax hasn't been abolished (an agenda item for some lobbyists).

A good valuation provision can fix the value of your ownership interest at an amount considerably lower than its market value at the time of your death. (And the lower the value your agreement provides, the lower your estate taxes.) Of course, for you to really save a bundle on estate taxes, the IRS must accept the value set in your buy-sell agreement. The key to getting the IRS to accept it is choosing the right valuation method. We discuss estate taxes in "Estate Tax Issues" in Chapter 9.

What Valuation Methods Are Based On

Sometimes new owners imagine that, if they were to leave their company after a few months or years, they'd get back exactly the money they invested (often called their capital contribution—see "Capital Accounts," below). This is rarely appropriate. Instead, a departing owner should get more than the initial investment if the business does well and less (possibly even nothing) if it does badly. After all, the point of investing is to make a gain, which, of course, means that you also have to take the risk of taking a loss.

Assets Versus Liabilities

The value of a new business is often closely tied to the net value of its assets (that is, the current fair market value of the company assets minus company liabilities).

EXAMPLE: Carol and Dick go into business together to clean and repair houses before the houses go on the real estate market. Carol plans on doing industrial-strength cleaning, interior painting, and yard work, while Dick will take care of any needed exterior painting, critical repairs, and, if called for, minor structural improvements. Each puts up $20,000 as a capital contribution.

Their first decision is to purchase a van. Rather than looking into the used van market, however, they buy a new vehicle from a dealer for almost $35,000 and have their company name, "Property Moppers," painted on the side. Dick also buys a high-powered washer, a power painter, and a set of tools for a total of $4,500. Carol buys what seems like a year's worth of cleaning supplies and paintbrushes for $500.

Six months into it, Property Moppers has had only three jobs, and, because of their inexperience, Dick and Carol spent more to fix up the houses than they were paid. Carol, knowing that it takes time to build a business reputation and get a system down, vows to hang in there. Dick, however, has no patience and tells Carol he already wants out. He demands that Carol pay him the $20,000 he put into the company. Carol can't afford to buy out Dick without taking out a home equity loan, something she is loath to do—at least before she finds someone to do Dick's work. Fearing she may just have to give up the business and sell the equipment, she tries to make a deal with Dick. Eventually, they agree to have an appraiser value the current worth of their business assets, with Dick accepting half of that amount for his share.

The appraisal is straightforward. Since Dick and Carol didn't buy anything on credit, the business has no liabilities. Since they don't have any customers, the business has no "goodwill." In short, the business is worth the current value of its assets. Although they bought the van for $35,000, the appraiser concludes it has already dropped in value by $10,000. Similarly, although they paid $4,500 for the tools new, the appraiser decides that their current market value is less than half that—$2,000. Finally, the appraiser sets the market value of Carol's remaining cleaning supplies at $20. Adding all the assets up, the appraiser values Property Moppers at $27,000, or $13,000 less than the sum of the owners' capital contributions! Under their agreement, Dick must accept half of that—$13,500— rather than his original $20,000 contribution.

In short, because the value of a company goes up and down depending on the success or failure of the business, most valuation formulas do not use capital contributions as the basis for a buyback price, but instead use information on sales, profits, or assets to come up with the current worth of the company.

Capital Accounts

The term capital account refers to the dollar value of a partner's or an LLC member's interest in the business (not counting depreciation or goodwill). An owner's capital account starts off with the value of her initial investment in the business (her capital contribution). Accounting additions and subtractions occur over time as the profits and losses of the company are recorded and as additional capital contributions or distributions are made.

Sometimes the value of these capital accounts is used as the basis for setting the amount each owner gets if the company ceases to do business and liquidates its assets ("dissolves"). Thus, if a business dissolves in a situation where all creditors of the business have been fully paid off and there's still money left in the business, each owner may be able to be paid back his capital investment. If there is insufficient cash left from a liquidated business to pay each owner the amount in his capital account, the relative percentage of each owner's capital account will be used to split whatever cash is left from the liquidated business (for example, a 50% owner should get 50% of the net cash of a liquidated business).

Since the value of capital accounts usually bears little relationship to the real worth of a business, our buyout agreement does not use capital accounts to put a price on ownership interests for buyouts and buybacks.

How Our Valuation Provisions Work

Throughout this book and in our buyout agreement itself, we refer to the price or formula you choose in your agreement as the Agreement Price. This price, which represents the value of the entire business, applies to most transfers under the buyout agreement. The Agreement Price can be updated at any time.

When the Agreement Price Applies

The Agreement Price will usually control whenever the company or the continuing owners buy an ownership interest, no matter why the buyout was triggered—death, retirement, divorce, disability, or any other reason listed in the agreement.

However, one part of your agreement may include a buyout provision that uses a different price. For instance, a Right-of-First-Refusal provision may require the company and the continuing owners to match the price an outsider has offered for an owner's interest, rather than the Agreement Price (as discussed in Chapter 2). If so, the outsider's price will take precedence over the general Agreement Price.

You might have provided that the full Agreement Price is not to be used, or is to be discounted, in other buyout situations as well. For example, as discussed in Chapter 3, your agreement might state that a co-owner who wants out in the first year or two may be eligible to receive only a fraction of the Agreement Price.

Explain Provisions to Family Members

It's fairly common for an owner's spouse or children or other relatives to object when a company eventually asserts its right to buy back the shares of a deceased, disabled, or divorced owner. Often, these family members have an unrealistically high expectation of the value of the company and are upset if the amount they will receive in a buyout is based on a conservative valuation formula.

Trouble of this sort is particularly likely when key family members have been kept in the dark about the terms of a buyout agreement. It follows that you can defuse most potential future problems by making sure that spouses, adult children, and any other family members likely to be affected by a future buyout clearly understand the valuation method described in your buyout agreement. At a minimum, make sure that the spouses of all owners read and sign your buyout agreement (we provide a specific spousal consent provision at the end of our agreement, to be signed by spouses).

The Price of an Individual Owner's Interest

For purposes of convenience, the price provisions in our buyout agreement set an Agreement Price that reflects the worth of the whole company. To come up with a price for any individual owner's interest, simply multiply the entire Agreement Price by that owner's ownership percentage. For example, if an owner owns 25% of his company, you'd multiply the Agreement Price by 25% to come up with the price of that owner's share.

Choosing a Valuation Provision

Our buyout agreement sets out five alternative valuation provisions. We discuss each below. Once you decide on the one you want, simply check the appropriate box in your agreement.

Updating the Valuation Provision

Having all the valuation provisions in your buyout agreement allows you to easily update your method of valuation should the need arise, without having to create a whole new agreement. Once you've been in business at least two or three years, you might want to choose a more complex valuation formula than you initially chose (for instance, a formula based on earnings rather than assets). Also, any time the type of business you run changes (for instance, your company changes from a products and service company to one that sells only products), you should revisit your valuation clause.

To change your valuation method at a later date, you can simply line-out your check mark for the valuation method you originally chose and place a new check mark in front of a different valuation alternative. You will want to date and have each owner initial each line-out and addition to your agreement. Or, if you saved it on your computer, you can just change your choice in the agreement and print out a clean copy for signature by the owners.

Agreeing on a Fixed Price (Valuation Method 1)

> **TIP**
>
> **Using a fixed price may not be the best method.** For a number of reasons, which we discuss below, adopting a valuation formula is often, but not always, a better approach than actually inserting a fixed price in your buyout agreement. In short, before getting enthusiastic about the first—or any other—valuation alternative, please read this entire chapter.

The most straightforward approach to nailing down a buyout price for your agreement is to agree upon an actual fixed-dollar price in your buyout agreement.

Advantages. The agreed-value, or fixed-price, method combines simplicity with certainty. By setting a fixed-dollar value yourself, there is no need to bother with appraisals, accountants, or earnings multiples when an owner's interest is being purchased. You simply take your buyout agreement out of its file, blow off the dust, and locate the fixed price in Section VI, Agreement Price.

The fixed-price method also gives a clear picture to the owners of what the future holds—specifically, how much they can expect to walk away from the company with. It also makes it easier for business owners to do estate planning, since they know exactly what the agreed value of their ownership interests will be when they die, and how much their estate might owe in estate taxes, if any. A fixed price also lets owners know how much life or disability insurance they need to buy.

> **TIP**
>
> **Don't tie the payment to insurance proceeds.** Your buyout agreement should not call for a lump-sum payment that is tied specifically to the amount of life or disability insurance proceeds (see the warning "Set buyout price independent of insurance," in Chapter 5, for reasons why). Our approach is to have the buyout agreement set a buyback price independent of the means used to fund the buyout.

Disadvantages. Pinpointing a fixed price as the true value of your company can be a difficult task. Using the fixed-price method requires that the owners have business acumen, or at least informed common sense, when it comes to valuing their company.

The major problem with establishing a fixed price in advance is that any value you pick for your business will almost surely be quickly outdated. Depending on your initial outlook and your actual success or failure, your fixed price should be adjusted up or down to keep pace with business profitability and owner expectations. And after several years of profitable operations, it may make sense to place a value on the ability of the company to draw customers or attract business (called "goodwill"). For example, a small architecture company that specializes in public safety buildings (police, fire, and emergency response) may, over the years, build up a valuable reputation that will help bring in a steady stream of profitable new jobs, thereby increasing the value of the company.

It follows that if you use the fixed-price method, you should periodically revise your agreement. We recommend that you make annual updates to change the agreed value shown in your agreement.

You can regularly update the fixed price either by preparing and signing a new agreement with a new value or by signing a separate statement. If you use separate statements to update your agreed value, make sure to attach copies to your buyout agreement for future reference. (See Chapter 8 for more on updating your agreement.)

TIP

Revisit the fixed price regularly. Even if you plan to annually update your company's agreed value, there is always the danger that this task will be overlooked. Although it's not an adequate substitute for meeting and agreeing on a new price, some co-owners include a backup clause in their agreement that will automatically adjust the Agreement Price up or down based on the consumer price index or another inflation-tracking mechanism in any year when the co-owners fail to update it.

Businesses Where an Agreed-Upon Price May Work

In some companies, an agreed-on price may be a simple and efficient way to provide for how much a business is worth.

- **Service businesses.** From computer repairs to cutting hair, new service businesses typically have few valuable assets beyond the energies and hopes of their owners. In this context, rather than bothering with trying to determine the worth of the business by more conventional means (for instance, book value, capitalization of earnings, appraisal), the owners may simply agree on what they think the business is worth and revise this figure periodically. Later, if the business grows and succeeds, they may wish to switch to one of the other valuation methods.

- **Closely held companies with just a few owners.** Another occasion where it may be appropriate to use the agreed-value method is for small, closely held companies where the owners want to maintain close, harmonious relationships. Since the price is set in advance, an individual being bought out is less likely to become paranoid and conclude that the company is manipulating a last-minute valuation process in order to establish an artificially low buyout value. And by establishing the buyout price in the agreement at a reasonably conservative figure—something that owners in smaller companies are likely to do—the company should be able to afford a buyout when the time comes to implement one.

- **Companies in their first year.** Choosing a conservative fixed price that all owners agree on is a simple way to provide an Agreement Price for the first year of business. This can be helpful if you try to obtain insurance funding in the first year (see Chapter 5). Many insurance companies won't cover a company in its first year, but some will for a low fixed price of, say, $100,000 or $250,000.

As you can see, there are can be problems with using a fixed-price, or agreed-value, provision. Because it's usually subjective—and often out of date—a fixed price can create arguments between the buyer of an owner's interest (the company or the continuing owners) and the seller (a departing owner or his spouse, his inheritors, or an estate representative). Its subjectivity and unreliability may even subject a fixed price to a court challenge by a departing owner or inheritor, and a judge may refuse to uphold it without real data to back it up.

Because of these drawbacks, the fixed-price method is less popular than several of the other methods discussed below, although it is sometimes used to set a low value for a new or small service business, at least until the business has been in operation long enough to make it sensible for the owners to switch to one of the other methods (see "Businesses Where an Agreed-Upon Price May Work," above).

If you do decide to use the fixed-price method, there are a few steps you can take to protect the company. First, be conservative when setting a value for your business. We all hope to be hugely successful, but few of us will really become multimillionaires because of small business ownership. Recognizing this, when you prepare your buyout agreement, it's wise to resist galloping optimism. Also consider that, although you will want to be paid a high price for your business interest if you will be the first to leave, the tables are turned if you and your co-owners must buy out someone else. If your business is highly overvalued, it might even have to be liquidated to pay off a departing owner.

The language of the agreed-value provision in our buyout agreement is shown below.

WORKSHEET

Turn to your worksheet. Check Valuation Method 1 if you wish to set an agreed value for your company. (Section VI, Valuation Method 1.) Insert the agreed value for the entire company in the blank.

Section VI: Agreement Price

Unless otherwise provided in this agreement, the undersigned agree that the method checked below for valuing the company shall be used to determine a price for ownership interests under this agreement.

☐ **Valuation Method 1: Agreed Value**

The agreed value of the company shall be $ [*insert agreed-upon price for entire company, such as "100,000"*], or such other amount as fixed by all owners of the company after the date of adoption of this agreement as specified in a written statement signed by each owner of the company. If more than one such statement is signed by the owners after the date of adoption of this agreement, the statement with the latest date shall control for purposes of fixing a price for the purchase of ownership interests under this agreement. The value of an individual owner's interest shall be the entire value for the company as determined under this paragraph, multiplied by his or her ownership percentage.

Using a Buyout Formula

Because valuing a business interest that will be sold in a future transaction is so difficult, using a valuation formula based on numbers such as the value of current assets, the level of sales, or the amount of profit can make a lot of sense. Because formulas use regularly updated, factual information, they tend to give a more accurate picture of your company's worth than using a fixed price. The trick is choosing the one of a half dozen or so common valuation methods that best represents the value of your company.

Start by understanding that some valuation methods are more appropriate for certain businesses than others. For instance, for a company that exists only to own real estate, it would make more sense to establish its worth by appraising the fair market value of its assets (the buildings and land it owns) and then subtracting its liabilities (the mortgages it owes on), rather than trying to value it based on a multiple of yearly earnings.

On the other hand, an assets-based method would work poorly for a small, organic honey company that has been profitably producing and marketing high-grade honey for the last 15 years. While the company's only assets might be a few boxes of bees and some mesh jumpsuits and smoke guns, valuing it based on its earnings history would surely be more appropriate.

Small service businesses are in a category all their own. Most of the value of these companies is tied up in the owners' hard work and their customers' personal goodwill toward them. If a service business's major asset consists of a customer or client list, and an owner who departs will likely take most of her own customers with her, there may be little value left in the business. In that case, the departing owner should be paid for little beyond any company assets and equipment. This is true for most service businesses where clientele and reputation are key, like those of tax preparers, interior decorators, or hairstylists.

> **EXAMPLE:** Abe, Emily, and Tanya start an interior design business. But when Abe tries to do every color scheme in deep purple, the two women say "enough" and decide to go their separate ways. Because each of the three decorator/owners has his or her own client list, the only property that needs to be divided consists of furniture and office equipment and, of course, liabilities (debts).

Here are some common valuation alternatives used by privately owned small businesses:

- book value
- multiple of book value
- capitalization of earnings method, and
- appraisal value.

Let's take a look at each one in turn.

Book Value (Valuation Method 2)

At least at the start, the value of a company's assets minus its liabilities is all many businesses are worth. Recognizing this, the first valuation formula we present uses a company's assets minus liabilities as shown on the most recent year-end balance sheet.

Commonly, this number is called a company's "book value," but it also goes under the names "net asset value" and "depreciated asset value." (Assets are listed on a company's balance sheet at their "depreciated" value—the cost of the asset minus depreciation taken on the asset.) Note that a balance sheet usually lists the net amount of assets minus liabilities as the "owners' equity" amount. Theoretically, this figure can be positive (if assets exceed liabilities) or negative (if liabilities exceed assets).

As you no doubt know, a balance sheet is basically a snapshot of a company's assets minus liabilities on a particular date. Assets listed on the balance sheet usually will include cash in the bank, real estate, business equipment and machinery, accounts receivable (money customers owe to the business), and other types of tangible assets. Liabilities usually consist of accounts payable (amounts owed to employees and suppliers) plus the remaining balances on any loans taken out by the company.

Advantages. A big advantage to choosing the book value method is that it uses figures that are readily available from the company's financial statements. Balance sheets are typically prepared as of the end of each fiscal (tax) year of a company, and are needed to prepare annual tax returns for the business. Because it is so easy to understand and implement, micro-businesses and start-ups often use the book value method.

> **EXAMPLE:** The balance sheet of Mega-Mania Computer Supplies, Inc., shows assets totaling $320,000 (after depreciation) and liabilities of $200,000. Thus, shareholders' (owners') equity is $120,000. It follows that if the company has issued 1,000 shares, and Joe owns 100 of them (Joe owns 10% of the company), the book value of his shares is one-tenth of total owners' equity, or $12,000.

Disadvantages. A big drawback to the "snapshot" aspect of the book value method, however, is that it does not give you information on the profitability of the business. Book value usually doesn't measure the value of certain intangible assets, such as a strong reputation or customer goodwill, which reflect the ability of the company to continue to earn a good profit—these assets are not reflected on the company's balance sheet.

As a result, of all the valuation formulas, the book value method usually results in the most conservative (lowest) valuation figure for a business. (Also, book value can result in a low figure because the depreciated value of assets—their original cost minus any depreciation—may be less than the resale value of the assets.)

For these reasons, book value is most often used by owners of new businesses that have yet to earn a profit or build up goodwill. It is also the best method to use when owners wish to put the company's ongoing survival interests ahead of any individual owner's interest in selling out for top value. Again, this can make excellent sense if a business is just getting off the ground and the owners are worried that the company (or its remaining owners) will be hard pressed to come up with money necessary to buy back a departing owner's interest under the buyout agreement.

> **EXAMPLE:** Louise, Danny, and Ari form their own company, Digi-Fix, which provides computer repair services. Each owns one-third of the company. After four years, Danny quits, deciding to turn his whitewater rafting hobby into a career as a full-time river guide. On its last fiscal year balance sheet, the company's assets included cash in the bank, depreciated fixed assets (mostly computers, tools, and equipment), and accounts receivable, totaling $95,000. Liabilities consisted of accounts payable plus the current remaining balance on a small business bank loan taken out by the company two years after its formation, totaling $60,000. The book value of the company—its owners' equity—is the difference between assets and liabilities, or $35,000. Using the book value method, each owner's third of the company is worth $11,666 ($35,000 ÷ 3). The company's cash reserves, though modest, are adequate to pay Danny $11,666 for his interest, so the company purchases Danny's interest and continues business operations with the two remaining owners.

The book value method, however, often does not make sense for long-term owners. People who work in a business for many years expect to be fairly compensated at retirement or death. Using book value to come up with a buyback price usually won't provide an adequate buyout price for a profitable, mature company. When your company reaches this point, it may be better to choose one of the other valuation methods below that provide a higher buyout price.

If You Own Real Estate

If your business owns considerable real estate (but does not use it mainly for rental income purposes), you may sensibly decide that valuing your company based on its assets (real estate) is more appropriate for your company than valuing it based on its earnings (rental income, for example). Just the same, you may not want to use a straight book value method to value the assets, because this method may not adequately represent the value of your property. Book value can be inappropriate for companies with real estate in particular, because real estate is usually worth more than its depreciated value as shown on the company balance sheet (in most geographical areas, anyway).

To come up with a formula that does a better job of valuing your real property, you may want to provide that real property be valued at its current market value.

> EXAMPLE: Let's revisit Digi-Fix. This time assume that, many years ago, the computer repair company bought the real estate where it does business. Since real estate has skyrocketed in their area, companies that bought real estate there years ago can be worth quite a bit. The book value method would surely not give any of the owners a fair buyout price, since that method doesn't reflect the current market value of real estate.

If your company owns real estate, select the appraisal method in your buyout agreement to value your company (discussed in "Appraisal Value," below). A professional will appraise your real estate at its fair market value at the time of a buyout.

EXAMPLE: Let's return to our Digi-Fix example, but assume now that it has been in operation ten more years. Thanks to several very profitable long-term service contracts, the three owners have been able to pay themselves salaries of $80,000 per year for the past few years while hiring repair people to do much of the work, allowing each owner to put in a three-day workweek.

This time, it's Louise who wants to leave, to spend more time with her two young children. The book value of Digi-Fix's assets on its last fiscal year balance sheet was $125,000, consisting of $60,000 in equipment, tools, and office furniture (after depreciation), $35,000 in repair fees owed to the company by customers (accounts receivable), and $30,000 cash. Liabilities totaled $50,000, consisting of $40,000 owed to the local bank, plus various accounts payable totaling $10,000. This means the total owners' equity is $75,000 ($125,000 − $50,000). According to the book value method, Louise's interest is worth $25,000—one-third of the total book value of $75,000. This is a pretty low buyout amount for someone who has been receiving $80,000 every year for three days of work! True, when Louise leaves, she will no longer have to work those three days per week, and the remaining owners may have to replace her. But surely they can do this for less than $80,000 per year. At any rate, using the book value method would be a poor choice in this situation.

If the book value method will result in too low a buyout figure—as it will for most successful businesses in the long term—consider adopting or switching to one of the other methods set out below.

The language that we use in our buyout agreement to establish the book value method is shown below.

☐ **Valuation Method 2: Book Value**

The value of the company shall be its book value (its assets minus its liabilities as shown on the balance sheet of the company) as of the end of the most recent fiscal year prior to the purchase of an ownership interest under this agreement. The value of an individual owner's interest shall be the entire value for the company as determined under this paragraph, multiplied by his or her ownership percentage.

Businesses Where the Book Value Method May Work

Valuing an owner's interest at book value is most appropriate for companies whose assets, rather than earnings potential, are the base, or strong point, of the business. As mentioned in the text, this applies to companies with low earnings and to companies just starting out, which probably don't have an established earnings record. Let's look at a couple of examples of which types of businesses this simple book value approach often works best for.

- **Start-up companies.** When a business is young and has not yet developed a reputation or turned a profit, the true value of the company may well be the amount of the depreciated value of assets less its liabilities. And because the book value method is based on the business's financial statement, it will not lead to any extra costs for accounting, legal, or appraisal fees.
- **Marginally profitable companies.** Especially in a highly competitive field, many companies just aren't able to make much of a profit above their ongoing expenses, such as salaries, rent, utilities, and advertising, meaning that an earnings-based valuation method would produce a low value. Nevertheless, the company may have a bright future if it can find a way to break away from the pack. In the meantime, the book value method may do a fairly accurate job of valuing the business.

WORKSHEET

Turn to your worksheet. Check Valuation Method 2 if you wish to use your company's book value (as of the end of the last fiscal year prior to a buyout) to value your ownership interests. (Section VI, Valuation Method 2.)

TIP

Use several years if your balance sheet numbers fluctuate from year to year. If your company has been in business several years but its balance sheet numbers tend to fluctuate widely year to year (for instance, because of large losses at the end of a year or the beginning of the next year), you may want to provide that the book value of your company be derived from several years' balance sheets, not just the balance sheet of the last fiscal year.

Multiple of Book Value (Valuation Method 3)

As we mentioned above, if a small business has been up and running successfully for several years, its real value is probably greater than its book value (the balance sheet value of its assets minus the balance sheet value of its liabilities). For an outside buyer, there can be considerable value in the fact that the owners of an ongoing business have already set up a profitable business (for instance, bought or leased equipment, installed a phone system, rented or bought a building, purchased inventory, developed a clientele, implemented a marketing program, trained employees, and established an accounting system).

Of course, most of the time, an outside buyer won't be involved in your buyout situation—the selling will be between the owners, between an owner and the company, or between the company and an owner's family. Nevertheless, knowing what an outsider would pay for a company can give you a good indication of its fair market value. That's why it can be sensible to use a valuation formula that treats your entire company as a candidate for sale—a formula that is likely to arrive at a dollar figure that better reflects what an outside buyer would pay for a profitable business.

Enter the "multiple of book value" method. While based on book value, this formula goes beyond measuring the book value of your company's tangible assets to take into account "intangible assets" and your company's value as a "going concern." These intangibles typically include things whose worth is hard to calculate, such as a desirable lease and the goodwill, or positive reputation, of the business. Other intangible assets that can add value to a company are its brand or trade names, its mailing lists, and the anticipated effect of long-term advertising campaigns.

The multiple of book value method calculates the worth of the company by taking the owners' equity figure from your balance sheet and multiplying it by a predetermined number, called a multiplier. This multiplier—which you and your co-owners will establish in your buy-sell agreement—should be greater than 1 (or greater than 100%, if you use a percentage). That's because the purpose of the multiplier is to increase the Agreement Price of your company beyond its book value to bring it closer to fair market value. Because it is so difficult to precisely value goodwill and other intangibles, picking the correct multiplier is at best an imprecise science.

EXAMPLE: Fit-Tite Jeans, Inc., a discount retailer of distressed, stretched-to-fit denim jeans, with a desirable location near a big university, has had ten years' worth of steadily increasing business. Most years, both sales volume and profits have jumped by 10% or more. Because customer satisfaction appears to be high, the owners of Fit-Tite expect business to remain good. An outside buyer would probably agree (though maybe not out loud) that customer goodwill should be taken into account when offering a fair price for the business.

Wanting to account for their company's goodwill, the Fit-Tite owners agree to change the book value formula they adopted as part of their original buy-sell agreement. They reason that it is only fair that any departing owner be bought out at an amount that reflects the hard work she's put in over the years and that better represents what an outside buyer would pay for the business. To accomplish this, the owners adopt a new agreement, selecting the multiple of book value method and inserting a multiplier of 2 (200%) to double the book value figure taken from the company's last balance sheet.

The language for the multiple of book value method used in our buyout agreement is shown below.

WORKSHEET

Turn to your worksheet. Check Valuation Method 3 if you wish to use a multiple of your company's book value (as of the end of the last fiscal year prior to a buyout) to value your company. (Section VI, Valuation Method 3.) Make sure to insert a multiplier (after consulting an expert, if necessary) in the blank.

The Value of Goodwill

Some profitable ongoing businesses are worth significantly more than the balance sheet value of assets minus liabilities, because they've earned a good business reputation. That reputation brings in a steady stream of regular business. This intangible asset, which business brokers call "the well-founded expectation of continued public patronage," or "going concern value," is more colloquially labeled goodwill. Taking goodwill into account when setting a buyout price rewards the owners for putting their skill and hard work into building up the company.

The concept of business goodwill is especially applicable for successful retail businesses—for example, a restaurant with a big following—but it is often less of a factor for businesses that depend primarily on personalized service. For instance, a carpenter, podiatrist, or dentist may have worked hard to acquire personal goodwill, but it's tricky—and sometimes impossible—to transfer this goodwill to another person when the business is sold. Or, put another way, when a person who provides individual service retires or dies, much of the value of the business disappears. And, of course, this is especially likely to be true if the owner leaves to open or join a competing business.

Although undoubtedly a real asset, the value of business goodwill is easily overestimated following a change in business ownership. Even loyal customers soon go elsewhere if the quality of a service or product diminishes. For example, the reputation of even the most established restaurant can quickly take a dive if new management takes over and the menu and service don't match previously met expectations. And as a rule, the more competition there is in a particular market, the less goodwill is worth—after all, in this age of the pampered consumer, people will quickly go elsewhere if offered even a slightly better service or price.

☐ **Valuation Method 3: Multiple of Book Value**

The value of the company shall be [*insert multiplier, one or higher, such as "two"*] times its book value (its assets minus its liabilities as shown on the balance sheet of the company) as of the end of the most recent fiscal year prior to the purchase of an ownership interest under this agreement. The value of an individual owner's interest shall be the entire value for the company as determined under this paragraph, multiplied by his or her ownership percentage.

TIP

Use additional years if your balance sheet fluctuates. As with the regular book value method, if your company has been in business several years but assets and liabilities tend to fluctuate fairly widely from one year to the next (for instance, because large expenses accrue at the end of a year or the beginning of the next year), you may want to provide that the book value figures from balance sheets of several years should be used to arrive at an average adjusted book value amount.

Capitalization of Earnings (Valuation Method 4)

SKIP AHEAD

For established companies only. This method measures a business's value by its average annual profits. If your company is just starting out, it's premature to value your ownership interests by using the capitalization of earnings method, since your business has no earnings history. Better to adopt another valuation provision for your first couple of years, then switch over to this valuation method later. While we recommend reading this section to get an idea of what may be in your future, if you're pressed for time, you may want to skip ahead to the appraisal method below.

Once a company produces a good profit for several years in a row and appears to have a promising future, it often makes sense to base its value on its average annual earnings. Earnings often better reflect a small, but established, company's value than its assets and liabilities do. A solid earnings history is often a pretty good predictor of how the company will perform in the future.

EXAMPLE: Two restaurants are each worth $175,000 according to the book value method (balance sheet assets minus liabilities). But their values diverge if you look at each restaurant's profit picture. After paying each of its three owners a salary of $50,000 per year, Peas and Carrots, Inc., has earned an annual profit averaging $10,000 over the last three years. But Mucho Mocha, Corp., which also has three owners and pays the same salaries, produces yearly profits averaging $80,000 per year. Clearly, pushing caffeine beats flogging legumes. Based on the likelihood that (in the immediate future, at least) both businesses' profits will stay near their three-year average, Mucho Mocha is probably worth more than Peas and Carrots. Thus, a book value valuation method, which results in a similar value for both companies, won't produce accurate results for Mucho Mocha, but the capitalization of earnings method, which takes into account Mucho Mocha's higher earning capacity, will produce a much fairer result.

Under the capitalization of earnings method, you first determine the company's annual earnings, or profit, by subtracting the cost of doing business from gross revenues. Next you multiply the earnings by a number —usually between two and ten—called a multiplier. The selection of a multiplier should depend, at least to some degree, on your company's industry as well as on general conditions. That's because once some types of businesses become solidly profitable, they are likely to stay that way, while other types of endeavors are much more likely to produce up-and-down profits. For example, a small educational publishing company with an established and defensible market niche may be valued at about ten times average annual profits. However, a small publisher of fiction—a much chancier venture—is likely to be valued at a much lower multiple of annual profits, perhaps two. (Choosing a multiplier is discussed further below.)

You apply your selected multiplier to the average annual earnings from several consecutive years—called the "base earnings period."

EXAMPLE: The four owners of Bean Bag Furniture, Inc., guessed right: They obtained a long-term, low-rent lease on a store in a rundown area that is rapidly becoming one of the trendiest shopping districts in town. After an initial period of marginal returns, their business is just plain booming. For the past three years, net profits, after paying each working owner a decent salary, have averaged $250,000. Now one owner has decided to retire. The owners' buy-sell agreement calls for arriving at the value of the business by multiplying its average net profits for the past three years by a multiplier of two. Thus, Bean Bag's value is $250,000 x 2, or $500,000. It follows that, since the retiring owner holds one-fourth of the total shares, her interest is worth $125,000 under the capitalization of earnings method.

Earnings Figure May Not Accurately Represent True Profit

Keep in mind that with a few adjustments, a balance sheet can make a business appear more or less profitable than it really is. For example, the owners' salaries or draws could be way more or way less than the industry averages. Or a business can temporarily show chunky profits by postponing major expenses.

If you think your balance sheet may need adjusting before it fairly states your profit, you may want to have a professional appraiser or an independent business valuation expert make appropriate adjustments (with appropriate disclosures that explain the adjustments) so that the numbers reflect the earning value of your company more realistically and accurately.

It's almost always a mistake to choose a base earnings period shorter than three years (and the IRS prefers to see figures that represent a five-year average), because doing so would risk an exceptionally good or bad year's skewing the results.

The capitalization of earnings method requires you to do a fair bit of research, or educated guessing, before you agree on the multiplier to insert in your buyout agreement. Many factors should go into choosing a multiplier, or capitalization rate, including:

- **General economic conditions.** For example, if yours is a tourist-based business and the economy is heading toward a recession, your multiplier should be lower than if the economy is growing fast and consumers have plenty of disposable income.

- **The nature of your business.** This includes the type of products and services you sell and whether customers are loyal to you or another co-owner. For example, if the service your business sells is highly personal, such as is often true for interior decorators, the company may not do well if a key co-owner leaves, meaning you'll probably want to choose a low multiplier.

- **The age of your business.** The longer your business has been profitable (especially if profits are stable or growing), the higher the multiplier you'll normally want to choose.

- **The risk—or lack thereof—inherent in operating your business.** For example, if your business is under assault by new competitors and profits are falling, it's probably worth a lot less than if the reverse is true, and you'll want to choose a low multiplier.

- **Multipliers used in similar sales.** Try to find out what multipliers have been used in recent sales of interests in similar small businesses. But make sure the comparable sales figures you look at are both current and truly comparable.

TIP
Capitalization rate is the same as a multiplier. In reading or talking with an expert about the capitalization of earnings method, you may come across the jargon "capitalization rate," or "cap rate." Don't be daunted—the term capitalization rate means exactly the same thing as a multiplier—thus, using a cap rate of ten simply means multiplying your earnings by ten.

Be realistic when you choose a multiplier. One experienced small business adviser we know recommends against using a multiplier higher than three. Anything more could cripple the business with too high a buyout price. However, some experts say that, for a larger business with a superb earnings history, a highly desirable market niche, and a solidly positive cash flow, it can sometimes make sense to pay as much as ten times earnings, which would make the selling owner quite happy.

Because there are so many factors that can affect the choice of a multiplier, using this method is often most sensible in an industry where the multiplier has been generally defined and accepted in the trade. Construction companies, retail stores, and restaurants are examples of businesses where it can be reasonably easy to obtain information on standard industry multipliers.

TIP

People who regularly buy and sell businesses are a good source of information. Business appraisers and brokers, especially those who specialize in a particular industry, often can tell you what sorts of multipliers are in general use in your type of business. Trade publications that report prices paid for businesses that change hands are another good source of information.

The capitalization of earnings clause in our buyout agreement is shown below.

☐ **Valuation Method 4: Capitalization of Earnings
(Adjusted for Income Taxes)**

The value of the company shall be determined on the basis of [*insert multiplier, one or higher, such as "two"*] times the average net earnings (annual gross revenues of the company minus annual expenses and minus any annual federal, state and local income taxes payable by the company) for the [*insert number of years, typically "three" or more*] fiscal years of the company (or the number of fiscal years the company has been in existence, if fewer) that have occurred prior to the purchase of an ownership interest under this agreement. The value of an individual owner's interest shall be the entire value for the company as determined under this paragraph, multiplied by his or her ownership percentage.

Rates of Return and Earnings Multipliers

To really understand how the capitalization of earnings method works, it helps to understand what the term "expected rate of return" means. This is the percentage of an investment that a buyer expects to get back each year. For instance, if you put $100,000 in a certificate of deposit (CD) with an interest rate of 5% (an optimistic rate used for this example), your rate of return on that investment would be 5%, meaning you'd make about $5,000 in interest each year.

In terms of buying a small business, to get a 5% rate of return on a purchase price of $100,000, the company would have to earn profits of $5,000 per year. If you, as an investor, had the option of putting your $100,000 into a guaranteed CD or into a small business to get the same annual profits of $5,000 per year, you'd probably take the CD. Why put your money in an inherently risky small business when you are guaranteed the same return from an insured bank? For that reason, a 5% rate of return on a business investment might be an unacceptably low rate if interest rates for safe investments are at 5%. An expected rate of 10% to 15% would be more reasonable, depending on economic conditions.

In valuing a business based on its earnings, the multiplier, or capitalization rate, varies inversely with the expected rate of return. For example, if a company uses a multiplier of 20 (20 times annual earnings), a buyer would only get a rate of return of 5% (100% ÷ 20). If the company uses the much lower multiplier of 5, a buyer would expect a more desirable 20% rate of return (100% ÷ 5). (Would-be buyers—the company and continuing owners—like low multipliers.)

Rate of Return	Multiplier/Cap Rate
5%	20
8%	12.5
10%	10
15%	6.67
20%	5
25%	4
30%	3.33
50%	2

Rates of Return and Earnings Multipliers (continued)

The rate of return paid by other investments will affect the multiplier you choose. That's because, as mentioned above, the rate of return a buyer will want to achieve when investing in a risky small business will be substantially above what he could get if he placed his money in a CD, a U.S. government bond, or other comparably safe investment.

The expected rate of return is also likely to be somewhat above the return a buyer would anticipate receiving by investing in the stock market. For example, if the stock market has averaged an 11% rate of return over the last few years (a very optimistic figure these days), an 8% rate of return from a small business (and thus a multiplier of 12.5) won't look nearly as good as it would if the stock market's recent average rate of return was 5%. In this case, an investor in a small business would probably be looking for at least a 20% rate of return (and thus a multiplier of no higher than 5)—for quick payback on his investment. On the other hand, if the stock market has been averaging 5% returns, or even negative returns, a 10% rate of return would look pretty good.

WORKSHEET

Turn to your worksheet. Check Valuation Method 4 if you wish to use the capitalization of earnings method to value your ownership interests. (Section VI, Valuation Method 4.) Also, insert the multiplier and the number of years to be used as the base earnings period into the blanks.

SEE AN EXPERT

Fine-tuning your formula. You can customize your earnings formula to be as complicated or as uncomplicated as you wish, but whichever method you choose, your price or formula should be reasonable, fair, and affordable. Depending on your company's circumstances, you may wish to provide for the earnings formula to do any of the following:

- Weigh your earnings average to reflect a recent upward earnings trend (counting the most recent year's earnings the most).

- Provide for a partial allocation of annual earnings in case an owner leaves in the middle of a fiscal year.

- Define earnings as operating earnings before the subtraction of interest, taxes, depreciation, and amortization (this EBITDA formula is commonly used in some industry sectors as the measure of earnings that is multiplied by the earnings multiplier to establish a value of a business). This option eliminates the effects of a business's financing and accounting decisions.

These adjustments must be made by someone who knows the particulars of your business. If you're interested in including them in your buyout agreement, we recommend you get an expert's help.

Appraisal Value (Valuation Method 5)

By now, it may seem that you have to be a financial wizard to come up with a fair buyout price or an appropriate valuation formula for a small business. Don't worry—there is an easy, if more expensive, way out: You can adopt a provision that simply provides for your business's value to be established by a professional business appraisal at the time of a buyout.

The appraisal method involves agreeing to hire one or more professional appraisers who will decide the value of your business for you at the time of a buyout. Here is the way our appraisal method works: As part of the buyout process, the buyer (usually the company or the continuing owners) and the seller (the departing owner, the representative of a deceased owner's estate, or the ex-spouse of a divorced owner) each choose an independent appraiser to value the company. If the appraisers come up with a similar price, often the parties can negotiate a mutually agreeable price. But if the appraisers arrive at very different values and cannot agree on a price, our buyout agreement requires the two appraisers to choose a third appraiser to make yet another appraisal, which is used as the Agreement Price. The appraised value is binding on all parties.

> **TIP**
>
> **Choose a knowledgeable appraiser.** One way to reduce the possibility of disputes and to hold down expenses is to agree on one appraiser that all owners have confidence in. Find an independent appraiser who intimately knows your industry and, preferably, your segment of it.

Although using an appraisal approach to value your company may seem like a safe, conventional approach, there are a few potential drawbacks. Here are several:

- **Cost.** Having an appraiser can reduce guesswork and, hopefully, conflict, but it can also be expensive and time-consuming. Business valuations usually cost a minimum of $1,000 and up to $2,500 for $100,000 companies, up to $5,000 for $500,000 businesses, and $10,000 and above for larger companies. Using two or three appraisers will double or triple these amounts. In short, for a small business, appraisal costs can eat up a chunk of cash.

- **Lack of predictability.** Unlike most other valuation methods, establishing your business's value based on a time-of-sale appraisal does not provide a valuation figure you can look to in advance of a buyout. This can mean an owner who is contemplating leaving the company or adopting an estate plan won't have essential information she needs. This also means the company or co-owners will not know how much life or disability insurance to take out or how much liquidity will be needed to fund a potential buyout. (See "Ongoing Appraisal Packages," below, for a way around these problems.)

- **Disputes.** It may be difficult, even for an independent professional appraiser, to subjectively but fairly value a small private company whose shares are not traded on any exchange, especially if one of the principals has died or is leaving the business. While naming an appraiser in your buyout agreement takes a big step toward avoiding conflict, if tension between owners is already present, the appraisal process can still be rancorous and political. You always take the risk that one party or another will contest the appraisal based on a claim that the appraiser unfairly favored the other side.

- **Delays.** It can take some time to get an appraiser's report, unless you have the good fortune of finding an appraiser who is both experienced in your line of business and prompt. To avoid delays, your agreement sets a certain period for the selection of an appraiser (this also prevents one of the owners from using the appraiser selection process as a delay tactic) and for the appraisal itself.

The appraisal valuation language in our agreement, shown below, provides for the mutual selection of one appraiser, or, if that doesn't work out, it provides a mechanism for choosing two or three appraisers.

☐ **Valuation Method 5: Appraised Value**

The value of the company shall be its fair market value as determined by an independent appraiser mutually selected by Buyer(s) and Seller of the ownership interest subject to purchase under this agreement. If Buyer(s) and Seller are unable to agree upon an independent appraiser within 30 days, Buyer(s) and Seller, within the next ten days, shall each select an independent appraiser. If the two selected appraisers are unable, within 60 days, to agree on the fair market value of the company, then the two appraisers shall select a third independent appraiser within the next ten days, who shall, within 30 days, determine the fair market value of the company. All costs of an appraiser mutually selected by Buyer(s) and Seller or of a third appraiser selected by two appraisers shall be shared equally by Buyer(s) and Seller. All costs of an individually selected appraiser shall be paid by the party selecting the appraiser. The value of an individual owner's interest shall be the entire value for the company as determined under this paragraph, multiplied by his or her ownership percentage.

WORKSHEET

Turn to your worksheet. Check Valuation Method 5 if you wish to use an appraisal (at the time of purchase of an ownership interest by your company or continuing owners) to set the agreement price for a buyout. (Section VI, Valuation Method 5.)

SEE AN EXPERT

There are many other ways to value your business. Although we include the most common types of valuation methods in our buyout agreement, there are many other different versions of each. And we obviously don't have the facts necessary to tailor our agreement to exactly match the needs of your business. Whether yours is a manufacturing, wholesale, retail, or service business, it's important to recognize that a more custom-tailored valuation method may lead to a more accurate estimation of the worth of ownership interests in your company. Talk to your legal and accounting advisers about their experiences and recommendations, and to other business owners in your field about how they would go about valuing their business. If you're still interested in learning about more elaborate, detailed formulas, you'll need to do more reading (we list several resources in Chapter 10) or see an expert.

Appraiser Credentials

Anyone can value a business—generally, there is no license requirement. We suggest, however, hiring an independent appraiser with professional *credentials*, who has been tested for proficiency and understanding of the fundamentals of appraisal concepts and ethics. As in many other fields, the business valuation industry has created its own professional designations. While many appraisers are also certified public accountants, the American Society of Appraisers (a widely respected private accreditation group) uses these designations:

- AM (Accredited Member): requires two years of full-time appraisal experience
- ASA (Accredited Senior Appraiser): requires five years of full-time appraisal experience, and
- FASA (Fellow Appraiser): an Accredited Senior Appraiser who has been recognized by ASA's International Board of Governors for outstanding services to the appraisal profession and/or the Society of Appraisers.

Another group, which accredits appraisers of closely held businesses according to education and experience qualifications, is the Institute of Business Appraisers—see their website at www.go-iba.org.

Ongoing Appraisal Packages

Some business appraisal firms offer an ongoing "buy-sell agreement service."
For a set price, they will perform annual valuation "checkups" on your
company, giving you and your co-owners a dependable annual valuation
that will normally withstand IRS scrutiny. It's helpful for insurance, estate
planning, and business planning reasons to have handy a reasonably recent
estimation of your company's value. As an added bonus, before any buybacks
actually occur, you'll get to know and trust your appraiser, and the appraiser
will get to know the strengths and weaknesses of your business.

Choosing Payment Terms for Buyouts

The payment terms in your buyout agreement control how and when a buyer must make payments to the seller under any buyout that arises under the buyout agreement. (For our purposes, the buyer will probably be the company or the continuing owners, or possibly an owner's child or a key employee. The seller will probably be a selling owner, his family members, or his estate representative.)

Lest you think that payment terms are just annoying financial details that can be handled quickly at the time of a buyout, consider that payment terms often can make or break a deal. Reasonable payment terms can make an otherwise unaffordable buyout affordable for the company or continuing owners.

Payment terms can also affect the most important aspect of a buyout—the price that the buyer is willing to pay and the seller is willing to accept. For instance, terms that are more favorable to the buyer, such as a low-interest installment plan that extends over five years, can allow the seller to receive a higher final price. In contrast, payment terms that favor the seller, such as an immediate, one-time, lump-sum cash payment, might lower the price the buyer is able to pay.

> **TIP**
>
> **Insurance payoffs can come in a series of payments.** It's possible to coordinate a payment plan with life insurance or disability insurance funding (see Chapter 5). Your agreement can provide for a series of payments that are tied to insurance payouts. If you choose to do this, make sure your payment plan meshes with the insurance policy's payout schedule.

Balancing the Interests of Buyer and Seller

Because payment terms can have a great effect on the success of any buyout that arises under your buyout agreement, you want to pick a payment plan that is perceived as fair to both buyer and seller. The seller, of course, usually will want to receive payment for his interest fairly quickly, while the buyer will probably want to make payments over as long a time as possible.

However, both sides have an interest in establishing terms that make it possible for your company or the continuing owners to exercise a buyout. If payment terms are too severe, the buying company or co-owners may not be able to afford them. For example, payment terms that require a 100% lump-sum cash payout right away can prevent even the most successful companies from buying back an owner's interest. Or, if the company does make the purchase, such harsh payment terms may harm or even destroy the business. Either way, the buyout can end up failing.

But in case you are tempted to provide extremely lenient buyout terms to benefit the buyer (for example, low payments over many years), remember to balance your concern for the continued well-being of the company with the need to minimize inconvenience to a departing owner—or her family, if the owner has died. (After all, this could be you or your family.)

Depending on the circumstances, a departing owner or her family normally has a legitimate interest in getting the buyback money reasonably fast. Aside from the obvious reasons of needing money for expenses, waiting a period of years to be paid off carries big risks. For example, if the remaining owners make bad business choices, they could render the business insolvent, with the result that the departing owner or her family may never receive all—or a substantial portion of—the buyout price. And, of course, how and when the payments occur can be of intense concern if the departing owner is pulling out precisely because she doesn't trust the others.

A good balance may be to require the buyer to pay a good chunk of the purchase price up front and require the seller to carry back only 20% to 30% of the purchase price to be paid over three to five years. (And if the seller never sees the rest of the money, at least he's received the lion's share of it.)

Your choice of payment terms may depend on where the funds to purchase an owner's interest will come from. If you opt to fund a buyout with life and/or disability insurance (discussed in Chapter 5), some buyout scenarios may be funded immediately.

Of course, you can't know ahead of time what payment terms will work for both parties in a particular buyout situation. But choosing a fair payment plan now will at least give you a starting point to negotiate from when an actual buyout looms.

> **TIP**
>
> **Payment terms are not written in stone.** Any payment term you adopt now can be changed if all owners agree. For instance, suppose you choose a five-year payment plan now, with interest at 10% per year on the unpaid balance. Now, suppose seven years after you sign your agreement, when your business is prosperous, a departing owner says, "You know, I'd like to get as much cash as I can now to invest in a new business. I propose that you pay me, right now, 50% of what I would have received over a five-year payment plan." If this seems fair to the remaining owners, all can agree to substitute the lump-sum payment for the five-year payment plan. You will want to get the unanimous written consent of all owners to any change of payment terms and place a copy of the signed consent in your company records book.

Following are several common ways to set up payment terms.

Lump-Sum Cash Payment

This method requires the buyer to pay the full amount of the buyback price in cash within a specified number of days from the date the buyer provides a Notice of Intent to Purchase to the seller.

Again, we believe requiring a lump-sum payment can be problematic, since the company or the continuing owners are unlikely to have sufficient cash on hand and, unless the business is extremely solvent, may be unable to obtain a loan from a bank to fund the cash buyout of the ownership interest. The unhappy result may be that the company or the continuing owners are unable to exercise their buyout rights to avoid having a new owner come on board. This means an owner's inheritor or ex-spouse—or an outsider—may be allowed to hold on to his ownership interests, just the result the buyout agreement is designed to avoid.

The lump-sum payment provision in our buy-sell agreement is shown below.

Section VII: Payment Terms

Unless otherwise provided in this agreement, the undersigned agree that the payment terms checked below shall be used for the purchase of ownership interests under this agreement.

☐ **Payment Terms Alternative 1:**
Full Cash Payment

Cash payment for the Seller's ownership interest shall be made by Buyer(s) to Seller within [*insert number of days, typically "30" or "60"*] days of the date the company provides a Notice of Intent to Purchase to the Seller under this agreement.

WORKSHEET

Turn to your worksheet. If you wish to choose the full cash payment alternative, check this provision on your worksheet. (Section VII, Payment Terms Alternative 1.) Insert in the blank the numbers of days (from the date of the company's Notice of Intent to Purchase) by which payment must be made.

Installment Plans

Typically, buyout agreements require a departing owner (or his estate or family members) to receive at least part of the purchase price in installment payments (to "carry back" part of the price) over several years. This method has a hidden advantage for the company and the continuing owners: It ensures the departing owner will take a continued interest in the financial health of the company until the debt is paid off.

If the installment period is more than two years, you might consider using a floating interest rate, perhaps prime rate or one point above prime. That way, your interest rate won't become outdated if rates increase or decrease in the years before a buyout occurs. The most commonly used index for the prime rate is *The Wall Street Journal*. If you wish to do this, rather than inserting an interest rate like "5%" in your agreement, you can insert something like "*Wall Street Journal* Prime, as published in *The Wall Street Journal* Money Rate section, adjusted monthly, plus 1%."

Equal Payments Under an Installment Plan

Using this approach, the company or the buying owners pay the purchase price, plus interest, in installments. This type of payment plan is not used often—most sellers want a good-sized portion of the purchase price up front. (See the next section for a payment plan that requires a down payment followed by installment payments.) However, in a family business situation where an owner is transferring ownership to her children, or perhaps a key employee, the owner may be willing to take regular payments without a big down payment up front. Another possible scenario where this installment plan could be used is when installment payments will be made with staggered insurance policy payouts (some buy-sell insurance policies pay out benefits in installments).

You can adopt any installment payment schedule that you and your co-owners conclude is most likely to meet your needs—perhaps providing for equal payments over two or three years. Of course, without a large down payment, the seller has an interest in receiving payments for his interest fairly quickly, perhaps over no more than one to three years.

The provision in our agreement that calls for equal payments over a specified term, with interest added, is shown below.

☐ **Payment Terms Alternative 2:**
Monthly Installments of Principal and Interest

Buyer(s) shall pay Seller the purchase price for an ownership interest in equal installments over a term of [*insert term for repayment in months, such as "24"*] months, with interest added to the amount of each installment computed at an annual rate of [*insert interest rate*] and compounded annually on the unpaid continuing balance of the purchase price of the ownership interest. The first installment payment shall be made to Seller by Buyer(s) on [*insert date of first installment payment*], and the continuing payments shall be made to Seller by Buyer(s) on the [*insert payment due day, typically "1st"*] of every month, until the full purchase price, together with any interest owed, is paid in full.

WORKSHEET

Turn to your worksheet. If you wish to provide in your buyout agreement for monthly payments of principal and interest, check this alternative on your worksheet. (Section VII, Payment Terms Alternative 2.) Insert in the blanks:

- the number of months over which payments will be made
- the interest rate
- the due date of the first installment, and
- the monthly installment due date.

TIP

You can customize your payments terms. It's possible to change this provision to provide for payments to increase or decrease over a number of years, perhaps tied to future levels of profits.

Down Payment Plus Installment Payments

This method specifies an initial cash down payment on the buyout date followed by periodic payments on a portion of the purchase price, plus interest, until the full amount is paid. A down payment of one-third to two-thirds of the buyout price is often required, followed by installment payments for three to five years. Of course, with a higher down payment, a longer installment period may be acceptable.

> **TIP**
>
> **Insurance proceeds can fund the down payment used to buy a deceased or disabled owner's interest.** You can use any life or disability insurance proceeds taken out on an owner to make the down payment on a disabled or deceased owner's interest (for a discussion of insurance funding, see Chapter 5). We don't specifically tie the down payment to the amount of insurance proceeds in our provision below, since this really isn't necessary—if insurance proceeds are available, you simply use them at the time of the buyout to fund the down payment.

The provision from our buyout agreement that calls for a cash down payment followed by the installment purchase of an ownership interest is shown below.

> **WORKSHEET**
>
> **Turn to your worksheet.** If you decide to use the combined cash and installment payment alternative, check this provision in your worksheet. (Section VII, Payment Terms Alternative 3.) Insert in the blanks:
> - the amount of the down payment
> - the number of days in which the down payment must be made
> - the number of months over which payments will be made
> - the interest rate
> - the due date of the first installment, and
> - the monthly installment due date.

☐ **Payment Terms Alternative 3:**
Partial Cash Payment, Followed by Monthly Installments of
Principal and Interest

The purchase of an ownership interest shall be accomplished as follows: An initial cash payment of [*insert the cash amount of the purchase price to be paid up front, such as "$40,000"*] shall be paid by Buyer(s) to Seller within [*insert number of days for down payment, such as "30"*] days of the date the company provides a Notice of Intent to Purchase to Seller. The remainder of the purchase price shall be paid by Buyer(s) to Seller in equal installments over a term of [*insert term for repayment in months, such as "24"*] months, with interest added to the amount of each installment computed at an annual rate of [*insert interest rate*]% and compounded annually on the unpaid continuing balance of the purchase price of the ownership interest. The first installment payment shall be made by Buyer(s) on [*insert date of first installment payment*], and the continuing payments shall be made by Buyer(s) on the [*insert payment due day, typically "1st"*] of every month, until the full balance of the purchase price, together with any interest owed, is paid in full.

Interest-Only Installment Payments

Using this payment method, payment of the purchase price is postponed until a future date. Until this future date, the company makes installment payments of interest only. We rarely recommend this approach, except possibly in the first year or two of a new business or in a family business situation where affluent members of an older generation are looking for a generous way to transfer ownership to their children without making an outright gift.

The provision in our buyout agreement that allows interest-only installment payments is shown below.

☐ **Payment Terms Alternative 4:**
Monthly Installments of Interest Only, With a Final Payment for the Full Purchase Price

Buyer(s) shall pay Seller the purchase price for an ownership interest on [*insert future date for full payment of purchase price*]. Until such date, Buyer(s) shall pay Seller monthly payments of interest, computed at an annual rate of [*insert interest rate*]% on the purchase price for the ownership interest. The first installment payment of interest shall be made by Buyer(s) on [*insert date of first installment payment*], and the continuing installment payments of interest shall be made by Buyer(s) on the [*insert payment due day, typically "1st"*] of every month, until payment of the full amount of the purchase price by Buyer(s) as specified above. On the date for full payment of the purchase price by Buyer(s), interest owed on the purchase price from the date of the last payment of interest by Buyer(s) to the date of payment of the purchase price shall be added to and included with the payment of the purchase price by Buyer(s).

WORKSHEET

Turn to your worksheet. If you wish to choose the interest-only installment alternative, check this provision in your worksheet. (Section VII, Payment Terms Alternative 4.) Insert in the blanks:

- the date for full payment of the purchase price
- the interest rate
- the date of the first installment payment, and
- the monthly installment due date.

TIP

At the time of a buyout, this method may be used as a temporary payment method. Occasionally, when a co-owner leaves, neither the company nor the co-owners can afford to make the payments required by their buyout agreement. If so, all may agree to substitute an interest-only agreement such as this one on an interim basis.

Customized Schedule of Payment

With this method, set amounts are paid at chosen times (for example, one-quarter of the purchase price, with interest, anytime during the following four calendar quarters). Obviously, the total of all payments should equal the full amount of the buyback price to be paid for the ownership interest, plus any interest charged on the financed amount. This might make sense for seasonal businesses or for businesses that make most of their annual income once a year.

WORKSHEET

Turn to your worksheet. If you are interested in customizing your own payment terms, make a notation on your worksheet now. Write down whatever terms you're thinking of, including dates for payment, any applicable interest rates, and the number of months over which payments will be made. You may need to ask a lawyer to draft these terms for you. (Section VII, Payment Terms Alternative 5.)

☐ **Payment Terms Alternative 5:**
Customized Schedule for Payment for Ownership Interest
Buyer(s) shall pay Seller the purchase price for the ownership interest according to the schedule and other terms included below:
[*specify the amount and dates of a customized payment schedule*]

Creative Ways to Pay

You and your co-owners may come up with any number of other ways to compensate a departing owner and ease the financial pain of future buyouts.

Consulting fees. Regardless of how you plan now to pay out the purchase price, how an actual buyout is paid for years from now might look very different. For instance, suppose you plan to fund a company buyout of a departing owner like this: one-third cash reserves, one-third bank loan, and one-third installment plan. When an owner gives notice that she wants to be bought out, but is willing to work for the company on an advisory basis, the company and the owner might agree that the owner will take half of the purchase price up front (which the company pays for with cash reserves and a loan), and the other half in the form of consulting fees.

> TIP
>
> **Paying consulting fees can lower the company's tax cost.** Like salaries, consulting fees can be tax-deducted by the company, but are treated as ordinary income to the departing owner (rather than as capital gains). (This is beneficial for the company as a whole but not so good for the departing owner.) The income tax consequences of buyouts are discussed further in Chapter 9.

Lease payments or licensing fees. Another creative way a company can deduct payments to the departing owner is to pay the departing owner lease payments or licensing fees. If the departing owner owns real estate or equipment that the business rents, the owner can receive these lease payments. Or, if a departing owner owns a copyright or patent, the company or continuing owners could pay the departing owner licensing fees or royalty payments for the intellectual property the owner leaves behind at the company.

Increased retirement funding. The company could set up a retirement fund before the departing owner leaves and contribute large amounts to it to compensate the owner for past services (the continuing owners may be able to opt out of the retirement plan for a time, or reduce their salaries or distributions, to pay for this). This gives the company a tax deduction on the payments, but the departing owner will owe taxes when money is taken out of the retirement fund.

Deferred compensation. Similarly, the company could set up a deferred compensation plan and arrange to pay the departing owner a "defined benefit." (A defined benefit plan can pay the departing owner a fixed amount at his departure or retirement from the company; for example, the departing owner might receive $20,000 per year for ten years.) The company would be able to deduct the deferred compensation payments to the departing owner, but they would be taxed to the departing owner as ordinary income.

Private annuity. Another creative way to structure and fund a buyout is to use a private annuity. The departing owner can opt to receive a "private annuity" in exchange for giving the company her ownership interest. The company would pay a fixed amount each year directly to the departing owner for the remainder of her life. The payments to the departing owner would be treated as capital gains. This comes with two tax advantages: The ownership interest would not appreciate during the departing owner's lifetime, and the departing owner could spread her capital gain out over her lifetime. When the business is in excellent financial shape, this approach can make sense. But in other circumstances, a private annuity can be risky, since if the business goes belly up, the departing owner probably won't get paid enough to cover the purchase price.

CAUTION

Funding a future buyout with a retirement plan, deferred compensation, or a private annuity is not for the do-it-yourselfer. If you're interested in finding out more about funding a future buyout with one of these methods, see a lawyer or pension specialist to set it up for you. (We cover finding and working with lawyers in Chapter 10.) ●

Completing and Updating Your Buyout Agreement

n this chapter, we cover the last few steps you'll need to take to finalize your agreement. We'll also explain the last few sections of our buyout agreement: resolving disputes, binding new owners to the agreement, and placing a legend on your ownership certificates.

For the future, we'll also let you know how to resolve conflicts that may come up during an actual buyout and how to update your agreement when your circumstances change.

Finalizing Your Buyout Agreement

Before you sign your agreement, you need to decide whether you'll keep your buyout provisions in a separate document or whether you'll insert them into an existing document, such as your corporate bylaws, your LLC operating agreement, or your partnership agreement. Because corporations, LLCs, and partnerships are such different animals, sometimes we have different advice for owners of these types of businesses. This is one of those times.

For Corporations

If you do business as a corporation, you can add your buyout provisions to your bylaws or you can adopt your buyout provisions as a separate agreement—often called a "shareholders' agreement" in the corporate context. This type of agreement is signed by all shareholders and is just as valid and binding on the owners of a corporation as the provisions of the corporate articles and bylaws.

We believe the latter approach—adopting a distinct agreement—is better. By keeping your agreement separate from your organizational documents and having each owner (and each owner's spouse or legally recognized domestic or civil partner) sign it, you emphasize the importance of its buyout provisions. With full disclosure thus assured, an owner can't later claim surprise when she wants to sell to an outsider and her co-owners invoke the terms of the buyout agreement to stop the transaction.

Creating a Separate Agreement

To adopt a separate buyout agreement, have all shareholders date and sign the agreement at the bottom, using the signature page included at the end of the buyout agreement.

> **TIP**
>
> **Refer to your buyout agreement in your bylaws.** If you adopt your buyout provisions in a separate buyout agreement, as we suggest, we recommend that you add a provision to your current bylaws that refers to the existence of your buyout agreement. (Legally, this tactic is called "incorporating your buyout agreement by reference" into your bylaws.) Doing this helps to cover all your legal bases and can help avoid a challenge to your buyout agreement from someone looking for a legal way out of its enforceability.
>
> To do this, amend your bylaws by adding a sentence that recognizes that a separate agreement exists to control and regulate the ownership of interests in the corporation. Here is one simple way to phrase this new bylaw provision.

The provisions of the agreement among the shareholders dated [*insert date of signing of your buy-sell agreement*], which regulates the transfer of ownership interests in the corporation and other related matters, is hereby incorporated by reference into these Bylaws and shall be binding on the corporation, its creditors, its shareholders and their assigns and successors, and other parties as provided in the agreement.

Adding the Buyout Provisions to Your Bylaws

If, instead, you decide to add your buyout provisions to your bylaws, simply cut and paste the buyout provisions from the file we provide into your existing bylaws (don't include the signature page from our buyout agreement).

We recommend that you add the buyout provisions to the end of your bylaws, but you can insert them anywhere you wish. When adding these provisions to the document, you will want to change the paragraph numbering or lettering of the buyout provisions to conform to the numbering or lettering scheme of your existing bylaws.

Remember to have all owners (and their spouses) sign the new bylaws.

Reviewing Your Bylaws

Whichever approach you take, you'll need to make sure that your buyout provisions do not conflict with the existing provisions of your articles and bylaws. Mostly, you want to check to make sure that an existing bylaw does not prohibit, or impose additional rules on, any of the procedures covered in your buyout provisions. For example, if your corporate bylaws completely prohibit the transfer of shares in your corporation, but your buyout provisions allow an owner to sell to an outside buyer under certain circumstances, you will want to amend your bylaws to delete the prohibition against transfers.

Approving Amendments to Your Bylaws

If you've amended your articles or bylaws—whether you've added the buyout provisions directly or you've just incorporated them by reference—the shareholders need to approve that amendment. You should meet any special voting requirements under state law and in your articles or bylaws for shareholder approval of such an amendment.

Shareholder approval to amend your articles or bylaws can be obtained in two ways: (1) at a formal shareholders meeting, documented by written minutes, or (2) by having each shareholder sign a written consent form that says he or she approves the buyout provisions attached to the written consent. While not always required under state law or corporate articles or bylaws, we also recommend that all directors of the corporation separately approve the amendment to the bylaws. Just hold a directors meeting or prepare a written consent for directors to sign as you did with your shareholders.

RESOURCE

If you need help with these corporate formalities or you want a ready-made minutes or consent form to use to approve your bylaws amendment, see *The Corporate Records Handbook*, by Anthony Mancuso (Nolo).

Placing a Legend on Your Certificates

Another task you'll need to perform after adopting your buyout provisions is to update your stock certificates to give notice of the buyout restrictions on the shares to potential creditors and buyers. Most states require you to add language to each certificate stating that the shares are subject to the terms of a shareholders' agreement. This statement is called a stock certificate "legend."

We believe the placement of a legend on certificates is essential to remind owners—and to give notice to others who may buy or receive ownership interests—that interests cannot be disposed of at will, but only under the terms of a buyout or shareholders' agreement. If you don't do this, you invite confusion and controversy from successors to ownership interests who claim ignorance of the existence of your buyout restrictions.

The language of Section IX of our buyout agreement requires the placement of a legend on certificates, as shown below. The legend says that your secretary or other equivalent officer of the company will provide a copy of the text of your agreement to any requesting person, whether an owner or not. Make sure to honor any such requests.

Here's how to comply with this section of the agreement:

- **Existing certificates.** The secretary of the company should gather up all the outstanding certificates issued to the company's existing owners and type the legend in capital letters on the front of all certificates.
- **New certificates.** The secretary should also type this legend on any new certificates issued to future owners. One way to ensure this happens is to type the legend on all blank certificates that remain in your corporate or LLC records binder. When these certificates are issued to new owners, the legend will already be on them, and you will not have to remember to perform this task.

Section IX: Placement of Notice of Transfer Restrictions on Certificates

(a) The following statement must appear conspicuously on each ownership certificate issued by the company:

THE INTERESTS REPRESENTED BY THIS CERTIFICATE ARE SUBJECT TO RESTRICTIONS UPON TRANSFER AND ARE REDEEMABLE PURSUANT TO PROVISIONS CONTAINED IN AN AGREEMENT AMONG THE OWNERS OF THE COMPANY. FOR A COPY OF THIS AGREEMENT, CONTACT THE SECRETARY OR EQUIVALENT OFFICER OF THE COMPANY AT THE PRINCIPAL OFFICE OF THE COMPANY AT [*insert company's address*].

(b) The secretary or other equivalent officer of the company shall provide to any owner or third person upon written request and without charge a copy of this agreement.

TIP

Order new certificates if the legend won't fit. If there is insufficient room on your current certificates to type the legend, or if you wish to have this legend printed on new certificates by a legal stationer, order new certificates. (Some states allow the legend to go on the back of certificates, but we don't like this idea—an owner may not flip the certificate over to read the language on the back.)

If you do this, you can exchange the new certificates bearing the printed legend with the old certificates held by your current owners. Make sure to note the cancellation of the old certificates and the issuance of the new certificates in your company's transfer ledger or records binder.

For LLCs and Partnerships

For general and limited partnerships, the partnership agreement, and for LLCs, the LLC operating agreement, are the primary agreements among the owners of the business. They set out the capital contributions of the owners and their rights and responsibilities with respect to each other. For these types of businesses, you may want to place your buyout provisions directly into the partnership or LLC operating agreement.

To accomplish this, simply cut and paste the buyout provisions from our agreement into the existing organizational document (leaving out the signature page). We recommend that you add them to the end of the existing document, but you can insert them anywhere you wish. When adding these provisions to the document, you will want to change the paragraph numbering or lettering of the buyout provisions to conform to the numbering or lettering scheme of your existing LLC operating agreement or partnership agreement.

Creating a Separate Agreement

If you wish to adopt a separate buyout agreement, have all owners (and each owner's spouse or legally recognized domestic or civil partner) date and sign the agreement at the bottom, using the signature page included at the end of the buyout agreement.

TIP

Refer to your buyout agreement in your partnership or LLC operating agreement. If you adopt your buyout provisions in a separate buyout agreement, as we suggest, we recommend that you add a provision to your partnership or operating agreement that refers to the existence of your buyout agreement. (Legally, this tactic is called "incorporating your buyout agreement by reference" into your partnership or operating agreement.) Doing this helps to cover your legal bases and can help avoid a challenge to your buyout agreement from someone looking for a legal way out of its enforceability.

To do this, amend your partnership or operating agreement by adding a sentence that recognizes that a separate agreement exists to control and regulate the ownership of interests in the corporation. Here is one simple way to phrase this new provision.

The provisions of the agreement among the owners dated [*insert date of signing of your buyout agreement*], which regulates the transfer of ownership interests in the [*partnership/LLC*] and other related matters, is hereby incorporated by reference into this [*partnership agreement/LLC operating agreement*] and shall be binding on the company, its creditors, its owners and their assigns and successors, and other parties as provided in the agreement.

Reviewing Your LLC or Partnership Agreement

Before finalizing your buyout provisions, you'll need to make sure they mesh well with the existing provisions of your partnership or LLC operating agreement. Mostly, you want to check to make sure that an existing provision in your partnership agreement or LLC operating agreement does not prohibit, or impose additional rules on, any of the procedures covered in your buyout provisions.

For example, if your partnership agreement completely prohibits the transfer of ownership interests, but your buyout provisions allow an owner to sell to an outside buyer under certain circumstances, you will want to amend your partnership agreement to delete the prohibition on transfers. Similarly, if your LLC operating agreement prohibits an LLC member from selling an LLC membership interest without the approval of all nonselling members, but your buyout provisions allow a deceased owner's estate to force the company to purchase the deceased owner's interest, you may want to remove the conflicting restriction on transfers from your LLC operating agreement.

Working out whether your buyout provisions are consistent with the other provisions in your partnership or operating agreement can get a bit legalistic. The reason for this is that state partnership and LLC laws contain default provisions—rules that apply in the absence of a contrary provision in the partnership or LLC operating agreement—that affect ownership transfer rights in a partnership or an LLC. Consequently, many partnership and LLC agreements have adopted specific clauses that override or repeat the default state law, and these clauses may conflict with your buyout provisions. Here are some of these special state-law-based provisions to look out for in a partnership or LLC operating agreement:

Restrictions on transfer of full ownership rights. One common state default rule is that, in the absence of a contrary provision in a partnership or an LLC agreement, a person who is transferred an ownership interest (the "transferee") receives only economic rights in the business—that is, a right to receive profits and any distribution of cash or property made by the partnership or LLC. The transferee does not get any voting or other management rights attached to the interest unless the nontransferring owners approve this at the time of transfer. You will most likely want future transferees to get full ownership rights—both economic and management rights—without having to obtain the consent of all owners at the time of transfer. If you find a clause in your partnership or operating agreement that requires the approval of all owners for transfers of management rights, you'll probably want to delete it (or have a lawyer make our buyout provisions mesh with that requirement).

Termination of business on dissociation of owner. This one is particularly legalistic. Under prior law in some states (which may be restated in partnership or LLC agreements that have not been updated), the business legally dissolves when an owner is "dissociated"—this means when an owner transfers an interest, dies, withdraws, is expelled, files for bankruptcy, or otherwise ceases to hold an ownership interest—unless the remaining owners vote to continue the business. If you find this type of clause in your partnership or LLC operating agreement, you probably will want to delete it (after asking a lawyer's advice, to be safe). Most state LLC laws no longer require this provision or mention it as a "default" LLC rule. If you keep it in your agreement, it will conflict with our buyout provision that says the company does not terminate when an owner is dissociated. If you have any questions about this provision, check with a small business lawyer.

SEE AN EXPERT

Pay a lawyer to help you check for legal consistency. Finding contradictions and inconsistencies between your buyout provisions and your partnership or LLC operating agreement is not always an easy task. This is one of the times when it may make sense to pay a lawyer to do the difficult work for you. When you ask a lawyer to review your draft buyout agreement, also give the lawyer a copy of your partnership or LLC operating agreement. The lawyer will know if there is any inconsistent language in your partnership or operating agreement that needs to be rooted out. You have to pay for this type of legal scrutiny, but we think it's worth it.

Approving Changes to Your LLC or Partnership Agreement

You and your co-owners will need to approve the additions to your partnership or LLC operating agreement. All current owners should date and sign the amended agreement. This new agreement that contains your buyout provisions will be your new partnership or operating agreement. If spouses of the owners or any additional nonowners (such as LLC managers) signed the original partnership or operating agreement, make sure they sign the new agreement as well.

RESOURCE

Need more information? For further information on partnership and LLC operating agreements, see Nolo's products *Form a Partnership: The Complete Legal Guide,* by Ralph Warner & Denis Clifford, and *Form Your Own Limited Liability Company,* by Anthony Mancuso.

Placing a Legend on Ownership Certificates

Another task you may need to perform after adopting your buyout provisions is to update your membership or ownership certificates. Usually, only corporations issue ownership (stock) certificates to their owners. However, some LLCs issue membership certificates to owners.

Most states require the placement of a notice, or legend, on ownership certificates whenever the interests they represent are subject to buyout provisions. This lets owners and outsiders know that interests in the company are subject to restrictions and may be bought back by the company and its owners pursuant to the buyout provisions that your company has adopted.

If your LLC issues membership certificates, for instructions on putting the required legend on your certificates, see "Placing a Legend on Your Certificates," under "For Corporations," above.

Signing Your Agreement

First, if you haven't already, you should read Chapter 9 on income and estate tax issues before making final decisions on your buyout provisions. Then, assuming you have filled out the worksheet as you read this book, you can now transfer the choices you marked on your worksheet to the buyout agreement available for free on this book's companion page on Nolo.com (see Appendix A for the link).

Next, we recommend you bring your draft agreement for review by a lawyer, tax expert, or other professional with experience in buyout agreements. (See Chapter 10 on how to find an expert.)

Finally, you've come to the last step in completing your agreement— signing it! On the last page of our buyout agreement, you'll find Section XI, which contains blank lines for the signatures of the owners and their spouses (or legally recognized domestic or civil partners). Have each owner and spouse (or partner) print his or her name and the date in the spaces provided, and then sign the agreement.

Resolving Buyout Disputes in the Future

Even the best buy-sell agreement—one that clearly and fairly covers every possible eventuality—can't guarantee a future free of disputes. Human nature being what it is, if business owners are not on good terms during a buyout situation, one owner (or his inheritors or his ex-spouse) may pick a fight with the others. And even if the owners are getting along personally, it's possible to disagree as to the value of a business interest. For example, a departing owner might assert the purchase price the company has offered to pay him is unfairly low because the valuation method in the agreement wasn't properly followed.

For these and other reasons, it makes sense to include a procedure in your agreement for resolving conflicts. Then, if the owners can't negotiate a solution or a compromise and a spat does ensue, all owners will have the security of knowing there is a method in place to resolve the dispute fairly and quickly and without having legal fees bankrupt all involved. To help meet these goals, our buyout agreement provides a way to resolve disputes using "alternative dispute resolution"—ADR for short.

ADR is a catchall term that describes a number of methods used to resolve disputes out of court, including negotiation, mediation, and arbitration. The common denominator of all ADR methods is that they are faster, less formal, cheaper, and often less adversarial than a court trial.

Our agreement utilizes the two most effective out-of-court mechanisms for resolving disputes: mediation and arbitration.

Litigation

First let's take a look at how regular court litigation works (or doesn't work), if only to demonstrate why it's often a poor choice for resolving small business disputes. First, if lawyers must be hired to represent each side in a small business conflict, the resources of the company and the involved owners may quickly be drained. Simply put, legal fees can be astronomical. To understand why, realize that business lawyers usually charge $150 to $350 per hour (and often more)—and a single case can take hundreds of hours of an attorney's time in depositions and other trial preparation before the case even goes to trial. In short, when you add up the legal expenses of both sides, going to court can, and often does, cost more than the dispute is worth.

Add to this the fact that litigation can drag on for months or even years, during which time your business may be in limbo, and you have a true recipe for disaster. In fact, many small businesses simply fall apart before the court fight is over.

Third, keeping conflicts out of a public courtroom can be important to small business owners. Understandably, some don't want to expose trade secrets or private financial information, or have to air their dirty laundry in public. For example, if you go to court over the buyout of a co-owner who has a drug or alcohol abuse problem, some very personal matters could be brought up, such as a recount of all the embarrassing things the owner did under the influence. Revealing such information to the public could affect your company's reputation, not to mention ruin your business partner's life. Likewise, if you rely on consumers to buy products or services from you, you'll want to keep up your public image. For instance, if one of your co-owners becomes disabled in a tragic accident, and you and the other co-owners attempt to buy him out, you could engender a wave of bad local publicity that could damage your business for years.

Fourth, filing a lawsuit is a hostile and aggressive act. So as not to jeopardize your case, your lawyers may forbid you to speak with opposing co-owners (even if you need and wish to cooperate to keep the business functioning). Also, your attorney may all but insist on using every means possible to win, even if it means showing your co-owner in the worst possible light or dragging his family through the mud. Of course, behavior like this is highly likely to cause your adversary to retaliate in kind. Continuing your business relationship in circumstances like these is all but impossible.

Fifth, many times small business disputes do not raise legal claims that can be effectively pursued in court. For example, if two partners are in a major disagreement about who should control different aspects of the business, but there has been no violation of the partnership agreement, chances are the co-owners won't be able to resolve their problem in court.

Lastly, small businesses are particularly vulnerable to losing a court case. They usually carry less comprehensive insurance and have less capital than larger companies. As a result, they are at an increased risk of being wiped out by even one oversized court award.

Mediation

Compared to litigation, mediation is inexpensive, quick, confidential, less risky, and almost always available for small business disputes. In a nutshell, mediation is a process where the parties to a dispute try to come to a voluntary agreement with the help of an outside, neutral third party: the mediator. A mediation session is an informal process that takes place without rules of evidence and other court-like protocols (though it does follow a defined structure—see "The Stages of Mediation," below). With the help of their mediator, the parties decide what issues need to be resolved and what procedure should be followed to solve their dispute.

TIP
All parties to a dispute must agree to mediation and be able to mediate. If one party refuses or perhaps isn't competent to participate in mediation, the dispute cannot be mediated. Particularly when one party may be mentally disabled, you'd be better off going to court, where a judge or lawyer can protect that party's interests.

The Stages of Mediation

Many people think that mediation is a totally unstructured process in which a friendly mediator chats with the disputants until they suddenly drop their hostilities and work together for the common good. In fact, mediation is a carefully designed process intended to help the disputing parties craft a detailed written solution to their problem. True, compared to the formalism of an American trial court, mediation is informal, but that's not a bad thing.

Stage 1: Mediator's Opening Statement. After the disputants are seated at a table, the mediator introduces everyone, explains the goals and rules of the mediation, and encourages each side to work cooperatively toward a settlement.

Stage 2: Disputants' Opening Statements. Each party is invited to tell, in his or her own words, what the dispute is about and how he or she has been affected by it, and to present some general ideas about resolving it. While one person is speaking, the other is not allowed to interrupt.

Stage 3: Joint Discussion. The mediator will try to get the parties to talk directly about what was said in the opening statements. This is the time to determine what issues need to be addressed.

Stage 4: Private Meetings With the Mediator (Called "Caucuses"). The private caucus is a chance for each party to meet privately with the mediator (usually in a nearby room) to discuss the strengths and weaknesses of his or her position and new ideas for settlement. The mediator may caucus with each side just once or several times, as needed. Often the mediator helps each party to focus on their real needs and to put aside less-essential issues. Although it may take hours or even days, this eventually causes the parties to abandon emotionally laden side issues and come to terms with the best way to resolve the major issues.

Stage 5: Joint Negotiation. After the private caucuses, the mediator may bring the parties back together to negotiate directly.

Stage 6: Closure. This is the end of the mediation. If an agreement has been reached and the parties are ready, they can write up and sign a legally binding contract. Otherwise, the mediator may draw up a written summary of their agreement and suggest they take it to lawyers for review. If no agreement was reached, the mediator will review whatever progress has been made and advise each party of their options, such as meeting again later or going to arbitration.

Precisely because a mediator has no power to impose a decision, but encourages the parties to arrive at their own compromised solution, participants are usually more open to creative proposals to resolve a dispute than in a courtroom. In fact, partly because of this, business ownership transition problems are quickly becoming a well-developed specialty in the private dispute resolution world. Here are just a few of the many other reasons why mediation is particularly well suited for business disputes:

- Mediation costs a lot less than litigation. Fees start at $1,200 or so per party for a full-day session, but can go higher, depending on how long mediation lasts, how specialized your dispute is, and which firm or mediator you choose. You should count on at least a couple of days for small business mediation, maybe as much as a week or two if your dispute is complicated. Still, the cost will be a pittance compared to taking the same dispute to court.

- Mediation spares the disputants the fear of the courtroom, where a judge or jury can stun one party with a big loss. Because the mediator has no authority to impose a decision, nothing can be decided unless both parties agree to it. Knowing this greatly reduces the tension felt by all parties—people in mediation tend to be more relaxed and open to compromise. (If for any reason you don't feel the mediation session is productive, you can call it off. For instance, if one party isn't cooperating—he insists that he's right and is not willing to hear the other side, he doesn't agree with the advantages of mediation, or he's just a loud-mouthed jerk—you may not want to waste any more time in mediation, and instead go straight to arbitration. See "Arbitration," below.)

- People who arrive at a joint decision are much more likely to abide by it than are people who have a decision imposed on them by a judge. This is key when an ongoing business is involved, since mediation greatly increases the likelihood that the solution will actually work.

- When you have to keep working with your co-owner (or a member of her family) and you want to remain on good terms, mediation is usually the best choice. Unlike a judge, a mediator will not place blame. Just the opposite: A mediator's job is to help both parties evaluate their goals and options in order to find a solution that works for everyone. For instance, during litigation, it's common to call a witness just to show the judge or jury the bad character of the person you're up against; in mediation this would be completely irrelevant, and therefore is almost never done. And since neither side needs to personally attack the other, each is able to save face and, hopefully, continue some sort of business and personal relationship with the other after the dispute is over.

- Unlike court, mediation is not limited to solving the dispute at hand. Often, issues are discussed in mediation that would not be legally relevant in court, but which are highly important to the parties. This allows the parties to address the issues that may have created the dispute in the first place, including problems that stem from different communication styles and clashing personalities. In short, if undiscovered or ongoing problems surface during mediation, the parties, with the help of the mediator, can work them out.

- Mediation can be particularly helpful if you're having trouble communicating and negotiating with the other party; the mediator will help you make your points and not allow the other side to intimidate you. In fact, even the experience of talking civilly to each other and working cooperatively toward a solution can help business owners restore their relationship; some consider mediation a kind of business therapy.

- Mediation is also a good choice when you don't want to air your company's and co-owners' dirty laundry. Mediators take a vow of confidentiality so you can be assured that you won't read about what your co-owner told your mediator about you in the local paper. Especially for family businesses—where a contested court case can tear a family apart—mediation is almost surely the better choice. Because of the privacy, the civility, and the encouragement it provides to co-owners to come to a compromise, mediation offers many distressed families a positive way to begin a healing process that will go beyond the particular dispute.

When and if the parties do come up with a solution, the mediator should help them put the agreement in writing, usually as a legally binding contract. The negotiated solution can include whatever you've agreed to, including issues not thought to be important when the mediation began. For example, the agreement can set up a plan for you and the departing owner to work together in the future (perhaps a retiring owner agrees to sell out as part of the settlement, but the company agrees that it will hire him to do consulting work for two years).

Choosing a Mediator

To find a mediator, ask for recommendations from colleagues or small business lawyers or associations, or look in your local yellow pages under Mediation Services for a private dispute resolution company.

It's important to choose a mediator with experience in small business disputes, in particular in disputes arising out of buy-sell agreements. And, in some situations, you may even want to seek out a mediator with more specialized knowledge. For example, if your conflict is over the value of an owner's interest, then experience in business valuation techniques or at least general financial know-how will be necessary. Likewise, if you're trying to structure a complicated installment payment plan with an eye toward minimizing taxes, the mediator should have some tax savvy. Or, if you and your co-owners are arguing over the worth of a patent, the mediator should have a technical background.

TIP

Use experts as consultants. Small business lawyers or tax experts can also be used in a consultative role as part of mediation. Often they make no appearances at the mediation session itself, but stand by to review settlement proposals. But be sure to have any experts you need lined up before you begin mediating. When proposals start flying, you may need to have your adviser at the ready to check them out, to recommend any necessary changes, and to consider any tax consequences.

Arbitration

Arbitration, another form of alternative dispute resolution, is more like court than like mediation. Like mediation, arbitration uses a neutral third party, called an arbitrator (or sometimes, there are several neutral parties that make up an arbitration panel). However, in binding arbitration, the parties themselves are not expected to arrive at a voluntary agreement (although, of course, they are always free to do so). Instead, each side presents its version of the dispute to the arbitrator, who then issues a written decision that is binding on the parties.

Although arbitration is more structured and trial-like than mediation, the fact that it uses relatively informal rules of evidence and procedure means that it's almost always faster than going to court. Also, arbitrators have a bit more leeway than judges to impose commonsense solutions, rather than being bound to follow the letter of the law. In short, arbitration is almost always quicker and less expensive than going to court, and definitely more private.

If an unhappy losing party decides to sue in court in an attempt to overturn the arbitrator's decision (in fact, such lawsuits occur infrequently), she is almost sure to lose. That's because the court will not overturn the arbitrator's decision unless the arbitrator was blatantly biased or unfair (for example, had an undisclosed conflict of interest). In other words, once the arbitrator makes a decision, the fight is over.

Our Solution

Arbitration is required by our buyout agreement only if negotiation and mediation prove unsuccessful. In other words, disputants are encouraged to mediate first, arbitrate second (if necessary), and litigate not at all. In fact, few disputes ever get past the mediation stage, because in mediation disputants are highly motivated to arrive at a compromise they can live with, rather than risk that an arbitrator will impose a less palatable one.

The language of the dispute resolution clause we use in our buy-sell agreement is shown below.

Section VIII: Resolution of Disputes

Mediation Followed by Arbitration

Except as may otherwise be provided in this agreement or a later one dated and signed by all owners, any dispute concerning the contents of this agreement, if it cannot be settled through direct negotiation, shall first be submitted to mediation according to the terms specified below. All parties agree to try in good faith to settle the dispute by mediation before resorting to arbitration or litigation.

(a) An owner, an owner's legal representative, the spouse or ex-spouse of an owner, the executor or administrator of a deceased owner's estate, or any other party with an interest in this company who wishes to have a dispute mediated shall submit a written request for mediation to each of the other owners of the company. Mediation shall commence within 15 days after the date of the written request for mediation.

(b) Any decision reached by mediation shall be reduced to writing, signed by all parties, and shall be binding on each party. The costs of mediation shall be shared equally by all parties to the dispute.

(c) Each party to the mediation process shall cooperate fully and fairly with the mediator in any attempt to reach a mutually satisfactory compromise to a dispute. If the dispute is not resolved within 30 days after it is referred to the mediator, the dispute shall be submitted for arbitration according to the terms specified below or on terms agreeable to all parties at the time the dispute is submitted to arbitration.

(d) Within 15 days of the delivery of the notice of intention to proceed to arbitration to all parties, each party shall reply in writing to the arbitrator, stating his or her views of the nature and appropriate outcome of the dispute.

(e) The arbitrator shall hold a hearing on the dispute within 15 days after replies have been received from all parties or, if all replies have not been received, no later than 30 days after the giving of notice of intention to proceed to arbitration.

Section VIII: Resolution of Disputes (continued)

(f) At the arbitration hearing, each party shall be entitled to present any oral or written statements he or she wishes and may present witnesses. The arbitrator shall make his or her decision in writing, and his or her decision shall be conclusive and binding on all parties to the dispute.

(g) The cost of arbitration, including any lawyer's fees, shall be borne by the parties to the dispute equally unless the arbitrator directs otherwise.

CAUTION

Our dispute resolution clause is not optional. We assume all readers will agree in their buyout agreement to attempt to mediate their disputes and, if mediation fails, to arbitrate instead of going directly to court. Of course, you can change this provision, for example, by not requiring arbitration if mediation fails, but we don't think this is the best course—for the reasons given earlier, a court case should be avoided if at all possible.

Binding Future Owners Under Your Buyout Agreement

The next section of our buyout agreement, Section X, tries to ensure that new owners in the company will be legally bound to the terms of the buyout agreement. While the agreement states that all future holders of ownership interests—whether they have received an interest by sale, gift, will or trust, or otherwise—will be subject to the terms of the buyout agreement, new owners must sign the agreement or they may not actually be legally bound to follow it.

EXAMPLE: George and Harry have owned and managed a mortuary for 40 years as a corporation. Having bought the building that houses the mortuary and owning a large share of a local cemetery, the business has come to be worth a lot of money. Getting on in years, George starts to gift shares to his children, hoping to avoid eventual estate taxes. George does not require his children to sign the company's shareholder (buy-sell) agreement before receiving shares. Soon after receiving shares in the corporation, George's son Michael decides he doesn't want to follow in his father's footsteps to become an undertaker, so he sells his shares to one of George and Harry's competitors. Since Michael never signed the agreement, it would be very hard, if not impossible, to get a judge to void the transfer of shares.

Other problems can arise if a recipient of an ownership interest never signs the agreement. If, for instance, Michael from the above example gets divorced and his spouse receives half of his ownership interest in a divorce settlement, the company cannot require the spouse to sell her ownership interest back to the company.

For this reason, any time family members receive interests in the company by gift, they, as well as their spouses, should be required to adopt the agreement.

Our agreement requires all new owners, and their spouses, to sign the buyout agreement before taking an ownership interest in the company. Section X from our buyout agreement is shown below.

Section X: Continuation of Restrictions

All heirs, successors and assigns to an ownership interest in the company will be bound by the terms of this agreement.

Before receiving a purchased, donated, or otherwise transferred interest from an owner or an owner's legal representative, the owner or the owner's legal representative will require any purchaser, donee or transferee, and his or her spouse, to sign this agreement, agreeing to be bound by its terms.

In the future, whenever a new owner joins your company, add this owner's name (and her spouse's name, if applicable) to your buyout agreement and have the new owner sign it. You can simply add a new date and signature line at the bottom of your original agreement for the new owner to date and sign, or you can prepare a new one, having all old and new owners sign it. This latter approach gives you a chance to review your agreement to make sure it still works for all owners. For example, if the economic circumstances of your corporation or the personal preferences of your owners have changed since the adoption of your agreement, you may want to change the valuation and payment alternatives in Sections VI and VII of the agreement. (See the next section for information on updating your agreement.)

Updating Your Agreement

As we have discussed elsewhere, it's important to review your agreement periodically to make sure it reflects the current economic realities of your company and the present expectations of your owners. It is particularly important to review Sections VI and VII of the agreement, where you check the methods to be used to value ownership interests and the payment terms to pay for them for purposes of a buyout under your agreement. Some experts recommend doing this each year, at the owners' annual meeting.

If all owners agree to make changes to the buyout agreement, you can date and have all owners initial changes on the original agreement itself, or you can prepare a new one and have it dated and signed by all owners.

Updating the Agreement Price

There's another way to update your valuation provision if you have selected the fixed-price valuation method (Valuation Method 1) in Section VI (see Chapter 6). This provision lets you change the buyout price to be paid for interests by having all owners sign a written statement that specifies a new agreed-upon price. Below is a sample statement you can copy and use for this purpose.

If you use a written statement like this, be sure to attach it to your agreement.

Owners' Consent to New Agreement Price for Interests in the Company

The undersigned owners of [*name of company*], representing all of the voting owners on the books of this company on the date shown below, agree that in any purchase or sale of ownership interests under the buy-sell agreement dated [*date of signing of your agreement*], unless otherwise stated in a provision of such agreement other than Section VI, for the purposes of determining the purchase price for individual ownership interests, the entire value of the company shall be $ [*insert agreed-upon price for entire company, such as "100,000"*]. The value of an individual owner's interest shall be the entire value for the company as determined under this paragraph, multiplied by his or her ownership percentage.

The price stated in this statement shall supersede any price specified in Section VI of the above-mentioned agreement, and shall supersede any price specified in any statement dated and signed by owners prior to the date of this statement, shown below.

Dated: _____

Signed: [*signatures of all current owners*]

TIP

Update your price whenever your financial outlook changes. Even if you and your co-owners do not sign a new statement annually, make sure to do so whenever financials in your business take a significant upturn or downturn (for instance, your payroll costs increase significantly, with a resulting reduction in owners' equity as shown on your last fiscal year-end balance sheet, or your annual profits go up significantly three quarters in a row and you expect this trend to continue).

Updating the Funding Method

If you revisit your agreement to add insurance funding in a few years, you may also need to change these parts of your agreement:

- Section III, Scenario 2 and/or Scenario 3 (buyout options)
- Section V (funding)
- Section VI (price), and
- Section VII (payment terms).

Make sure your agreement coincides with the terms of your insurance policy, or you may have trouble with the insurance payoff.

> **RELATED TOPIC**
>
> **Don't forget to add new owners to your agreement, as discussed in "Binding Future Owners Under Your Buyout Agreement," above.** You can simply add a new date and signature line at the bottom of your original agreement for the new owner to date and sign, or you can prepare a new one, having all old and new owners sign it. ●

Income and Estate Tax Issues

Tax consequences are obviously important whenever business interests are transferred. And the adoption of particular provisions in your buyout agreement as well as the actual buyout of an owner's interest according to those provisions can have important income and estate tax consequences. For this reason, it is important to have your buyout agreement reviewed by a skilled tax adviser to make sure that a buyout will have the appropriate tax consequences for the seller, buyers, inheritors, and other people intended to benefit from a buyout under your agreement.

In this chapter, we flag some of the basic federal income and estate tax issues involved with buyouts of ownership interests in partnerships, LLCs, and corporations and try to explain them. The tax implications of buyout provisions and the tax consequences of using a particular buyout method are complicated, and we don't cover all the rules and exceptions—just enough to give you a good start when seeking more specific, individually tailored, and up-to-date advice from your tax or financial adviser. And remember, even the basic rules here are subject to change.

Income Tax Issues

Let's start by looking at some of the fundamental income tax issues surrounding a buyout of an owner's interest.

Before we get into the tax treatment of buyouts, let's define a technical tax term that you need to know—the concept of "income tax basis" in an ownership interest. Then we'll discuss how the continuing owners, the selling owner, and the company are taxed following a buyout.

Tax Basis and Capital Gains

As you may or may not know, the term income tax basis, or simply basis, refers to the value assigned to property for the purposes of determining the taxable gain or loss from it after it is sold. When you sell an ownership interest, calculating your exact basis (with the help of a tax adviser) is crucial, because this is the number that the IRS uses to determine if you've made a profit ("recognized a gain," in IRS-speak).

Generally, your income tax basis in an ownership interest is the cash amount you pay, along with your current basis in any property you transfer, to buy the interest. If you transfer property that's subject to a debt that the business assumes—for example, you transfer real estate subject to a mortgage—your basis in your interest is decreased by the amount of the assumed debt. In addition, in a partnership or an LLC, if the business has any outstanding accounts payable or other business debts when you make your capital contribution, your share of these liabilities is added to your basis (since you are personally liable for the debts of the business).

Over time, this original basis in your ownership interest is adjusted up or down. For example, in a partnership or an LLC, your basis in your ownership interest is increased when profits are allocated to you and decreased when losses are allocated. These allocations occur automatically at the end of the tax year of the partnership or LLC whether or not profits are actually paid out, and are known as each owner's "distributive share." In addition, your basis in an LLC or partnership interest is decreased whenever you receive a cash distribution from the business—for example, when profits are actually paid to you (unless the distributions exceed your basis in your interest). In addition, your basis normally increases whenever the business incurs additional liabilities (for example, takes out a loan).

Obviously, figuring your basis in an ownership interest during the course of its operations or at the time of a buyout of your ownership interest is anything but obvious to most of us, and this is just one of the important tasks that should be referred to a tax adviser.

 TIP

There are different types of bases in partnership and LLC ownership interests. In a partnership or an LLC, there are two types of basis: the owner's individual basis in an ownership interest—called the "outside basis"—and the partnership or LLC's separate basis in its assets—called its "inside basis." In our discussion of basis in this section, when we refer to partners' or LLC members' bases in their ownership interests, we mean the partners' or LLC members' "outside bases" in their interests.

Your gain when you sell your ownership interest is calculated by subtracting your tax basis in your ownership interest (your original basis plus or minus adjustments) from your sale proceeds. In general, the higher your basis, the lower your gain will be for tax purposes.

EXAMPLE: Barbara is a shareholder and vice president of Biz Wiz, a small corporation with four other owners. As part of its initial stock issuance, Barbara's company issues her 3,000 shares in exchange for her cash payment of $70,000 plus the patent she owns for *Biz Wiz* software. Her starting basis consists of her patents of $30,000 plus her cash payment of $70,000: $100,000. When Barbara leaves the company four years later, no adjustments have been made to her original basis in her shares. Under the terms of the buyout provisions in the shareholder agreement signed by Barbara and her co-owners, her ownership interests are appraised and purchased by the company for $125,000. Barbara recognizes a gain of $25,000—the $125,000 sales price minus her basis of $100,000 in her shares.

You can expect to pay a tax on any gain you make when you sell your ownership interest. In most cases, your profit should be eligible to be taxed at capital gains tax rates. The capital gains rates vary according to how long you owned your ownership interest—for the long term (currently defined as more than one year) or for the short term (one year or less). Without listing the various capital gains rates, which depend on your personal income tax bracket and are subject to change, the main point is this: Long-term capital gains rates are normally lower than ordinary individual income rates paid by the owners, so it's usually an advantage to have the profit from a sale of an ownership interest taxed at long-term capital gains rates.

EXAMPLE: Let's revisit Barbara's situation. After owning her Biz Wiz shares (in which her tax basis is $100,000) for several years, Barbara sells them back to Biz Wiz for $125,000. Her $25,000 profit is eligible for long-term capital gains treatment, rather than ordinary income tax treatment. Had Barbara's sale not qualified for capital gains tax rates, she would have been taxed on the sale proceeds at her higher personal income tax rate.

Capital Accounts

The term capital account refers to the dollar value of a partner's or an LLC member's interest in the business (not counting any depreciation or goodwill). It's easy to confuse capital account balances with other accounting and tax terms, such as an owner's basis in an ownership interest or an owner's distributive share of profits and losses. To avoid this, just think of a capital account balance as the amount that an owner can expect to be paid if the business is liquidated and split up among the owners (assuming sufficient cash is left after all creditors have been paid).

When partners or LLC members contribute cash or property to a company, their capital accounts are credited with the cash amount or fair market value of the contribution. When profits are allocated to the owners at the end of the tax year of a partnership or an LLC, their capital account balances go up (the business owes the owner this money); as distributions are made, such as payments of draws, or profits, their capital account balances go down (the business no longer owes this money).

In fact, an owner's capital account balance may be used in a partnership or an LLC operating agreement as the price an owner receives for a buyout of the owner's interest (though we don't use this method for the reasons stated in the "Capital Accounts" section in Chapter 6). But if the assets of the partnership or LLC are appraised and adjusted on the company's balance sheet just prior to the buyout (for example, an increase in assets results in proportionate increases to the balances in the owners' capital accounts), payment of the capital account balance to a departing owner might represent a fair value for their interest. If you're interested in using this approach to value ownership interests in an LLC or a partnership, choose the appraisal method in Chapter 6—a professional appraiser can handle these calculations for you.

SEE AN EXPERT

Special exclusions may be available. Shareholders in qualifying active C corporations may be able to exclude some or all of the capital gain realized from selling originally issued shares if they were held for more than five years. If you are a shareholder of a C corporation, ask your tax adviser about this possibility. This exclusion is covered in IRC Section 1202.

Okay, we've established that capital gains tax treatment is normally the way to go when selling an ownership interest. And we've also seen that having a higher basis in your ownership interest results in the recognition of less capital gain and, therefore, the payment of less tax when the interest is sold. Below, we discuss special IRS rules that affect the basis of an ownership interest and your eligibility for capital gains tax treatment when your ownership interest is bought out under a buyout agreement.

Tax Treatment for Continuing Owners

In Chapter 4, we discussed why our buyout agreement allows the company and then the continuing owners the opportunity to purchase a departing owner's interest. A big advantage of this approach is that the decision as to who will make the purchase doesn't have to be made until a particular buyout situation presents itself. This allows the owners of the company to evaluate the tax advantages and disadvantages of several different buyout scenarios. The decision as to whether to have the company or the continuing owners purchase an ownership interest can have significant tax consequences. We look briefly at some of these tax consequences below.

Continuing Owners as Buyers

Let's start by focusing on a simple truth: When the continuing owners buy a departing co-owner's interest, they have spent additional personal funds to increase their ownership interest in their company, and their percentages of ownership in the company increase accordingly.

> **EXAMPLE:** Amanda, Beth, Chris, and their father each own 15,000 shares in Shortcuts, Inc. They each own 25% of the company. When their father decides to retire, Amanda, Beth, and Chris buy his 15,000 shares (the corporation does not buy any shares itself). According to their buy-sell agreement, the children split the purchase of the shares equally, buying 5,000 shares apiece. Amanda, Beth, and Chris now each own 20,000 shares. They each own 33% of the company, instead of 25%.

It follows that the continuing owners' tax basis in their ownership interests will increase by the amount of cash they paid to buy the departing owner's shares.

> **EXAMPLE:** Let's fill in the details of the Shortcuts example above. Amanda, Beth, and Chris each have a basis of $15,000 in their original shares—that is, each paid $15,000 to buy their original 15,000 shares. When their father decides to retire, Amanda, Beth, and Chris each pay him $5,000 for 5,000 of his shares. Amanda, Beth, and Chris now own 20,000 shares each (33% of the company), and each has a basis of $20,000 in her larger ownership interests.

This type of direct purchase by the continuing owners lets the owners increase their bases in their ownership interests so that in the future, when one of them wants to sell the shares, there will be less of a taxable gain (less difference between tax basis and the sales price) and therefore less capital gains tax to pay.

Of course, unless life and disability insurance will fund a buyout, the continuing owners will normally have to use personal funds or borrow money to purchase a departing owner's interest. Or, if a shareholder has to take dividends from the corporation to fund the buyout, the funds will be subject to double taxation—once as income to the corporation, and again when received by the shareholder. Similarly, partners or LLC members will be taxed when taking draws from their businesses to fund buyouts (a draw is an advance distribution of profits by a partnership or an LLC and is taxed to owners at their individual income tax rates). In short, these additional considerations demonstrate that the decision as to who buys a departing ownership interest—the company or the continuing owners—is a complex one where input from a tax expert is necessary.

Company as Buyer

When the company itself buys a co-owner's interest, it's a slightly different story, although the continuing owners' percentages of ownership in the company increase just the same. Let's see what happens to Amanda, Beth, and Chris in this situation.

> **EXAMPLE:** Amanda, Beth, Chris, and their father each own 15,000 shares in Shortcuts, Inc., or 25% of the company. When their father decides to retire, the corporation buys back (redeems) the father's 15,000 shares and cancels them. Although Amanda, Beth, and Chris still only own 15,000 shares apiece, they now each own 33% of the company.

When a company buys back a departing owner's interest, whether it's a corporation, an LLC, or a partnership, each continuing owner ends up owning a larger fraction of the company, since there are fewer owners. And, assuming the business stays on a steady course, each owner's larger share can be sold for more than would have been true before one owner sold out.

However, from a tax point of view, when the company itself buys a departing owner's interest, the continuing owners' tax bases do not go up, since the owners did not actually purchase any part of an interest or invest more dollars. The result is that the continuing owners may owe higher capital gains taxes when they eventually sell their interests than if they had personally bought the departing owner's interest themselves.

For this reason, if a co-owner wants to be bought out, you and your co-owners may want to buy the co-owner's share yourselves, rather than having the company pay for it. But this decision isn't usually this simple. After all, the higher capital gains taxes could well be less than the money the continuing owners would save by not purchasing the departing owner's interest themselves.

Also key to the decision of whether the company or the continuing owners should purchase a departing or deceased owner's interest is whether the sale proceeds will be taxed as a capital gain to the *seller*. We look at this issue in the next section.

Tax Treatment for the Selling Owner

First, the good news: Generally, when an owner sells an ownership interest, whether it be shares in a corporation or an ownership interest in a partnership or an LLC, the sale is eligible for capital gains tax treatment (which saves tax dollars, as discussed above). But, of course, there are technical tax requirements and exceptions to this rule. When the time comes for a buyout, you will want to talk to a tax adviser to make sure your sale or purchase of an interest actually qualifies for long-term capital gains treatment. Let's look at some of the general rules for corporations, partnerships, and LLCs.

Buyouts of Partnerships and LLC Interests

While most buyouts by the continuing owners qualify the selling owner for capital gains tax treatment, when the partnership or LLC buys out an owner, things aren't so certain.

Continuing owners as buyers. When the continuing owners buy out a departing owner in a partnership or an LLC, any gain on the sale is normally taxed to the selling owner at (hopefully long-term) capital gains tax rates. Also included in the sale and taxed to the selling owner is the owner's share of any partnership or LLC liabilities. Finally, at the time of sale the basis of a partner or an LLC member is adjusted up or down for the amount of profit or loss allocable to the owner for the portion of the tax year prior to the sale.

> EXAMPLE: Maria sells her partnership interest to her partner for $25,000. Her basis in her interest was $15,000, and her half of partnership liabilities is $5,000. At the time of the sale, Maria's share of partnership profits for the current tax year is $1,000. Maria's adjusted basis is $16,000—her $15,000 basis adjusted up by $1,000 for her share of current-year profits. Her taxable gain is thus $14,000 ($25,000 selling price plus her $5,000 share of partnership liabilities, minus her $16,000 adjusted basis). Maria will owe capital gains taxes on $14,000.

> (!) CAUTION
>
> **Exceptions to capital gains rules.** If a portion of the purchase price is allocated to "unrealized receivables" (rights to payments by the business for past or future services) or substantially appreciated inventory (inventory whose market value exceeds 120% of its basis), that portion is taxed at ordinary income rates to the selling owner, rather than given capital gains treatment. Also, if any portion of the purchase price is a payment for the goodwill of the business, it will be taxed at ordinary income tax rates, unless a written agreement specifically provides for the payment of goodwill.

Company as buyer. When the business itself—not the continuing owners—purchases the interest of a departing owner (called a "liquidation" of the owner's interest), capital gains treatment for the seller's gain is not a sure thing. Selling owners may be eligible for capital gains tax treatment on their gains from the sale or they may have to pay ordinary income taxes on the sale proceeds. Tax analysts see this as a tax flexibility afforded partnerships and LLCs—the business can structure the liquidation of an owner's interest by the partnership or LLC any way it wants to. But sellers who have to pay a high tax rate on the sale proceeds may be less thrilled at that prospect.

Here's a quick look at the three ways a partnership or an LLC can treat buyouts for tax purposes when the business itself buys the interest:

- If a buyout of the interest of a retiring or deceased owner qualifies under Internal Revenue Code (IRC) Section 736(b) as an "exchange for an interest," the payment should receive capital gains treatment. Capital gains taxes are due on the amount by which the sales price exceeds the owner's basis in the interest.

- If the payments for an ownership interest are determined with reference to the income of the business, they may be considered to be payments to sellings owners of their distributive shares—that is, their shares of the profits in the partnership or LLC. In this case, selling owners (or their estates) will owe ordinary income taxes on the entire sales price. The distributive shares allocable to the remaining partners are reduced (this is similar to the partnership getting a deduction for the payment).

- If the sale is considered by the IRS as a "guaranteed payment," the selling owner pays ordinary income taxes on *all* of the sale proceeds (not just the amount by which the purchase price exceeds the owner's basis). The partnership is entitled to a deduction for the amount paid.

We won't cover the technical requirements and exceptions to the above rules. Just make sure to have your tax adviser analyze potential and future buyouts under your buyout provisions to make sure you will obtain the desired tax result when and if the time comes for the buyout of an owner's interest by your partnership or LLC.

CAUTION

Ask your tax adviser about goodwill payments. If you plan to include goodwill in your buyout price, you may want to amend your partnership or LLC operating agreement to specifically provide for a reasonable payment to a selling owner for their share of goodwill in the business. (This way, a selling owner shouldn't have to pay ordinary income tax rates on the portion of the buyout price allocated to goodwill.)

Your tax adviser can help you decide if you should do this and can add the necessary language to your agreement to meet the tax rules. (Even though courts have allowed retroactive amendments to partnership agreements to include this language after a buyout, we recommend you make any necessary changes prior to effecting a buyout under your buyout provisions.)

Buyouts of Corporate Shares

The good news is that most buyouts of a corporate shareholder's entire ownership interest should qualify for capital gains tax treatment by the owner (or their estate). But, again, there are technical exceptions you should go over with a tax adviser if you think they may apply to you.

Continuing owners as buyers. When the continuing shareholders buy out a departing owner, the transaction should qualify for capital gains tax treatment: The selling owner pays capital gains taxes on the excess of the sales price over their basis in the interest.

Corporation as buyer. There are more than a few tax wrinkles that arise if the corporation is the buyer. When the corporation itself buys a departing or deceased owner's shares, it is called a "redemption."

Here's the basic rule: If a redemption by the corporation of an owner's shares qualifies under IRC Section 302 as an "exchange," then capital gains tax rules apply. The selling owner (or their estate) pays capital gains taxes on the amount by which the sales proceeds exceed their basis in the transferred shares.

If the buyout does not qualify as an exchange, the payout is treated and taxed as a dividend. Even though the long-term capital gains rate and the dividends rate are currently the same, dividend treatment is a disadvantage because the entire dividend payment is subject to tax. (In an exchange, only the amount of the sales proceeds that exceeds the seller's basis is subject to tax.) Therefore, sellers or their estates will no doubt want buyouts to qualify as exchanges under the tax rules.

Fortunately, most buyout scenarios qualify as exchanges and are therefore eligible for capital gains tax treatment. But watch out for either of the following circumstances when your corporation redeems stock under your buyout agreement:

- **The corporation buys less than all of an owner's interest.** This could happen if your corporation is exercising its Right of First Refusal under your agreement to purchase shares offered by a shareholder to an outsider, but the outsider is planning to buy less than all of the shareholder's stock. In this case, the corporation has a right to buy less than all the shares of the selling shareholder. This purchase would not automatically qualify as an exchange. Also, if the continuing shareholders buy some of a departing owner's shares, the corporation is buying less than all the shares of an owner, and the transaction won't automatically qualify as an exchange.

- **The corporation is a family business.** Even if the corporation purchases all the shares of a departing owner, it might not be purchasing the owner's entire interest under the technical definition of an exchange. That's because the rules say that shares owned by an owner's relatives (spouse, children, grandchildren, and parents) will be attributed to the owner. Unless the corporation buys out all of the owner's shares plus all shares owned by the owner's relatives, the redemption does not automatically qualify as an exchange.

If you're concerned about a corporate buyout of shares not automatically qualifying as an exchange—because the corporation is buying less than all the owner's shares or because relatives of the owner will own shares in the corporation after the buyout, talk to your tax adviser. Some special rules still allow the purchase to qualify as an exchange (for example, a partial buyout of a deceased shareholder's shares to pay estate taxes may qualify for capital gains treatment). We discuss this exception further in "Partial Buybacks to Pay Estate Taxes," below. We won't go into the details of these other special rules here. Just be aware of the basic requirement for capital gains treatment stated above and, if you anticipate problems or want more information, ask your tax adviser for more information about these special tax rules.

Estate Planning

SEE AN EXPERT

In this section we provide an overview of basic estate tax rules as they relate to small businesses, but estate tax rules do change, and they can get complicated fast. Before settling on an estate tax strategy, see a knowledgeable tax adviser to learn about the best approach for your situation.

While most estate planning relating to buyouts involves avoiding estate taxes, which we'll discuss later, you can also save your heirs income taxes by leaving your business interest to them in a tax-savvy way.

In general, assuming your business interest has appreciated since you formed your business or bought into it, it can be smarter to leave your business interest to your inheritors upon your death rather than selling or giving it to them shortly before your death. Here's why.

Stepped-Up Basis at Death of Owner

When you leave a business interest to someone at death, either by will or by a probate-avoiding living trust, the inheritor's tax basis in the property becomes equal to its fair market value as of the date of your death. Because fair market value at the date of your death is likely to be higher than your original tax basis in the interest (assuming appreciation over the years), it is often said that at death the tax basis of a business interest is "stepped up" to its fair market value. (This is actually a simplification of the rule, because the basis of inherited property is adjusted up or down to its fair market value as of the date of death.) This adjusted-value rule can save your heirs a lot in taxes.

> **EXAMPLE:** Bill paid $25,000 for an ownership interest in BJB, a company he owns along with his wife and her brother. His company's buy-sell agreement allows an owner to leave his ownership interest to whomever he wishes in his will, and that inheritor has the right to force BJB to buy back the ownership interest at its current fair market value (to be established by a professional appraiser). Bill dies, leaving his ownership interests to his daughter, Amy.
>
> Forty days after her father's death, Amy demands that BJB buy back the interest she recently inherited. BJB gets an appraisal for Bill's interest for $200,000 and buys it from Amy for this amount. Amy does not owe any capital gains or income taxes, since at Bill's death her income tax basis in the ownership interest was automatically stepped up to the fair market value of $200,000, and her sale proceeds were also $200,000. (If her basis in the ownership interest had not been stepped up, but had stayed at Bill's original basis of $25,000, Amy would have had to report and pay taxes on capital gains of $175,000 when she sold her ownership interest back to BJB.)

⊙ CAUTION

Other issues may be important in the sale or transfer of your business interest. Here we just demonstrated the general rule that property receives a stepped-up basis at death. But, in some cases, if a business is very valuable today but faces much uncertainty in the years ahead, waiting to transfer an ownership interest at death in order to save on taxes may be a poor choice. In short, you'll need to assess your business prospects, family needs, and tax situation to decide the optimum time and manner to sell or transfer your small business interest.

No Change of Basis for Gifts of Interests

When you give away an ownership interest, you give it away at *your* tax basis, not at the interest's fair market value when you make the gift. Unfortunately, the stepped-up basis rule does not apply to gifts. If you give away all or part of your business interest during your lifetime, the person who receives the interest will take it at the same tax basis as yours was when you made the gift.

> EXAMPLE: Let's go back to Bill and Amy's situation. Imagine that instead of waiting to leave his ownership interest in BJB to Amy upon his death, Bill gives it to Amy while he's living. Amy takes the interest at Bill's basis of $25,000. Several years later, after Bill dies, Amy sells her interest for $200,000. Unfortunately, instead of owing no capital gains tax, as would be true if Bill had waited and left his share of BJB to Amy at his death (her tax basis in BJB would have been stepped up to its current market value of $200,000), Amy owes a whopping capital gains tax. In the eyes of the IRS, she has realized a taxable gain of $175,000 ($200,000 − $25,000).

It follows that, if you're an elderly owner, it may not make sense to give away interests in your business to family members during your lifetime. Instead, it may make better sense to wait until your death to leave your ownership interest to your heirs, who will then inherit it with a basis equal to its stepped-up fair market value (subject to any limits in place at the time of your death). If they sell it soon after receiving it, they may not have to pay capital gains tax.

However, if your children work in the business and plan to succeed you some day, this may not apply. In this case, they'll be taking over their share of the company on a long-term basis, and no capital gains tax will be due for many years.

SEE AN EXPERT

Don't ignore state tax issues. Some states tax transfers of ownership interests. In a few states, a sales tax may even apply to sales of business assets. And, of course, many states and localities impose transfer taxes on real estate or other assets. Be sure to ask your tax adviser about your state's taxes.

Estate Tax Issues

If your enterprise is profitable, your estate—that's all the real estate and personal property you own when you die, including your business ownership interest—may be subject to estate tax. This may make you a candidate to engage in at least basic estate planning, which simply means planning how to pass along your property at death in the most efficient and cost-effective way. Often, the primary estate planning concern for small business owners is passing their ownership interest to the next generation with the least amount of red tape and taxes.

However, before we get too far into estate tax planning, you should know that the federal estate tax comes with a personal estate tax exclusion, currently set at $12.06 million.

In other words, the federal estate tax affects only those whose estates are worth more than the exclusion amount. And keep in mind that if you and your co-owners are young, you may buy and sell many businesses in your lifetime, so the business you own now may not affect your estate taxes at all. In short, younger readers will probably be wise not to sweat estate taxes too much. On the other hand, if you're in your 50s or 60s—and especially if you are older—you may want to pay more attention to this chapter.

 SEE AN EXPERT

Estate planning—and especially estate taxes—are complicated areas. In this chapter we provide only basic information about general estate tax rules. Once you understand the basics, you will be better positioned to further discuss these issues and the latest rates and exclusion amounts with your tax adviser.

Also, remember, in this book we've focused on how owners of a small business can limit and control the transfer of ownership interests to spouses, family members, inheritors, and outside purchasers. Please realize that this is a different goal from how business owners can best plan their estates to minimize probate costs and estate taxes and to ensure the orderly and efficient passing of property to heirs upon the owner's death.

No Income Taxes on Inheritance

Some people worry that their heirs will have to pay income taxes on the business interest or money they receive after their death. This should not happen. Specifically, any property your inheritors receive from your estate at your death will not be considered income, so your inheritors will not owe ordinary income taxes. However, if your inheritors sell inherited property, they may owe capital gains taxes. How these taxes are calculated is affected by the stepped-up basis rules discussed at the beginning of "Estate Planning," above.

Estate Tax Basics

Here's what you need to know: When you die, the government may impose a tax on the property you leave behind, if you leave over a certain amount. The federal estate tax affects only people who die leaving a taxable estate (including business property, personal property, and real estate) of more than the exclusion amount. This threshold, sometimes called the personal exemption, is adjusted annually for inflation. Property left in an estate above this threshold amount is taxed at a special estate tax rate (currently, 40%).

For the majority of Americans, the personal estate tax exemption is high enough that they don't have to worry about estate taxes. But you, as a successful small business owner, may not be able to rest as easily. If the value of your estate is higher than the exemption amount in the year you die, your estate will owe estate taxes, unless you leave your property in one of the few ways that qualify it for a deduction.

Marital deduction. The major way most people get a deduction on their estate tax is by leaving property to their spouses. Any property, including a business interest, that you leave to your spouse passes free of estate tax, under what's called the marital deduction.

Portability of spouse's deduction. If the second spouse dies owning all of the couple's property and it's worth more than the exemption amount, a somewhat recent change in the law allows the second spouse's estate to use the first spouse's estate/gift tax exemption (or what's left of it, if part of it was used for the first spouse's estate). Essentially, spouses can combine their estate tax exemptions. This feature is called the "portability" of the estate tax exemption.

For instance, if each spouse owns a few million in assets, and the first one to die leaves everything to the other, no estate tax is owed because property left to a spouse is tax-free (thanks to the marital deduction discussed above). When the second spouse dies and leaves double the amount that the first spouse left (the second spouse hadn't spent any of the couple's money), no estate tax will be due as long as the total amount is under the combined exemption amount, since the state can use both spouses' exemptions.

EXAMPLE: Walt and Helen are partners with another couple in a resort in Utah. Each person's interest is worth $7 million. Walt dies and leaves his share of the resort to his wife. Walt's estate does not owe federal estate taxes on his ownership interest because of the marital deduction. With the addition of Walt's ownership interest, Helen's estate increases from $7 to $14 million.

Helen dies when the personal estate tax exemption is $12.06 million. Her $14 million estate exceeds the exemption amount for one person. Without "portability," estate taxes would be levied on the excess of the exemption amount for one person ($14 million − $12.06 million) at estate tax rates that currently go up to 40%. Fortunately, the combined exemption amount for Helen and Walt is over $24 million, so no taxes are owed.

Caveat: To use the portability feature, the estate of the first spouse to die must file an estate tax return within nine months of death, even if the estate does not owe estate taxes. This portability feature means that AB trusts are no longer needed to be able to use both spouses' federal tax exemptions, since all married couples are entitled to use the two exemptions as long as federal estate tax returns are filed.

Family succession. If you plan to leave your business interest to your children to carry on the business, you may need to do some estate planning. If you don't, and you leave your share of a valuable business to your heirs with the expectation that they'll take over for you, you could be saddling them with such a hefty federal estate tax bill that they may have to sell the business just to have the cash to pay the estate taxes.

For example, assume that Eric owns a business worth $14 million, which he manages with his two children. His goal is to leave the business to his kids, who have expressed a desire to continue the business. But there's a potential problem: Without planning to avoid estate taxes, if Eric dies when the estate tax exemption is $12.06 million, his estate will owe estate taxes. In order to pay these taxes, Eric's kids may need to sell all or part of the business.

Ways to Avoid Estate Taxes

Before we describe how you may be able to use your buyout agreement to lower your eventual estate tax liability, we offer a thumbnail sketch of the primary estate planning devices used to avoid estate taxes—because these techniques may well prove to be more useful to you.

Making Gifts of Your Ownership Interest

Giving away part of your ownership interest during your life can help you save eventual estate taxes because it decreases the value of your eventual estate, but you have to pay attention to the gift tax rules. Otherwise, gifts you make during your life can be taxed when you die, at the same rates as the estate tax. (The government taxes gifts this way so that people can't pass their estates to their heirs tax-free before they die.)

Annual gift tax exclusion. First, know that currently you can make an unlimited number of $16,000 gifts (to different recipients) of cash or other property each calendar year, completely tax-free. (The property in the trust gets to use the personal exemption of the first spouse to die.)

> EXAMPLE: Each year for the rest of your life you can give your son and your daughter $16,000 each, without incurring estate or gift taxes or eating into your personal estate and gift tax exemption. Your spouse can also give $16,000 per year to each child tax free. And both of you can also make tax-exempt gifts to your children's spouses and kids.

(Note that $16,000 is the current amount of the annual gift tax exclusion at the time of this edition. Check Nolo's website or ask your tax adviser for the latest annual gift tax exclusion.)

In addition, gifts to your spouse, donations to qualified tax-exempt nonprofit organizations (such as charities), and payments for school tuition and medical expenses for family members are tax free.

Any other time you give away money or property worth over the exclusion amount—in other words, any time you make a taxable gift— you have to file a gift tax return. But you will owe a gift tax only once you have given away or left more than the federal estate and gift tax exemption amount ($12.06 million) in taxable gifts at your death. So, the idea is to make tax-free gifts of your ownership interest—to give it away to your heirs in $16,000, nontaxable units.

The $16,000 annual gift tax exemption is the basis for many long-term estate tax-saving strategies. This makes sense when you realize you and your spouse can give the exclusion amount to four people each year without being taxed, and you can repeat this act of generosity every year. But keep in mind that as far as business interests go, this technique may be helpful only to family businesses. After all, if your heirs don't plan to carry on your business, your co-owners may not want you giving away your ownership interest to your children.

Giving away an ownership interest free of gift tax can get complicated fast, but here goes. A common method used by many business owners is to give their children small interests (valued at $16,000 or less) in the business each year over many years. Typically, to keep control of the business, owners give away less than a majority of their interests (or, give away only nonvoting interests).

Unless your business is quite small, you may wonder if giving away small portions of your share will work to save a significant amount of estate tax. Because of a tax concept that allows you to discount the value of small ownership interests, the answer is often yes.

Family Limited Partnerships and LLCs

Family limited partnerships (or "family limited liability companies") are sometimes used as tax-savings vehicles, although they have come under recent fire from the IRS. These business structures are really no different from regular limited partnerships and LLCs, except that the partners and members are all family members.

Here is how these structures work: The owners of closely held businesses create family limited partnerships and LLCs, keeping the controlling interest to themselves and giving the nonvoting ownership interests (limited partner interests in limited partnerships or nonmanaging membership interests in LLCs) to family members.

Because these noncontrolling business interests can be subject to valuation discounts, a larger share of the business can be transferred to family members under the $16,000 annual gift tax exemption amount. By combining discounts for lack of marketability, minority ownership, and lack of control over management and income, the value of a limited partnership or LLC interest can be valued at a much lower amount than would be the case for the same interest in a publicly traded corporation.

The IRS attempts to disallow any family limited partnership whose sole purpose appears to be to reduce taxes. In short, any downward adjustments made to the value of a limited partnership interest must have valid business reasons. Also note that there is increased federal interest in recent years in limiting the ability of owners of family-owned businesses to use valuation discounts. Ask your tax adviser for information on the latest rules and regulations.

Discounts. "Valuation discounts" allow a business owner to give away more of the business in one year while staying under the $16,000 annual gift tax exemption threshold. Essentially, owners can lower the value of certain types of ownership interests for tax purposes, in order to be able to give more ownership interest away every year.

The value of an ownership interest can be discounted for tax purposes based on certain characteristics that seem to make it less valuable in the marketplace generally. One of these discounts is given to minority interests (an interest controlling 49% or less of a company's voting interests). Based on the fact that minority interests are often worth much less when a business is sold, they are valued by the IRS at a discount.

Buyout agreement provisions that restrict the transfer of ownership interests can themselves make an ownership interest less valuable—this is called a valuation discount for "lack of marketability." The rationale for this discount is that outside buyers might not want to pay as much for an ownership interest with transfer restrictions on it as they would for an interest that's freely sellable.

What all this adds up to is that when either a restricted or minority interest in a business is given away, it can be valued at about 20% to 40% less than if it were a nonrestricted or controlling interest. And when the discounts are combined (when a minority interest can't be freely sold), the interest may be worth 30% to 60% less.

How do discounts help when it comes to gifting a portion of your ownership interest? Simple: The lower the value of one percentage point of a company (or share, in the case of a corporation), the more percentage points (or shares) of the company that will fit under the $16,000 annual gift tax exclusion amount. For example, if one percentage point of a company is worth $16,000 without discounts, an owner could transfer only one percentage point (1%) of the company per year to a child before exceeding the annual $16,000 gift tax exemption. But if the ownership interest is eligible for a combined valuation discount of, say, 50%, each percentage point of the company can be valued at $8,000 for IRS purposes, meaning that the owner could transfer two percentage points of the company ($32,000 in undiscounted value) per year to a child before exceeding the annual $16,000 gift tax exemption.

EXAMPLE: A husband and wife can each transfer $32,000 (in undiscounted value) of their company to each of their two children each year, meaning that each child will get $64,000 worth of the company each year (assuming a 50%

discount). Over six years, the couple can transfer $768,000 of the company's undiscounted value. (Without using discounts, the parents would only be able to transfer $384,000 in six years.) The parents can do this until they have transferred 48% or 49% of the company to their kids and still remain in control of the business.

SEE AN EXPERT

The IRS examines valuation discounts very closely. Due to the opportunity for abuse, the IRS pays close attention to these discounts. We strongly suggest that you seek the advice of a tax expert before using a valuation discount on your gift tax return. When you do, be prepared to explain to the IRS why the discounts are justified. Also note that proposed federal regulations would limit the use of valuation discounts for family-owned businesses; check with a tax expert to see if these regulations have been adopted.

Appreciation. As an added bonus, the portion of the company that is given away during life will appreciate in the children's hands, not the parents', meaning that the children won't have to pay estate taxes on its increase in value, as would be the case if the parents waited to give their interest to their kids until after their death.

It follows that if the worth of your business is likely to increase a great deal in the near future, you might not be better off giving away your interest to your children in $16,000 increments over the years. Instead, you could come out ahead by giving them a large chunk now (if you plan on giving them the business eventually, that is). Here's why: If the value of your company skyrockets, your ownership interest will be worth much more in years to come than it is now, making it much harder to give away a significant portion of your ownership interest in $16,000 increments. If, instead, you make a gift now, you may have to pay a gift tax, but you'll do so based on your business's current, comparatively low, value. Savings can result because, by the time the business goes up in value, it will already be owned by your kids—meaning that at your death no estate tax will be due on the increase.

Generation-Skipping Transfer Tax

Years ago, the federal government caught on to the fact that the affluent would sometimes try to escape estate taxes by giving lots of property directly to grandkids or even great-grandkids. The idea was to pay just one gift tax, instead of two or three rounds of estate taxes when each generation died. To clamp down, Congress enacted what's called the "generation-skipping transfer tax." Now the government places an extra tax (up to 40%) on property left or given to a grandchild or other young relative. You can, however, give up to the annual exclusion amount (in total) directly to your grandchildren without triggering the extra tax. Of course, this property is still subject to regular estate taxes when you die (just not when the middle generation dies).

Lessening the Pain of Paying Estate Taxes

If your estate owes estate taxes when you die, but your heirs want to hang onto the share of your business you left them, they may have trouble finding the cash to pay the estate tax bill. Fortunately, the IRS allows some creative ways to pay federal estate taxes.

 SEE AN EXPERT

The rules summarized here are complex and subject to change. Check with your tax adviser for current information on these methods of paying estate taxes.

Alternate Valuation Date

The IRS provides that the executor of your estate can elect to value your estate for estate tax purposes six months after the date of your death (called the alternate valuation date). Thus, if your business doesn't do as well without you, and it's worth less six months after your death than it was on the date of your death, your executor can choose to use the alternate valuation date. The IRS may limit the use of this option in the future. This is covered in IRC Section 2032.

Deferral and Installment Payments

> SKIP AHEAD
>
> **For family businesses only.** This deferral, under IRC Section 6166, is only available for heirs who are going to hold onto the business interests they inherit. If your family members won't hold onto your ownership interest for at least 15 years—for instance, your business partners will buy out your share upon your death—your estate won't be allowed to defer its tax bill.

The inheritors of qualifying small business interests can delay the payment of estate taxes for five years so that they can prudently plan for such a big expense. During those five years, interest accrues on the estate tax bill at a low rate. Once the five years are up, the estate taxes may be paid off in up to ten equal annual installments.

If your heirs wish to use this option, they can't sell 50% or more of their interest before the tax is paid off. If they do, the entire amount of estate tax becomes due immediately.

To qualify for deferral and installment payments, the following requirements must be met:

- the value of the business interest must exceed 35% of the deceased owner's total estate, and either:
  - the business must have had 15 owners or fewer (when the deceased owner was alive), or
  - the deceased owner must have owned at least 20% of the company.

> CAUTION
>
> **Watch out for installment sales.** The IRS will not allow an estate to use the estate tax installment plan if the ownership interest has been sold to the company for a 15-year promissory note whose payments are set to coincide with estate tax payments. The IRS treats this as a sale of 50% or more of the interest. Your estate could be obligated to pay the estate taxes in full immediately, even though you are receiving payments for the sale of your ownership interest over 15 years. You may instead want to schedule a series of smaller buybacks over a period of years.

Alternate Real Estate Valuation

> **SKIP AHEAD**
>
> **For family businesses only.** These special rules are only available for heirs who are going to hold onto the business interests they inherit. If your family members won't hold onto your ownership interest for at least 15 years—for instance, your business partners will buy out your share upon your death—your estate won't be allowed to value their property using these rules.

In a nutshell, real estate used in a family business can be valued for estate tax purposes at its value for its *present* use, rather than its "highest and best" use. For example, if your business uses an old warehouse on the edge of town as a storage facility, the warehouse doesn't have to be valued for its worth as a strip mall. The same goes for farmland.

The difference between the property's present use value and its fair market value is limited to a specified amount that is indexed for inflation (at the time of this writing, the limit is a little over $1 million).

Several requirements must be met for the rule to apply:

- The value of the family business must be at least 50% of the deceased owner's overall estate.
- The value of the real estate of that business must be at least 25% of the deceased owner's overall estate.
- The deceased owner must have left the business to a family member.
- The deceased owner (or members of their family) must have used the real estate for the business for at least five of the eight years preceding the owner's death.

There are restrictions on the sale and use of the real estate for ten years (and, in some cases, 15 years) after the estate tax break. During this time, the family must agree to notify the IRS if the property is sold or no longer used for the business, and may be required to repay some or all of the estate taxes if the ownership or use of the real estate changes.

This "special use valuation" is covered in IRC Section 2032A.

Partial Buybacks to Pay Estate Taxes

> **SKIP AHEAD**
>
> **This method is only available for corporations.** If your business is not a corporation, skip ahead to the next section.

The IRS allows a deceased shareholder's estate to sell just enough of the shareholder's ownership interest to the corporation to meet estate taxes, funeral expenses, final bills, and probate and other fees—using what is called a "Section 303 redemption" under the IRC.

There are two requirements here:

- The value of the ownership interest must make up at least 35% of the estate of the deceased owner (after expenses and deductions).
- The estate or the heirs (whoever is selling off part of the ownership interest) must be responsible for paying the estate taxes and other final costs. (They are not, however, actually required to use the buyout money for this purpose.)

However, in "Income Tax Issues," above, we discussed that a redemption of a shareholder's stock must qualify as an exchange in order to give the selling owner capital gains treatment. Normally, to qualify as an exchange, the corporation must buy *all* of the shareholder's stock. Fortunately, a partial buyout of a deceased shareholder's shares to pay estate taxes under Section 303 may qualify for capital gains treatment.

For a deceased owner's estate or inheritors to be able to force a sale of only part of the deceased owner's interest, your buyout agreement must specifically state that an owner's estate or inheritors can force a partial buyout of a deceased owner's interest. The key here is partial—often buyout agreements (ours included) are written to allow the estate or inheritors to be able to force the company or the continuing owners only to buy *all* of the deceased owner's interest.

If you think your inheritors will want to keep their ownership interest and continue in your company, and the company and your buyout agreement will allow this, you can provide for this. By slightly changing our provision called Right of Estate, Trust, or Inheritors to Force a Sale, you can easily allow a partial redemption to pay estate taxes. Go to Section III, Scenario 3, Option 2, of the contract; the first sentence in Subsection (a) is shown below. Simply cross out "all, but not less than all," and add "any."

☐ **Option 2: Right of Estate, Trust, or Inheritors to Force a Sale**

(a) When an owner dies, the executor or administrator of the deceased owner's estate, or the trustee of a trust holding the deceased owner's ownership interest, or the deceased owner's inheritors can require the company and the continuing

any ~~owners to buy~~ all, but not less than all, of the deceased owner's ownership interest by delivering to the company within 60 days a notice of intention to force a sale ("Notice of Intent to Force a Sale") in writing. The notice shall include …

WORKSHEET

Turn to your worksheet. If you are interested in providing for partial redemptions, make a note on your worksheet to change the above language in Section III, Scenario 3, Option 2.

Buying Life Insurance

One way to protect your heirs from an estate tax squeeze is by purchasing life insurance to be paid to your inheritors upon your death. Your heirs can then use the proceeds to pay any debts, taxes, and bills your estate may owe. However, you shouldn't be the owner of the policy—if you are, the policy payout will be included in your estate at death, needlessly raising your estate taxes.

One obvious solution is for your children to buy the insurance on your life and own the policies. But you must be extremely careful to avoid having any "incidents of ownership" in the policy, meaning that there can be no record of your making the premium payments for the life insurance.

How Buyout Agreements Affect Estate Taxes

SKIP AHEAD

If you or one of your co-owners does not plan on being succeeded by a family member when you die or retire, this section may not interest you. Why? Paying estate taxes is less of a burden for heirs who do not plan on taking over the family business—that is, for those heirs who are bought out. After all, an heir who receives $1 million in cash for your ownership interest and gives the government one-third of it is still getting a good sum of money. If this describes you and your business partners, you may wish to skip ahead to Chapter 10.

If you're an owner of an intergenerational family business, and, after investigating the personal exemption, the marital deduction, portability, and gift tax exemption rules, you've found that your ownership interest may still be subject to the federal estate tax, you may be able to craft your buyout agreement to lower your eventual estate tax liability. By "intergenerational family business," we mean a business where at least one or more co-owners will leave their interests to heirs who will keep ownership of the business interests and work in or help manage the business for more than a few years. We include this section to help you pass your business on to your children or other relatives without being overburdened by estate taxes.

The Problem

For small business owners whose heirs will succeed them, drafting a buyout agreement with an eye toward estate tax concerns can be important. Here's why: If the bulk of the property you leave to your heirs consists of a largely nonliquid (not readily changeable into cash) interest in a small business (for example, one-third of a large furniture rental company), your heirs may not have any available resources to pay the estate tax bill. If your estate tax debt is large enough, your heirs might even have to sell the ownership interest and pay the taxes out of the receipts. Or, if they try to hold on to the business and pay estate taxes at the same time, they might have trouble keeping the company afloat.

EXAMPLE: Dick, with the help of his three sons, Dan, Bob, and Jonathan, had built up a successful custom glass manufacturing business by the time he died. His sons inherit the business, but little other property. Before filing an estate tax return, they hire a CPA to do an appraisal of the business, which comes out to $2 million over the estate tax exemption amount. As a result, Dick's estate owes about $800,000 in estate taxes (the current maximum estate tax rate is 40%).

The glass company has few liquid assets—its capital is tied up in equipment and inventory, its profits routinely paid out as salaries and bonuses. And Dick's sons, who are in the process of educating their children, don't have an extra $800,000 lying around. Rather than trying to make hefty payments to the IRS for years, which could hobble the company, the sons sell the glass outfit to pay off the taxes. Because their dad hadn't done any estate tax planning, they paid a lot of estate taxes and had to sell the family business and find other work.

The Solution

This is where buyout agreements can help. To avoid an estate tax squeeze, in some circumstances you can structure your agreement to legally minimize taxes. Here's how: As we discussed in Chapter 6, your buyout agreement will normally specify a price, or a formula for setting the price, for your ownership interest. The key for estate tax planning is choosing a conservative price or valuation formula (such as book value) in your agreement. This can set the value of your ownership interest at an amount considerably lower than its market value at the time of your death.

The lower your Agreement Price, the lower your estate taxes could be. Keep in mind that this will set the price not only for estate tax purposes, but also for any sales arising under the buyout agreement.

SEE AN EXPERT

Please realize that using your buyout agreement to avoid estate taxes is a relatively sophisticated form of tax planning and can be a tricky business. If you (possibly with your family members) own 50% or more of your business, the IRS may think that your reason for adopting a buyout agreement is to lower your estate taxes, not to set up transfer restrictions and buyback procedures. Since the IRS audits many family business transfers from one generation to the next, it's doubly important to see a tax expert in this case.

The IRS may accept the value your buyout agreement places on your business at the time of your death if the price or formula you used in your agreement represented the fair market value of the business at the time you created your agreement. This is true even if this value is below fair market value when you die.

CAUTION

Setting a low price can be detrimental. There's a danger to establishing a low valuation of your business in an effort to save on estate taxes. It could be counterproductive for at least one, and often several, reasons. For one, if you have to retire early, perhaps because you or a family member has health problems, you would want to be able to sell your interest back to the company for a price that represents its current fair value (not a price tied to the value of the interest at the time of your agreement to save on estate taxes). Also, if your heirs decide they do not want to take over the business after all, but want to sell the interest they inherit, a low Agreement Price may hurt them. In this case, they might be better off receiving a higher price for the interest and paying proportionately higher estate taxes.

The IRS will do what it can to prevent you from unfairly using an artificially low Agreement Price to reduce estate taxes. The IRS will accept your Agreement Price only if your agreement satisfies six rules:

- **Rule 1: Your buyout agreement must give the company or the continuing owners an option to purchase deceased owners' interests from their estate** (whether or not they ever exercise the buyback right). This is a very common buyout provision. In our agreement it's called an Option to Purchase a Deceased Owner's Interest and is discussed in Chapter 3. Many, if not most, business owners include this option in their buyout agreements for nontax reasons.

- **Rule 2: The Agreement Price must be "determinable and reasonable."** Your Agreement Price must be able to be calculated easily and objectively from your agreement. In practice, this means you must use a fixed price or an objective formula (like book value or capitalization of earnings) as a way to determine the price of the ownership interests. (We discuss the various valuation methods in Chapter 6.)

- **Rule 3: Under the agreement, owners cannot sell their ownership interests at a price higher than the general Agreement Price.** Your buyout agreement may not allow owners to sell their ownership interests at a higher price during their lifetime, at least without offering them to the company or the other owners first at the Agreement Price. This means that the price that is applicable after an owner's death must be used in all ownership transfer situations, such as when an owner wants to be bought out of the business—with the exception of a Right-of-First-Refusal provision. A right to first refusal is okay only if it gives the company or the continuing owners the option to buy a selling owner's interest at the Agreement Price, not at the price an outsider has offered (discussed in Chapter 2).

  Of course, just because your buyout agreement does not specifically say that a sale of ownership interests at a higher price is okay doesn't mean that it can't be done—when all owners agree, any provision in the buyout agreement can be rewritten or ignored. But if the buyout agreement is ignored and the IRS finds out, you can say goodbye to being able to use the Agreement Price for estate tax purposes. Likewise, if one owner (a majority owner, for instance) has the sole authority to change the agreement at any time, the IRS may decide that the owner wasn't really bound by the agreement during the owner's lifetime.

- **Rule 4: Your buyout agreement must not be merely a "device" to transfer your business interest to your heirs without paying estate taxes.** If the IRS finds that your intent in creating your buyout agreement was to lower estate taxes, it will ignore your Agreement Price and appraise the property itself. However, if the buyout provisions accomplish a valid nontax purpose—namely, keeping ownership interests within the control of the founders of a small, closely held company—then it may be okay if they have the collateral tax result of fixing the value of shares at a price lower than their future market value.

CAUTION

Agreements made late in life are risky. If you or a co-owner is in poor health or advanced years when you make your buyout agreement, your estate is likely to be subject to more intense scrutiny than otherwise. The IRS is likely to think that you created your agreement only for the purpose of passing on your ownership interest free of as much tax as possible.

- **Rule 5: Your buyout agreement must be a "bona fide business arrangement."** This requirement—which is very similar to the last one—says that your buyout agreement must have been adopted for a valid business purpose, such as to limit ownership and control of the company to the original group, or to ensure continuity of management. In other words, a set of buyout provisions that have no "teeth" (that are discretionary) will not look like the real thing to the IRS. Also, this rule means that your buyout agreement must be enforceable against all of the co-owners. For example, a buyout agreement that requires the estate of a deceased minority owner to sell the owner's interest back to the company while allowing the heirs of a majority owner to hold onto their interest would be risky.

- **Rule 6: Your buyout agreement must be similar to fair business arrangements entered into by unrelated persons in the same industry.** If you use a standard measure of value—such as book value or a multiple of earnings—that's commonly used in your type of business, you should be okay, even if your interest could fetch more in the open market. But if your buyout provisions contain a low fixed price that bears no relationship to reality, you may have problems with the IRS.

CAUTION

The value of goodwill should not be ignored. If your company has been around long enough for it to develop a good reputation and a reliable customer base, and possibly even recognizable brand names and trademarks, it's a poor idea to use a formula that completely ignores these factors. For instance, the book value method, which will undoubtedly give you a low Agreement Price, is likely to be questioned by the IRS if other successful businesses like yours are typically valued and bought and sold at market values in excess of book value. A formula such as capitalization of earnings is more acceptable for an established, successful company.

SEE AN EXPERT

Beware penalties for undervaluing your business interest. The IRS can slap your estate with a sharp penalty if it discovers that your buyout agreement grossly undervalued your business interest. If the IRS concludes your business interest was undervalued by 50% or more, the IRS can penalize your estate 20% of the unpaid tax. And if your business interest was undervalued by 75% or more, the IRS can penalize your estate as high as 40% of the unpaid tax. This is in addition to having to pay the readjusted tax itself, not to mention possible interest owed, court costs, and lawyers' fees. Again, do yourself a favor and see an experienced lawyer and tax adviser if you want to use your agreement to set the value of your business for estate tax purposes. ●

Lawyers, Tax Specialists, and Resources

Much of the work involved in creating a buyout agreement involves considering and discussing your options with your co-owners and then filling in the blanks. Most knowledgeable and motivated business owners can competently do the work themselves. But there are several issues that we've flagged throughout the book, and especially in Chapter 9, "Income and Estate Tax Issues," that may need the expertise of a tax planner. Other decisions involve a mix of financial and legal savvy and are likely to be best made with the input of an experienced small business lawyer or a tax attorney. In the sections below, we provide a few tips to help you in your search for competent expert information, assistance, and advice.

How to Find the Right Lawyer

Many small businesses can't afford to hire a lawyer to create a buyout agreement from scratch. Often a knowledgeable business owner can sensibly accomplish the whole task. Other times, it makes sense to briefly consult with a lawyer about your buyout agreement at an interim stage or have the paperwork reviewed upon completion.

You already have taken one positive step in the direction of making your legal life affordable by deciding to use this book to prepare your buyout agreement. Depending on the size of your business and the complexity of your agreement, your next step may be to find a cooperative lawyer who will answer whatever questions you may have and perhaps draft a customized clause here or there for your agreement.

You obviously don't want a lawyer who wants to draw up an overly legalistic agreement from scratch, while running up billable hours as fast as possible. Instead, you need what we call a "legal coach"—someone who is willing to work with you, not just for you. Under this model, the lawyer works to help you create your own agreement.

Look for Potential Lawyers

When you go looking for a lawyer, don't start with phone books or advertisements. Asking for a referral to an attorney from someone you trust can be a good way to find legal help. Talk to people in your community who own or operate businesses you respect. Ask them about their lawyer and what they think of that person's work. If you talk to half a dozen businesspeople, chances are you'll come away with several good leads. Other people, such as your banker, accountant, insurance agent, or real estate broker, may be able to provide the names of lawyers they trust to help them with business matters. Friends, relatives, and business associates within your own company may also have names of possible lawyers.

Two sites that are part of the Nolo family, Lawyers.com and Avvo.com, provide excellent and free lawyer directories. These directories allow you to search by location and area of law, and they list detailed information about the lawyers as well as reviews of many lawyers from their clients. You can visit www.lawyers.com/find-a-lawyer or www.avvo.com/find-a-lawyer to find out more.

In addition, Martindale.com offers an advanced search option that allows you to sort not only by practice area and location, but also by criteria like law school. Whether you look for lawyers by name or by expertise, you'll find listings with detailed background information, peer and client ratings, and even profile visibility.

Don't Ask a Lawyer for Tax Advice

When it comes to the tax implications of buy-sell agreements, accountants often have a better grasp of the issues than most lawyers (except for tax attorneys, who may have a special tax law degree). And an added bonus is that although tax advice doesn't come cheap, accountants often charge less than lawyers.

Interview the Lawyer

When you call potential lawyers, announce your intentions in advance—that you're looking for someone who is willing to answer a few questions or review your buyout (buy-sell) agreement. Ask the lawyers if they have experience in drafting buy-sell agreements—most lawyers (including small business lawyers) do not have experience with this area of the law. The ideal lawyer should have experience with small businesses, taxes, and estate planning.

If the lawyer seems agreeable to this arrangement, ask if you can come in to meet with her for a half hour or so. Although many lawyers will not charge you for this introductory appointment, it's often a good idea to offer to pay for it. You want to establish that you are looking for someone to help you help yourself, not for a free ride.

At the interview, reemphasize that you are looking for a legal coach, not for someone to draft a buy-sell agreement for you from scratch for $2,000 to $2,500 or more. Many lawyers will find this unappealing—for example, saying they don't feel comfortable reviewing documents you have drafted using self-help materials. If so, thank the person for being frank and keep interviewing other lawyers. You'll also want to discuss other important issues in this initial interview, such as the lawyer's customary charges for services, as explained further, below.

Pay particular attention to the rapport between you and your lawyer. Remember—you are looking for a legal coach who will work with you. Trust your instincts and seek a lawyer whose personality and business sense are compatible with your own.

Discuss the Cost of Services

Especially at the beginning of your relationship, when you bring a big job to a lawyer, ask specifically about what it will cost. If you feel it's too much, don't hesitate to negotiate.

Get a clear understanding about how fees will be computed. Some lawyers bill a flat amount for document review; others bill to the nearest six-, ten-, or 20-minute interval. Whatever the lawyer's system, you need to understand it.

It's a good idea to get all fee arrangements—especially those for good-sized jobs—in writing. In several states, fee agreements between lawyers and clients must be in writing if the expected fee is $1,000 or more. But whether required or not, it's a good idea to get it in writing.

How Lawyers Charge for Legal Services

There are no across-the-board rules on how lawyers' fees are to be charged. Expect to be charged by one of the following methods:

- **By the hour.** In many parts of the United States, you can get competent services for your small business for $150 to $250 an hour. Newer attorneys still in the process of building a practice may be available for paperwork review, legal research, and other types of legal work at lower rates.
- **Flat fee for a specific job.** Under this arrangement, you pay the agreed-upon amount for a given project, regardless of how much or how little time the lawyer spends. Particularly when you first begin working with a lawyer and are worried about hourly costs getting out of control, negotiating a flat fee for a specific job can make sense. For example, the lawyer may draw up a simple real estate purchase agreement for $500 or review and finalize your buy-sell agreement for $1,000.
- **Retainer.** Some corporations can afford to pay relatively modest amounts to keep a business lawyer on retainer for ongoing phone or in-person consultations, routine premeeting minutes review or resolution preparation, and other business matters during the year. Of course, your retainer won't cover a full-blown legal crisis, but it can help you take care of ongoing minutes and other legal paperwork (for example, contract or special real estate paperwork) when you need a hand.

Confront Any Problems Head-On

If you have any questions about your lawyer's bill or the quality of their services, speak up. Buying legal help should be just like purchasing any other consumer service—if you are dissatisfied, seek a reduction in your bill or make it clear that the work needs to be redone properly (a buy-sell agreement that addresses your particular problem, a more comprehensive lease, and so on). Lawyers who run a decent business will promptly deal with your concerns. If you don't get an acceptable response, find another lawyer, pronto. If you switch lawyers, you are entitled to get your documents back from the first lawyer.

Even if you fire your first lawyer, you may still feel unjustly wronged. If you can't get satisfaction from the lawyer, write to the client grievance office of your state bar association (with a copy to the lawyer, of course). Often, a phone call from this office to the lawyer will bring the desired results.

Finding the Right Tax Adviser

Buyout scenarios necessarily involve tax issues and questions, such as, "Is it more tax advantageous to have the company itself or the continuing owners buy a departing owner's interest?" Fortunately, many of these issues won't raise their ugly heads until it's time for an actual buyout. But while you're forming your buyout agreement, you may have concerns about the tax aspects of the various buyout provisions we provide. To get good answers in these areas, you may require the expert advice of a tax adviser. Depending on the issue before you, this adviser may be a certified public accountant, a financial or investment adviser, or a buy-sell agreement specialist.

Whatever your arrangement, consider the same issues for finding, choosing, and using a tax professional as those discussed above for legal services. Shop around for someone who is recommended by small business owners you respect, or who is otherwise known to you as qualified for the task. Again, you may be able to take advantage of the lower rates offered by newer local practitioners or firms. Your tax person should be available over the phone to answer routine questions, or by mail or fax to handle paperwork and correspondence, with a minimum of formality or ritual. It is likely that you will spend much more time dealing with your tax adviser than your legal adviser, so be particularly attentive to the personal side of this relationship.

Tax issues are often cloudy and subject to a range of interpretations and strategies, so it is absolutely essential that you discuss and agree to the level of tax aggressiveness you expect from your adviser. Some small business owners want to live on the edge, saving every possible tax dollar even at the risk that their tax practices will be challenged by the IRS or state tax agents. Others are willing to pay a bit more in taxes to gain an extra measure of peace of mind. Whatever your tax strategy, make sure you find a tax adviser who feels the same way you do, or is willing to defer to your more liberal or conservative tax tendencies.

As with legal issues that affect your business, it pays to learn the basics about business and employment taxation. Not only will you have to buy less help from professionals, but you'll be in a good position to make good financial and tax planning decisions. IRS forms, business and law library publications, trade groups, and countless other sources provide accessible information on business tax issues. Your accountant or other tax adviser should be able to help you put your hands on some good materials.

Legal Resources

Law is information, not magic. If you can look up necessary information yourself, you need not purchase it from a lawyer—although if it involves important issues, you may wish to check your conclusions with a lawyer or use one as a sounding board for your intended course of action.

Much of the research necessary to understand your state's business law can be done without a lawyer by spending some time in a local law or business library. Even if you need to go to a lawyer to sort out a particular legal question, you can give yourself a leg up on understanding the legal issues surrounding your question by going to law and business libraries and reading practice manuals prepared for lawyers and law students.

How do you find a law library open to the public? In many states, you need to look only as far as your county courthouse or, failing that, your state capitol. In addition, publicly funded law schools generally permit the public to use their libraries, and some private law schools grant limited access to their libraries—sometimes for a modest user's fee. If you're lucky enough to have access to several law libraries, select one that has a reference librarian to assist you. Also look through the business or reference department of a major city or county public library. These often carry state business statutes as well as books on business law and taxation useful to the small business owner.

In doing legal research for a corporation or other type of business, there are a number of sources for legal rules, procedures, and issues that you may wish to examine. Here are a few:

- **Federal laws.** These include the tax laws and procedures found in the Internal Revenue Code and the Treasury regulations implementing these code sections.

- **Administrative rules and regulations.** Issued by federal and state administrative agencies charged with implementing statutes, state and federal statutes are often supplemented with regulations that clarify the statute and contain administrative rules for an agency to follow in implementing and enforcing the statute.

- **Case law.** Case law refers to all federal and state court decisions, which interpret statutes and sometimes make new law, known as "common law."

- **Secondary sources.** Also important in researching corporate and business law are sources that provide background information on particular areas of law. One example is this book. Other secondary sources are commonly found in the business, legal, or reference section of your local bookstore. You can find practice guides on many subjects in most law libraries.

Tax Resources

Unfortunately, tax law is not as easy to learn as some other areas of business law. The present tax code contains over 3,000 pages of very fine print and changes from year to year. So, in many cases, going straight to a tax expert will save you a lot of time and frustration. If you do have a specific question you'd like to find the answer to and you're very brave, here are a few tips to follow.

- You can find the tax code itself (Title 26 of the United States Code) at https://uscode.house.gov.

- The IRS interprets the tax code through a series of regulations, and federal court decisions further interpret the law. You can access the Treasury regulations on the IRS website at www.irs.gov or in the law library. For court decisions, ask your law librarian for *United States Tax Court Reports.*
- Your law library should have a good selection of secondary sources, among them *Federal Taxation of Income, Estates and Gifts* (Thomson Reuters) and *Ernst & Young Tax Guide* (Wiley).
- Uncle Fed's Tax Board, a website maintained by private tax professionals at www.unclefed.com, contains helpful tax articles and a directory of tax professionals.
- You can find IRS publications at www.irs.gov.

Resources From Nolo

Below are a few titles published by Nolo that we believe offer valuable information to the small business owner:
- *Legal Guide for Starting & Running a Small Business,* by Fred S. Steingold. This book is an essential resource for every small business owner, whether you are just starting out or are already established. Find information to negotiate a favorable lease, hire and fire employees, write contracts, and resolve business disputes.
- *Tax Savvy for Small Business,* by Frederick W. Daily. Gives business owners information they need about federal taxes and shows them how to make the best tax decisions for their businesses, maximize their profits, and stay out of trouble with the IRS.
- *How to Write a Business Plan,* by Mike McKeever. If you're thinking of starting a business or raising money to expand an existing one, this book will show you how to write the business plan and loan package necessary to finance your business and make it work. Includes up-to-date sources of financing.

Resources for Valuation Methods

If you decide you want to explore valuation methods beyond the basics we presented in Chapter 6, you can research any one of a number of alternative routes. (But keep in mind that other valuation methods will probably be more complicated, and the more complicated your method gets, the more sense it makes to use a time-of-sale appraisal.) There are a number of good books that concentrate on business valuation techniques for small businesses, including *Valuing Your Privately Held Business*, by Irving L. Blackman (McGraw Hill), and *The Handbook of Business Valuation*, by Thomas L. West and Jeffrey D. Jones (Wiley & Sons).

How to Access the Buyout Forms

This book comes with files containing a buyout worksheet and a buyout agreement that you can download here:

www.nolo.com/back-of-book/BSAG.html

Here is a list of types of files provided by this book, as well as the software programs you'll need to access them:

- **RTF.** You can open, edit, print, and save these form files with most word processing programs, such as Microsoft *Word*, Windows *WordPad*, and recent versions of *WordPerfect*.

- **PDF.** You can view these files with Adobe *Reader*, free software from www.adobe.com. Government PDFs are sometimes fillable using your computer, but most PDFs are designed to be printed out and completed by hand.

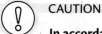 CAUTION

In accordance with U.S. copyright laws, the forms provided by this book are for your personal use only.

The following files are in rich text format (RTF):

Form Title	File Name
Buyout Worksheet	Worksheet.rtf
Buyout Agreement	Agreement.rtf

The following files are in Adobe Acrobat PDF Format:

Form Title	File Name
Buyout Worksheet	Worksheet.pdf
Buyout Agreement	Agreement.pdf

Buyout Worksheet

Buyout Worksheet

Section I: Introduction

When you're ready to draft your agreement, insert into the blanks in Section I of the agreement this information in the following order:

- Date you'll sign your agreement
- City and state in which you'll sign your agreement
- Names of the owners
- Your company's name

Section II: Limiting the Transfer of Ownership Interests

Refer to Chapter 2.

☐ **Option 1: Right of First Refusal**

    ☐ **Option 1a: Price and terms in offer**

    ☐ **Option 1b: Price and terms in agreement**

    ☐ **Option 1c: Right of First Refusal applies to sales to current owners**

    ☐ **Option 1d: Right of First Refusal does not apply to sales to current owners**

☐ **Option 2: Transfers to Relatives Can Be Made Without Restriction or Approval Notwithstanding Any Other Provision in This Agreement**

Notes: _____

_____

_____

_____

_____

_____

_____

_____

_____

_____

Section III: Providing the Right to Force Buyouts

Refer to Chapter 3.

Scenario 1. When an Active Owner Retires or Quits the Company's Employ

☐ **Option 1: Option of Company and Continuing Owners to Purchase a Retiring Owner's Interest**

☐ **Option 2: Right of Retiring Owner to Force a Sale**

  ☐ **Option 2a: Disincentive period, with illness/injury exception**

  Number of years _____

  Disincentive percentage _____

  ☐ **Option 2b: Disincentive period, without illness/injury exception**

  Number of years _____

  Disincentive percentage _____

Scenario 2. When an Owner Becomes Disabled

☐ **Option 1: Option of Company and Continuing Owners to Purchase a Disabled Owner's Interest**

Number of months _____

  ☐ **Option 1a: Date disabled owner stops working**

  ☐ **Option 1b: Date of buyout**

☐ **Option 2: Right of Disabled Owner to Force a Sale**

Number of months _____

  ☐ **Option 2a: Date disabled owner stops working**

  ☐ **Option 2b: Date of buyout**

Notes: _____

_____

_____

_____

_____

_____

_____

_____

Scenario 3. When an Owner Dies

☐ **Option 1:** Option of Company and Continuing Owners to Purchase a Deceased Owner's Interest

☐ **Option 2:** Right of Estate, Trust or Inheritors to Force a Sale

Scenario 4. When an Owner's Interest Is Transferred to His or Her Former Spouse

☐ **Option 1:** Option of Company and Continuing Owners to Purchase Former Spouse's Interest

Scenario 5. When an Owner Loses His or Her Professional License

☐ **Option 1:** Option of Company and Continuing Owners to Purchase Interest of an Owner Who Has Lost His or Her Professional License

☐ **Option 1a:** The full Agreement Price according to Section VI of this agreement

☐ **Option 1b:** Decided by an independent appraisal, according to the Appraised Value Method in Section VI of this agreement

☐ **Option 1c:** The Agreement Price as established in Section VI of this agreement, decreased by _____ %

Percentage agreement price will be decreased by _____

Notes: _____

_____

_____

_____

_____

_____

_____

_____

_____

_____

_____

_____

_____

_____

_____

_____

Scenario 6. When an Owner Files for Personal Bankruptcy

☐ **Option 1:** **Option of Company and Continuing Owners to Purchase Interest of an Owner Who Has Filed for Bankruptcy**

Number of days' notice required before bankruptcy _____

Scenario 7. Encumbrance of Interest

☐ **Option 1:** **Encumbrances Allowed Subject to Option of Company and Continuing Owners to Purchase Encumbered Interest**

☐ **Option 2:** **No Encumbrance Allowed**

Scenario 8. Expulsion of Owner

☐ **Option 1:** **Option of Company and Continuing Owners to Purchase an Expelled Owner's Interest**

☐ **Option 1a:** **Any criminal conduct against the company (such as embezzlement)**

☐ **Option 1b:** **A serious breach of the owner's duties or of any written policy of the company**

☐ **Option 1c:** _____ .

Additional reason for expulsion

☐ **Option 1d:** **The full Agreement Price according to Section VI of this agreement**

☐ **Option 1e:** **Decided by an independent appraisal, according to the Appraised Value Method in Section VI of this agreement**

☐ **Option 1f:** **The Agreement Price as established in Section VI of this agreement, decreased by _____%**

Percentage agreement price will be decreased by _____

Notes: _____

_____

_____

_____

_____

_____

_____

_____

_____

_____

Section IV: Buyout Procedure

Refer to Chapter 4.

(1) Option of Company and Continuing Owners to Purchase an Interest

    (b) Number of days that your company will have to make its buyback decision _____

    (c) Number of days that the continuing owners will have to make their individual buyback decisions _____

(2) Right to Force a Sale

    (b) Number of days that your company will have to make its buyback decision

    (c) Number of days that the continuing owners will have to make their individual buyback decisions _____

Section V: Funding

Refer to Chapter 5.

(1) Life Insurance

    ☐ **Option 1: Company-Purchased Life Insurance**

    ☐ **Option 2: Owner-Purchased Life Insurance**

(2) Disability Insurance

    ☐ **Option 1: Company-Purchased Disability Insurance**

    ☐ **Option 2: Owner-Purchased Disability Insurance**

Notes: _____

_____

_____

_____

_____

_____

_____

_____

_____

_____

_____

_____

_____

Section VI: Agreement Price

Refer to Chapter 6.

☐ **Valuation Method 1: Agreed Value**

Price for the entire company _____

☐ **Valuation Method 2: Book Value**

☐ **Valuation Method 3: Multiple of Book Value**

Multiplier _____

☐ **Valuation Method 4: Capitalization of Earnings (Adjusted for Income Taxes)**

Multiplier _____

Number of years that earnings will be based on _____

☐ **Valuation Method 5: Appraised Value**

Notes: _____

_____

_____

_____

_____

_____

_____

_____

_____

_____

_____

_____

_____

_____

_____

_____

_____

_____

Section VII: Payment Terms

Refer to Chapter 7.

☐ **Payment Terms Alternative 1:**
Full Cash Payment

Number of days when full payment will be due _____

☐ **Payment Terms Alternative 2:**
Monthly Installments of Principal and Interest

Term for repayment (in months) _____

Annual interest rate _____

Date first installment payment will be due _____

Payment due day (day of the month) _____

☐ **Payment Terms Alternative 3:**
Partial Cash Payment, Followed by Monthly
Installments of Principal and Interest

Down payment _____

Number of days when full payment will be due _____

Term for repayment (in months) _____

Annual interest rate _____

Date first installment payment will be due _____

Payment due day (day of the month) _____

☐ **Payment Terms Alternative 4:**
Monthly Installments of Interest Only, With a Final
Payment for the Full Purchase Price

Future date for full payment of purchase price _____

Interest rate _____

Date first interest payment will be due _____

Interest payment day (day of the month) _____

☐ **Payment Terms Alternative 5:**
   Customized Schedule for Payment for Ownership Interest

   Dates and amounts to be paid under a customized payment schedule

   _____

   _____

   _____

Section VIII: Resolution of Disputes

Refer to Chapter 8.

Be sure to read this provision before signing the agreement.

Section IX: Placement of Notice of Transfer Restrictions on Certificates

Refer to Chapter 8.

Be sure to read this provision before signing the agreement.

Section X: Continuation of Restrictions

Refer to Chapter 8.

Be sure to read this provision before signing the agreement.

Section XI: Signatures

Refer to Chapter 8.

You may wish to review your buyout agreement with your tax adviser or small business lawyer before you date and sign the agreement. Make sure that all married owners have their spouses sign the agreement (and that all owners with legally recognized domestic or civil partners have their partners sign the agreement).

Notes:

_____

_____

_____

_____

_____

_____

_____

Buyout Agreement

Buyout Agreement

Section I: Introduction

This agreement ("agreement") is made on _____, at

_____,

among _____,

_____, and

_____ ("owners"),

and _____ ("company").

    Owners wish to restrict the ownership of the company to the present owners and to persons with whom they may comfortably and easily deal, and to provide for the purchase of the ownership interest of any owner who dies or otherwise withdraws under the terms of this agreement.

    The legal existence of the company shall not terminate upon the addition of a new owner or the transfer of an owner's interest under this agreement, or the death, withdrawal, bankruptcy, or expulsion of an owner.

    "Seller" refers to an owner who is selling an ownership interest; or the estate representative, trustee, or family member of a deceased owner; or the ex-spouse of a divorced owner; or another seller under this agreement.

    "Buyer" refers to the company and/or the continuing owners who are purchasing an ownership interest.

    "Agreement Price" refers to the dollar amount that results from the use of the option checked in Section VI of this agreement at the time of the proposed sale.

    "Available interest" refers to the owner's interest that has become available for purchase by the company or continuing owners of the company as a result of a provision in this agreement.

    It is hereby agreed:

Section II: Limiting the Transfer of Ownership Interests

Check Option 1 below if you want the company and continuing owners to have a Right of First Refusal when an owner considers transferring his or her ownership interest.

☐ **Option 1: Right of First Refusal**

    (a) No owner ("transferring owner") shall have the right to sell, transfer, or dispose of in any way any or all of his or her ownership interest, for consideration or otherwise, unless he or she delivers to the company written Notice of Intent to Transfer the interest stating the name and the address of the proposed transferee and the terms and conditions of the proposed transfer. Delivery of this notice shall be deemed an offer by the transferring owner to sell to the company and the continuing owners the interest proposed to be transferred.

If the proposed transfer is a sale of the owner's interest, these terms shall include the price to be paid for the interest by the proposed transferee, and a copy of the offer to purchase the interest on these terms, dated and signed by the proposed transferee, shall be attached to the notice.

(b) The company and the nontransferring owners then have an option, but not an obligation (unless otherwise stated in this agreement), to purchase the interest proposed for transfer, and may do so within the time and according to the procedure in Section IV, Provision 1 of this agreement.

If the company and the nontransferring owners do not elect to purchase all of the interest stated in the notice, the transferring owner may then transfer his or her interest to the proposed transferee stated in the notice within 60 days after the end of the nontransferring owners' purchase option, according to the procedure in Section IV, Provision 1 of this agreement.

(c) Price and terms

You must check either Option 1a or Option 1b below if you checked Option 1, "Right of First Refusal," above.

☐ **Option 1a: Price and terms in offer**

If the proposed transfer is a sale of the owner's interest, the company and the nontransferring owners shall have the right to purchase the interest of the transferring owner only at the purchase price and payment terms stated in the Notice of Intent to Transfer submitted to the company by the transferring owner. The price and terms in this notice override the general Agreement Price selected in Section VI of this agreement and the agreement terms selected in Section VII.

If the proposed transfer is a gift of the owner's interest, the company and the nontransferring owners shall have the right to purchase the interest of the transferring owner at the Agreement Price selected in Section VI and according to the manner of payments and other terms of the purchase as established in Section VII of this agreement.

☐ **Option 1b: Price and terms in agreement**

The company and the nontransferring owners shall have the right to purchase the interest of the transferring owner at the Agreement Price selected in Section VI and according to the manner of payments and other terms of the purchase as established in Section VII of this agreement.

(d) Potential transferees

You must check either Option 1c or Option 1d below if you checked Option 1, "Right of First Refusal," above.

☐ **Option 1c: Right of first refusal applies to sales to current owners**

The Right-of-First-Refusal clause in this agreement shall apply to all potential transferees, whether they are current owners of any interests in the company or not.

☐ **Option 1d: Right of first refusal does not apply to sales to current owners**

The Right-of-First-Refusal clause in this agreement shall only apply to those potential transferees who are not current owners of any interests in the company.

(e) This Right-of-First-Refusal clause shall not apply to an owner's transfer of an ownership interest to a trust as long as the following conditions are met:

(i) the power to revoke the trust remains with the grantor (the owner of the interest), and

(ii) the grantor (the owner of the interest) is a trustee of the trust.

If either of the above conditions ceases to be true, this change will subject the ownership interest to this Right-of-First-Refusal.

Check Option 2 below if you want an owner to be able to give away an ownership interest freely without being subject to a Right of First Refusal. Of course, this option can be checked in addition to Option 1, above.

☐ **Option 2:   Transfers to Relatives Can Be Made Without Restriction or Approval Notwithstanding Any Other Provision in This Agreement**

Section III: Providing the Right to Force Buyouts

Scenario 1.   When an Active Owner Retires or Quits the Company's Employ

You may check Option 1 and/or Option 2 (or neither) below.

Check Option 1 below if you want the company and continuing owners to have the option to buy a retiring owner's interest.

☐ **Option 1:   Option of Company and Continuing Owners to Purchase a Retiring Owner's Interest**

(a) When an owner voluntarily retires or quits the company's employ, he or she is deemed to have offered his or her ownership interest to the company and the continuing owners for sale. The company and the continuing owners shall then have an option, but not an obligation (unless otherwise stated in this agreement), to purchase all or part of the ownership interest within the time and according to the procedure in Section IV, Provision 1 of this agreement. The price to be paid, the manner of payments, and other terms of the purchase shall be according to Sections VI and VII of this agreement. An owner who stops working for the company is referred to as a "retiring owner" below.

Check Option 2 below if you want a retiring owner to be able to force the company to buy his or her interest. This right can be in addition to Option 1 (company and continuing owners' option to purchase) above.

☐ **Option 2: Right of Retiring Owner to Force a Sale**

(a) When an owner voluntarily retires or quits the company's employ, he or she can require the company and the continuing owners to buy all, but not less than all, of his or her ownership interest by delivering to the company at least 60 days before his or her departure a notice of intention to force a sale ("Notice of Intent to Force a Sale"). The notice shall include the date of departure, the name and address of the owner, a description and amount of the owner's interest in the company, and a statement that the owner wishes to force a sale due to the owner's retirement as provided in this provision. The procedure for purchase of the ownership interest shall be according to Section IV, Provision 2 of this agreement. The price to be paid, the manner of payments and other terms of the purchase shall be according to this section and Sections VI and VII of this agreement. An owner who requests that his interest be purchased is referred to as a "retiring owner" below.

(b) Disincentive option

If you checked Option 2, "Right of Retiring Owner to Force a Sale," above, you may check Option 2a or 2b, below, if you want to discount the Agreement Price if an owner retires or quits within a certain period of time. If you check Option 2a or 2b, also insert the time period required for payment of the full Agreement Price and the penalty that will be taken off the Agreement Price for retirement within that time period.

☐ **Option 2a: Disincentive period, with illness/injury exception**

If a retiring owner gives notice that he or she wishes his or her ownership interest to be bought before the end of _____ months of ownership of the company, he or she is entitled to receive only _____% of the Agreement Price for the sale of ownership interests in this company under this agreement, unless he or she is required to leave because of serious personal illness or injury or the serious illness or injury of a spouse, parent, or child, in which case he or she is entitled to 100% of the Agreement Price.

☐ **Option 2b: Disincentive period, without illness/injury exception**

If a retiring owner gives notice that he or she wishes his or her ownership interest to be bought before the end of _____ months of ownership of the company, he or she is entitled to receive only _____% of the Agreement Price for the sale of ownership interests in this company under this agreement.

Scenario 2. When an Owner Becomes Disabled

You may check Option 1 and/or Option 2 (or neither) below.

Check Option 1 below if you want the company and continuing owners to have the option to buy a disabled owner's interest. If you check Option 1, also insert the amount of time an owner must be disabled before the company or the continuing owners can purchase his interest.

☐ **Option 1: Option of Company and Continuing Owners to Purchase a Disabled Owner's Interest**

(a) When an owner becomes permanently and totally disabled, and such disability lasts at least _____ months (the "waiting period"), either consecutively or cumulatively, he or she is deemed to have offered his or her ownership interest to the company and the continuing owners for sale. The company and the continuing owners shall then have an option, but not an obligation (unless otherwise stated in this agreement), to purchase all or part of the ownership interest within the time and according to the procedure in Section IV, Provision 1 of this agreement. The price to be paid, the manner of payments and other terms of the purchase shall be according to this section and Sections V and VI of this agreement.

An owner is considered disabled when he or she is unable to perform his or her regular duties. If disability insurance is used to fund a buyout under this provision, the insurance company shall establish whether an owner is disabled; without disability insurance, the owner's doctor will establish whether an owner is disabled. An owner who becomes disabled according to this section is referred to as a "disabled owner" below.

(b) Price

You must check either Option 1a or Option 1b below if you checked Option 1 above.

☐ **Option 1a: Date disabled owner stops working**

The Agreement Price as selected in Section VI of this agreement shall be established as of the date the disabled owner first stopped working.

☐ **Option 1b: Date of buyout**

The Agreement Price as selected in Section VI of this agreement shall be established as of the date of the proposed buyout of the disabled owner's interest.

Check Option 2 below if you want a disabled owner to be able to force the company to buy his or her interest. This right can be in addition to Option 1 (company and continuing owners' option to purchase) above. If you check Option 2, also insert the amount of time an owner must be disabled before he or she can force the company to purchase his or her interest.

☐ **Option 2:   Right of Disabled Owner to Force a Sale**

(a) When an owner becomes permanently and totally disabled, and such disability lasts at least _____ months (the "waiting period"), either consecutively or cumulatively, he or she can require the company and the continuing owners to buy all, but not less than all, of his or her ownership interest by delivering to the company, within 30 days of the expiration of the waiting period, a notice of intention to force a sale ("Notice of Intent to Force a Sale") in writing. The notice shall include the name and address of the owner, a description and amount of the owner's interest in the company, and a statement that the owner wishes to force a sale due to disability as provided in this provision. The procedure for purchase of the ownership interest shall be according to Section IV, Provision 2 of this agreement. The price to be paid, the manner of payments and other terms of the purchase shall be according to this section and Sections VI and VII of this agreement.

An owner is considered disabled when he or she is unable to perform his or her regular duties. If disability insurance is used to fund a buyout under this provision, the insurance company shall establish whether an owner is disabled; without disability insurance, the owner's doctor will establish whether an owner is disabled. An owner who becomes disabled according to this section is referred to as a "disabled owner" below.

(b) Price

You must check either Option 2a or Option 2b below if you checked Option 2 above.

☐ **Option 2a: Date disabled owner stops working**

The Agreement Price as selected in Section VI of this agreement shall be established as of the date the disabled owner first stopped working.

☐ **Option 2b: Date of buyout**

The Agreement Price as selected in Section VI of this agreement shall be established as of the date of the proposed buyout of the disabled owner's interest.

Scenario 3.   When an Owner Dies

You may check Option 1 and/or Option 2 (or neither) below.

Check Option 1 below if you want the company and continuing owners to have the right to buy a deceased owner's interest.

☐ **Option 1: Option of Company and Continuing Owners to Purchase a Deceased Owner's Interest**

(a) When an owner dies, he or she, and the executor or administrator of his or her estate or the trustee of a trust holding his or her ownership interest, are deemed to have offered the deceased owner's ownership interest to the company and the continuing owners for sale as of the date of the notice of death received orally or in writing by the company. The company and the continuing owners shall then have an option, but not an obligation (unless otherwise stated in this agreement), to purchase all or part of the ownership interest within the time and according to the procedure in Section IV, Provision 1 of this agreement. The price to be paid, the manner of payments and other terms of the purchase shall be according to Sections VI and VII of this agreement. An owner who has died is referred to as a "deceased owner" below.

Check Option 2 below if you want the estate, trust, or inheritors of a deceased owner to be able to force the company to buy his or her interest. This right can be in addition to Option 1 (company and continuing owners' right to purchase) above.

☐ **Option 2: Right of Estate, Trust, or Inheritors to Force a Sale**

(a) When an owner dies, the executor or administrator of the deceased owner's estate, or the trustee of a trust holding the deceased owner's ownership interest, or the deceased owner's inheritors can require the company and the continuing owners to buy all, but not less than all, of the deceased owner's ownership interest by delivering to the company within 60 days a notice of intention to force a sale ("Notice of Intent to Force a Sale") in writing. The notice shall include the name and address of the deceased owner, the date of death, a description and amount of the owner's interest in the company, the name and address of the person exercising the right to force the sale, and a statement that this person wishes to force a sale of the interest due to the owner's death as provided in this provision. The procedure for purchase of the ownership interest shall be according to Section IV, Provision 2 of this agreement. The price to be paid, the manner of payments and other terms of the purchase shall be according to Sections VI and VII of this agreement. An owner who has died is referred to as a "deceased owner" below.

Scenario 4. When an Owner's Interest Is Transferred to His or Her Former Spouse

You may check Option 1 below if you want the company and owners to have the right to buy a divorced owner's interest from his or her former spouse.

☐ **Option 1: Option of Company and Continuing Owners to Purchase Former Spouse's Interest**

(a) If, in connection with the divorce or dissolution of the marriage of an owner, a court issues a decree or order that transfers, confirms, or awards part or all of an ownership interest to a divorced owner's former spouse, the former spouse is deemed to have offered his or her newly acquired ownership interest to the divorced owner for purchase on the date of the court award or settlement, according to the terms of this agreement. If the divorced owner does not elect to make such purchase within 30 days of the date of the court award or settlement, the former spouse of the divorced owner is deemed to have offered his or her newly acquired ownership interest to the company and the co-owners (including the divorced owner) for purchase, according to the terms of this agreement. The divorced owner must send notice to the company, in writing, that his or her former spouse now owns an ownership interest in the company. The notice shall state the name and address of the owner, the name and address of the divorced owner's former spouse, a description and amount of the interest awarded to the former spouse, and the date of the court award. If no notice is received by the company from the divorced owner, an offer to the company and the co-owners is deemed to have occurred when the company actually receives notice orally or in writing of the court award or settlement transferring the divorced owner's interest to the owner's former spouse. The company and the co-owners (including the divorced owner) shall then have an option, but not an obligation (unless otherwise stated in this agreement), to purchase all or part of the ownership interest within the time and according to the procedure in Section IV, Provision 1 of this agreement. The price to be paid, the manner of payments and other terms of the purchase shall be according to Sections VI and VII of this agreement.

(b) A former spouse who sells his or her ownership interest back to the company or continuing owners agrees to be responsible for any taxes owed on his or her sales proceeds.

Scenario 5. When an Owner Loses His or Her Professional License

You may check Option 1 below if you want the company and owners to have the right to buy an owner's interest when he or she has lost his or her professional or vocational license. If you check Option 1, also check and/or fill in Options 1a through 1c.

☐ **Option 1: Option of Company and Continuing Owners to Purchase Interest of an Owner Who Has Lost His or Her Professional License**

(a) If an owner suffers the surrender, revocation, or suspension, which will stand for at least three months, of his or her license to perform services essential to the business purposes of the company, that surrender, revocation, or suspension of the license shall be deemed to constitute an offer by the owner to sell his or her interest to the company or the other owners. The owner shall notify the company in writing of such surrender, revocation, or suspension. The notice shall include the name and address of the owner, a description and amount of the owner's interest in the company, and a description and effective date of the decision that resulted in the surrender, revocation, or suspension of the owner's license. If no notice is received by the company, an offer is deemed to have occurred when the company actually learns of the decision to surrender, revoke, or suspend the owner's license. The company and the continuing owners shall then have an option, but not an obligation (unless otherwise stated in this agreement), to purchase all or part of the ownership interest within the time and according to the procedure in Section IV, Provision 1 of this agreement. The price to be paid shall be as specified in this section; if not so specified, then according to Section VI of this agreement. The manner of payments and other terms of the purchase shall be according to Section VII of this agreement.

(b) If an owner's license is surrendered, revoked, or suspended, the price that the company and/or the continuing owners will pay for the expelled owner's ownership interest will be:

☐ **Option 1a:** **The full Agreement Price according to Section VI of this agreement**

☐ **Option 1b:** **Decided by an independent appraisal, according to the Appraised Value Method in Section VI of this agreement**

☐ **Option 1c:** **The Agreement Price as established in Section VI of this agreement, decreased by** _____ **%.**

Scenario 6. When an Owner Files for Personal Bankruptcy

You may check Option 1 below if you want the company and owners to have the right to buy an owner's interest when he or she has filed for personal bankruptcy. If you check Option 1, also insert the number of days' notice that the owner must give to the company before filing for bankruptcy.

☐ **Option 1:** **Option of Company and Continuing Owners to Purchase Interest of an Owner Who Has Filed for Bankruptcy**

(a) When an owner is planning to file for bankruptcy, he or she must give notice to the company, in writing, _____ days before he or she files for bankruptcy. The notice shall state the name and address of the owner, a description and amount of the owner's interest and the expected date of filing by the owner for bankruptcy. This notice shall be deemed to constitute an offer by the owner to sell his or her interest to the company or the other owners. If an owner files for bankruptcy without giving notice, the date when the company learns of the filing for bankruptcy will be deemed to be the date of this notice. The company and the continuing owners shall then have an option, but not an obligation (unless otherwise stated in this agreement), to purchase all or part of the ownership interest within the time and according to the procedure in Section IV, Provision 1 of this agreement. The price to be paid, the manner of payments and other terms of the purchase shall be according to Sections VI and VII of this agreement. An owner who has filed for bankruptcy is referred to as a "bankrupt owner" below.

Scenario 7. Encumbrance of Interest

You must check either Option 1 or Option 2 below.

Check Option 1 below if you want to allow owners to use their ownership interest as collateral for personal loans or encumber their interest in other ways, subject to the option of the company and the continuing owners to purchase that interest in case of default.

☐ **Option 1: Encumbrances Allowed Subject to Option of Company and Continuing Owners to Purchase Encumbered Interest**

(a) Any owner may encumber any or all of his or her ownership interest in the company in connection with any debt, but any such encumbrance is subject to the following condition:

(b) If an owner defaults on a debt secured by his or her ownership interest, he or she must promptly give notice in writing to the company. The notice shall include the name and address of the owner, a description and amount of the owner's interest in the company, the date and description of the encumbrance on the owner's interest, and the date and description of any action taken by creditors as a result of the default. If no notice is provided by the owner, notice shall be considered given to the company on the date the company learns of the owner's default or of any action by a creditor as a result of the default. (An owner who defaults on a debt secured by his or her ownership interest is referred to as a "defaulting owner" below.) The company and the continuing owners shall then have an option, but not an obligation (unless otherwise stated in this agreement), to pay off the debt and to take title to the interest.

(c) If the amount paid to the creditor (debt plus any interest) is less than the Agreement Price selected in Section VI of this agreement, the remainder of the Agreement Price shall be paid to the defaulting owner by the buyer of his or her ownership interest. If the amount paid to the creditor (debt plus any interest) is more than the Agreement Price selected in Section VI of this agreement, the defaulting owner shall owe the difference to the buyer of his or her ownership interest.

(d) If the company and/or the other owners do not cure the default as provided in Subsection (b) above, the creditor may pursue any and all legal and equitable remedies.

Check Option 2 below if you want to prohibit owners from using their ownership interest as collateral for personal loans or encumbering their interest in any other way.

☐ **Option 2:   No Encumbrance Allowed**

No owner may encumber any or all of his or her ownership interest in the company in connection with any debt, guarantee, or other personal undertaking.

Scenario 8.   Expulsion of Owner

Check Option 1 below if you want to give the company and the continuing owners the option to purchase an expelled owner's interest. If you check Option 1, also check and/or fill in Options 1a through 1f.

☐ **Option 1:   Option of Company and Continuing Owners to Purchase an Expelled Owner's Interest**

(a) At a time when the company has three or more owners, situations may arise in which a group of owners wish to expel another owner. An owner may be expelled upon a unanimous vote of all other owners for adequate cause. Upon such expulsion, the expelled owner is deemed to have offered to sell all of his or her interest to the company and the continuing owners. The company and the continuing owners shall then have an option, but not an obligation (unless otherwise stated in this agreement), to purchase all or part of the ownership interest within the time and according to the procedure in Section IV, Provision 1 of this agreement. The price to be paid shall be as specified in this section; if not so specified, then according to Section VI of this agreement. The manner of payments and other terms of the purchase shall be according to Section VII of this agreement. An owner who has been expelled is referred to as an "expelled owner" below.

(b) Adequate cause includes, but is not limited to:

☐ **Option 1a: Any criminal conduct against the company (such as embezzlement)**

☐ **Option 1b: A serious breach of the owner's duties or of any written policy of the company**

☐ **Option 1c:** _____

(c) If an owner is expelled for a reason listed in Subsection (b), the price that the company and/or the continuing owners will pay for the expelled owner's ownership interest will be:

☐ **Option 1d:** The full Agreement Price according to Section VI of this agreement

☐ **Option 1e:** Decided by an independent appraisal, according to the Appraised Value Method in Section VI of this agreement

☐ **Option 1f:** The Agreement Price as established in Section VI of this agreement, decreased by _____%

Section IV: Buyout Procedure

Fill in the blanks in Subsections (b) and (c) below, if you checked Option 1 anywhere in Sections II or III of this agreement.

(1) Option of Company and Continuing Owners to Purchase an Interest

(a) This provision is triggered upon receipt of notice by the company according to Section II or the notification of any of the events checked in Section III where the company and/or the continuing owners have an option, but not an obligation (unless otherwise stated in this agreement), to purchase the interest that is the subject of the notice (called the "available interest").

(b) The company shall have an option to purchase any or all of the available interest within _____ days after the date on which the company receives notice or becomes aware of the event triggering the Option to Purchase.

(c) If the company does not decide to purchase all of the available interest within the time allowed, it shall immediately and, in all cases, no later than the date of expiration of the company's right to exercise its purchase option of the available interest, notify the continuing owners of their right to purchase the available interest not purchased by the company. This notice by the company to the continuing owners shall state:

1) the amount and description of the interest available for purchase by the continuing owners

2) the date by which the continuing owner must respond in writing to the company that he or she wishes to purchase any or all of the available interest, which date shall be _____ days after the date of the expiration of the company's purchase option, and

3) that any purchase by a continuing owner must be according to the terms of this buyout agreement.

A copy of this buyout agreement shall be immediately furnished to any continuing owner who requests a copy.

(d) Each continuing owner may exercise his or her option to purchase any or all of the available interest in writing by delivering or mailing to the company an individual

Notice of Intent to Purchase. This notice shall be sent to the secretary or equivalent officer of the company, and shall show the name and address of the continuing owner who wishes to purchase part or all of the available interest and the amount and a description of the interest that the continuing owner wishes to purchase.

(e) If the total amount of interest specified in the notices by the continuing owners to the company exceeds the amount of the interest available for purchase by them, each continuing owner shall be entitled, up to the amount of interest specified in his or her individual Notice of Intent to Purchase, to purchase a fraction of the available interest, in the same proportion that the amount of the interest he or she currently owns bears to the total amount of the company's interest owned by all continuing owners electing to purchase.

(f) If the company or any continuing owner exercises their option to purchase a part or all of the available interest, the company shall deliver or mail to the current owner or, if different, the current holder of the available interest, no later than five business days after the expiration of the period to exercise their option to purchase the available interest, a Notice of Intent to Purchase that includes the following information:

- the name and address of the company, and the name and title of the officer or employee who can be contacted at the company
- a description and the amount of ownership interest to be purchased by the company and/or each of the continuing owners, and the name and address of each such continuing owner
- the total amount of the interest to be purchased by the company and the continuing owners
- the terms of the purchase according to Section VII of this agreement
- a copy of this agreement, and
- if the interest to be purchased is represented by certificates, such as share certificates, a request for the surrender of the share certificates to the company.

(g) The company and the continuing owners shall purchase the portion or all of the available interest each has exercised an option to purchase in the Notice of Intent to Purchase, according to the terms specified in Section VII of this agreement, each making payment for the interest to be purchased and complying with other terms as appropriate. The sale shall be considered final when the company and the continuing owners make payment to the owner or holder of the interest or, if payment is made over time, when all paperwork necessary to the sale has been executed by the company, the continuing owners, and the owner or holder of the interest to be purchased.

(2) Right to Force a Sale

If you checked Option 2 in Scenarios 1, 2, or 3 in Section III of this agreement, fill in the blanks in Subsections (b) and (c) below.

(a) This provision is triggered upon receipt by the company of a Notice of Intent to Force a Sale according to Section III, where the company and the continuing owners have an obligation to purchase the interest that is the subject of the notice (called the "available interest").

(b) The company shall have an option to purchase any or all of the available interest within _____ days after the date on which the company receives the Notice of Intent to Force a Sale.

(c) If the company does not decide to purchase all of the available interest within the time allowed, it shall immediately and, in all cases, no later than the date of expiration of the company's right to exercise its purchase option of the available interest, notify the continuing owners of their right to purchase the available interest not purchased by the company. This notice by the company to the continuing owners shall state:

   1) the amount and description of the interest available for purchase by the continuing owners

   2) the date by which the continuing owner must respond in writing to the company that he or she wishes to purchase any or all of the available interest, which date shall be _____ days after the date of the expiration of the company's purchase option, and

   3) that any purchase by a continuing owner must be according to the terms of this agreement.

      A copy of this agreement shall be immediately furnished to any continuing owner who requests a copy.

(d) Each continuing owner may individually exercise his or her option to purchase any or all of the available interest in writing by delivering or mailing to the company a Notice of Intent to Purchase. This notice shall be sent to the secretary or equivalent officer of the company, and shall show the name and address of the continuing owner who wishes to purchase part or all of the available interest and the amount and a description of the interest that the continuing owner wishes to purchase.

(e) If the total amount of interest specified in the continuing owners' notices exceeds the amount of the available interest, each continuing owner shall be entitled to purchase a fraction of the available interest, up to the amount of interest specified in his or her Notice of Intent to Purchase, in the same proportion that the amount of the interest he or she holds bears to the total amount of the company's interest held by all owners electing to purchase.

(f) If the continuing owners decline to purchase all of the available interest that remains, the company shall purchase the amount of available interest not purchased by the continuing owners.

(g) The company shall deliver or mail to the current owner or, if different, current holder of the available interest, no later than five business days after the expiration of the continuing owner's period to exercise their option to purchase the available interest, a Notice of Intent to Purchase that includes the following information:

- the name and address of the company, and the name and title of the officer or employee who can be contacted at the company
- a description and the amount of ownership interest to be purchased by the company and/or each of the continuing owners, and the name and address of each such continuing owner
- the total amount of the interest to be purchased by the company and the continuing owners
- the terms of the purchase according to Section VII of this agreement
- a copy of this agreement, and
- if the interest to be purchased is represented by certificates, such as share certificates, the notice should request their surrender to the company.

(h) The company and the continuing owners shall purchase the available interest each has exercised an option to purchase according to the terms specified in Section VII of this agreement, each making payment for the interest to be purchased and complying with other terms as appropriate. The sale shall be considered final when the company and the continuing owners make payment to the owner or holder of the interest or, if payment is made over time, when all paperwork necessary to the sale has been executed by the company, the continuing owners and the owner or holder of the interest to be purchased.

Section V: Funding

(1) Life Insurance

You may check Option 1 or Option 2 (or neither) below if you checked Option 1 or Option 2 under Section III, Scenario 3, Death, above. Check Option 1 for company-purchased life insurance, Option 2 for owner-purchased life insurance.

☐ **Option 1: Company-Purchased Life Insurance**

The company will apply for, own, and be the beneficiary of a life insurance policy on the life of each owner. The company will take any actions necessary to maintain in force all of the insurance policies it is required to maintain under this section, including paying all premiums, and will not cancel them or allow them to lapse. The policy benefits shall be applied to the purchase price in a buyout of a deceased owner.

☐ **Option 2: Owner-Purchased Life Insurance**

Each owner will apply for, own, and be the beneficiary of a life insurance policy on the life of each other owner. Each owner will take any actions necessary to maintain in force all of the insurance policies he or she is required to maintain under this section, including paying all premiums, and will not cancel them or allow them to lapse. The policy benefits shall be applied to the purchase price in a buyout of a deceased owner.

(2)   Disability Insurance

You may check Option 1 or Option 2 (or neither) below if you checked Option 1 or Option 2 under Section III, Scenario 2, Disability, above. Check Option 1 for company-purchased disability insurance, Option 2 for owner-purchased disability insurance.

☐ **Option 1: Company-Purchased Disability Insurance**

The company will apply for, own, and be the beneficiary of a disability insurance policy for each owner. The company will take any actions necessary to maintain in force all of the insurance policies it is required to maintain under this section, including paying all premiums, and will not cancel them or allow them to lapse. The policy benefits shall be applied to the purchase price in a buyout of a disabled owner.

☐ **Option 2: Owner-Purchased Disability Insurance**

Each owner will apply for, own, and be the beneficiary of a disability insurance policy for each other owner. Each owner will take any actions necessary to maintain in force all of the insurance policies he or she is required to maintain under this section, including paying all premiums, and will not cancel them or allow them to lapse. The policy benefits shall be applied to the purchase price in a buyout of a disabled owner.

Section VI: Agreement Price

Unless otherwise provided in this agreement, the undersigned agree that the method checked below for valuing the company shall be used to determine a price for ownership interests under this agreement.

You must check one and only one of the valuation methods below:

☐ **Valuation Method 1: Agreed Value**

The agreed value of the company shall be $_____, or such other amount as fixed by all owners of the company after the date of adoption of this agreement as specified in a written statement signed by each owner of the company. If more than one such statement is signed by the owners after the date of adoption of this agreement, the statement with the latest date shall control for purposes of fixing a price for the purchase of ownership interests under this agreement. The value of an individual owner's interest shall be the entire value for the company as determined under this paragraph, multiplied by his or her ownership percentage.

☐ **Valuation Method 2: Book Value**

The value of the company shall be its book value (its assets minus its liabilities as shown on the balance sheet of the company) as of the end of the most recent fiscal year prior to the purchase of an ownership interest under this agreement. The value of an individual owner's interest shall be the entire value for the company as determined under this paragraph, multiplied by his or her ownership percentage.

☐ **Valuation Method 3: Multiple of Book Value**

The value of the company shall be _____ times its book value (its assets minus its liabilities as shown on the balance sheet of the company) as of the end of the most recent fiscal year prior to the purchase of an ownership interest under this agreement. The value of an individual owner's interest shall be the entire value for the company as determined under this paragraph, multiplied by his or her ownership percentage.

☐ **Valuation Method 4: Capitalization of Earnings (Adjusted for Income Taxes)**

The value of the company shall be determined on the basis of _____ times the average net earnings (annual gross revenues of the company minus annual expenses and minus any annual federal, state, and local income taxes payable by the company) for the _____ fiscal years of the company (or the number of fiscal years the company has been in existence, if fewer) that have occurred prior to the purchase of an ownership interest under this agreement. The value of an individual owner's interest shall be the entire value for the company as determined under this paragraph, multiplied by his or her ownership percentage.

☐ **Valuation Method 5: Appraised Value**

The value of the company shall be its fair market value as determined by an independent appraiser mutually selected by Buyer(s) and Seller of the ownership interest subject to purchase under this agreement. If Buyer(s) and Seller are unable to agree upon an independent appraiser within 30 days, Buyer(s) and Seller, within the next ten days, shall each select an independent appraiser. If the two selected appraisers are unable, within 60 days, to agree on the fair market value of the company, then the two appraisers shall select a third independent appraiser within the next ten days, who shall, within 30 days, determine the fair market value of the company. All costs of an appraiser mutually selected by Buyer(s) and Seller or of a third appraiser selected by two appraisers shall be shared equally by Buyer(s) and Seller. All costs of an individually selected appraiser shall be paid by the party selecting the appraiser. The value of an individual owner's interest shall be the entire value for the company as determined under this paragraph, multiplied by his or her ownership percentage.

Section VII: Payment Terms

Unless otherwise provided in this agreement, the undersigned agree that the payment terms checked below shall be used for the purchase of ownership interests under this agreement.

You must check one and only one of the payment terms alternatives below:

☐ **Payment Terms Alternative 1:   Full Cash Payment**

Cash payment for the Seller's ownership interest shall be made by Buyer(s) to Seller within _____ days of the date the company provides a Notice of Intent to Purchase to the Seller under this agreement.

☐ **Payment Terms Alternative 2:   Monthly Installments of Principal and Interest**

Buyer(s) shall pay Seller the purchase price for an ownership interest in equal installments over a term of _____ months, with interest added to the amount of each installment computed at an annual rate of _____ and compounded annually on the unpaid continuing balance of the purchase price of the ownership interest. The first installment payment shall be made to Seller by Buyer(s) on _____ , and the continuing payments shall be made to Seller by Buyer(s) on the _____ of every month, until the full purchase price, together with any interest owed, is paid in full.

☐ **Payment Terms Alternative 3:   Partial Cash Payment, Followed by Monthly Installments of Principal and Interest**

The purchase of an ownership interest shall be accomplished as follows: An initial cash payment of _____ shall be paid by Buyer(s) to Seller within _____ days of the date the company provides a Notice of Intent to Purchase to Seller. The remainder of the purchase price shall be paid by Buyer(s) to Seller in equal installments over a term of _____ months, with interest added to the amount of each installment computed at an annual rate of _____% and compounded annually on the unpaid continuing balance of the purchase price of the ownership interest. The first installment payment shall be made by Buyer(s) on _____, and the continuing payments shall be made by Buyer(s) on the _____ of every month, until the full balance of the purchase price, together with any interest owed, is paid in full.

☐ **Payment Terms Alternative 4:   Monthly Installments of Interest Only, With a Final Payment for the Full Purchase Price**

Buyer(s) shall pay Seller the purchase price for an ownership interest on _____ . Until such date, Buyer(s) shall pay Seller monthly payments of interest, computed at an annual rate of _____% on the purchase price for the ownership interest. The first installment payment of interest shall be made by Buyer(s) on _____ , and the continuing installment payments of interest shall be made by Buyer(s) on the _____ of every month, until payment of the full amount of the purchase price by Buyer(s) as specified above. On the date for full payment of the purchase price by Buyer(s), interest owed on the purchase price from the date of the last payment of interest by Buyer(s) to the date of payment of the purchase price shall be added to and included with the payment of the purchase price by Buyer(s).

☐ **Payment Terms Alternative 5:   Customized Schedule for Payment for Ownership Interest**

Buyer(s) shall pay Seller the purchase price for the ownership interest according to the schedule and other terms included below:

_____

_____

_____

_____

_____

_____

_____

_____

Section VIII: Resolution of Disputes

Mediation Followed by Arbitration

Except as may otherwise be provided in this agreement or a later one dated and signed by all owners, any dispute concerning the contents of this agreement, if it cannot be settled through direct negotiation, shall first be submitted to mediation according to the terms specified below. All parties agree to try in good faith to settle the dispute by mediation before resorting to arbitration or litigation.

(a) An owner, an owner's legal representative, the spouse or ex-spouse of an owner, the executor or administrator of a deceased owner's estate, or any other party with an interest in this company who wishes to have a dispute mediated shall submit a written request for mediation to each of the other owners of the company. Mediation shall commence within 15 days after the date of the written request for mediation.

(b) Any decision reached by mediation shall be reduced to writing, signed by all parties, and shall be binding on each party. The costs of mediation shall be shared equally by all parties to the dispute.

(c) Each party to the mediation process shall cooperate fully and fairly with the mediator in any attempt to reach a mutually satisfactory compromise to a dispute. If the dispute is not resolved within 30 days after it is referred to the mediator, the dispute shall be submitted for arbitration according to the terms specified below or on terms agreeable to all parties at the time the dispute is submitted to arbitration.

(d) Within 15 days of the delivery of the notice of intention to proceed to arbitration to all parties, each party shall reply in writing to the arbitrator, stating his or her views of the nature and appropriate outcome of the dispute.

(e) The arbitrator shall hold a hearing on the dispute within 15 days after replies have been received from all parties or, if all replies have not been received, no later than 30 days after the giving of notice of intention to proceed to arbitration.

(f) At the arbitration hearing, each party shall be entitled to present any oral or written statements he or she wishes and may present witnesses. The arbitrator shall make his or her decision in writing, and his or her decision shall be conclusive and binding on all parties to the dispute.

(g) The cost of arbitration, including any lawyer's fees, shall be borne by the parties to the dispute equally unless the arbitrator directs otherwise.

Section IX: Placement of Notice of Transfer Restrictions on Certificates

(a)   The following statement must appear conspicuously on each ownership certificate issued by the company:

THE INTERESTS REPRESENTED BY THIS CERTIFICATE ARE SUBJECT TO RESTRICTIONS UPON TRANSFER AND ARE REDEEMABLE PURSUANT TO PROVISIONS CONTAINED IN AN AGREEMENT AMONG THE OWNERS OF THE COMPANY. FOR A COPY OF THIS AGREEMENT, CONTACT THE SECRETARY OR EQUIVALENT OFFICER OF THE COMPANY AT THE PRINCIPAL OFFICE OF THE COMPANY AT _____ _____ .

(b)   The secretary or other equivalent officer of the company shall provide to any owner or third person upon written request and without charge a copy of this agreement.

Section X: Continuation of Restrictions

All heirs, successors, and assigns to an ownership interest in the company will be bound by the terms of this agreement.

Before receiving a purchased, donated, or otherwise transferred interest from an owner or an owner's legal representative, the owner or the owner's legal representative will require any purchaser, donee, or transferee, and his or her spouse, to sign this agreement, agreeing to be bound by its terms.

Section XI: Signatures

1)   Signatures of Owners

Each undersigned owner of the company acknowledges that he or she has read and understands the restrictions, limitations, conditions, and other terms and provisions contained in the above agreement. Each has had the opportunity to consult with independent counsel. Each hereby expressly agrees to be bound by these restrictions, limitations, conditions, and other terms and provisions, including terms for the valuation and sale of shares of the company.

Signature of Owner _____ Date _____

Printed Name of Owner _____

Signature of Owner _____ Date _____

Printed Name of Owner _____

Signature of Owner _____ Date _____

Printed Name of Owner _____

Signature of Owner _____ Date _____

Printed Name of Owner _____

2) Signatures of Spouses

Each undersigned spouse of an owner of the company acknowledges that he or she has read and understands the restrictions, limitations, conditions, and other terms and provisions contained in the above agreement. Each has had the opportunity to consult with independent counsel. Each hereby expressly agrees to be bound by these restrictions, limitations, conditions, and other terms and provisions, including terms for the valuation and sale of shares of the company.

Signature of Spouse/Partner _____ Date _____

Printed Name of Spouse/Partner _____

Signature of Spouse/Partner _____ Date _____

Printed Name of Spouse/Partner _____

Signature of Spouse/Partner _____ Date _____

Printed Name of Spouse/Partner _____

Signature of Spouse/Partner _____ Date _____

Printed Name of Spouse/Partner _____

Index

 **More from Nolo**

Nolo.com offers a large library of legal solutions and forms, created by Nolo's in-house legal editors. These reliable documents can be prepared in minutes.

Create a Document Online

Incorporation. Incorporate your business in any state.

LLC Formation. Gain asset protection and pass-through tax status in any state.

Will. Nolo has helped people make over 2 million wills. Is it time to make or revise yours?

Living Trust (avoid probate). Plan now to save your family the cost, delays, and hassle of probate.

Provisional Patent. Preserve your right to obtain a patent by claiming "patent pending" status.

Download Useful Legal Forms

Nolo.com has hundreds of top quality legal forms available for download:

- bill of sale
- promissory note
- nondisclosure agreement
- LLC operating agreement
- corporate minutes
- commercial lease and sublease
- motor vehicle bill of sale
- consignment agreement
- and many more.

www.nolo.com

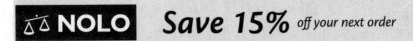

NOLO *Save 15%* off your next order

Register your Nolo purchase, and we'll send you a **coupon for 15% off** your next Nolo.com order!

Nolo.com/customer-support/productregistration

On Nolo.com you'll also find:

Books & Software
Nolo publishes hundreds of great books and software programs for consumers and business owners. Order a copy, or download an ebook version instantly, at Nolo.com.

Online Forms
You can quickly and easily make a will or living trust, form an LLC or corporation, apply for a provisional patent, or make hundreds of other forms—online.

Free Legal Information
Thousands of articles answer common questions about everyday legal issues, including wills, bankruptcy, small business formation, divorce, patents, employment, and much more.

Plain-English Legal Dictionary
Stumped by jargon? Look it up in America's most up-to-date source for definitions of legal terms, free at Nolo.com.

Lawyer Directory
Nolo's consumer-friendly lawyer directory provides in-depth profiles of lawyers all over America. You'll find information you need to choose the right lawyer.

BSAG9